Tim

Many [...] [...]

for Christmas 2001.

All our love

Mum + Dave
xx

Thos. F. Hedley, Esq.,

With Regards of

His Nephew

F. Y. Hedley

# MARCHING THROUGH GEORGIA

Since publication I have discovered that the author married Mary Elizabeth Harlan at Carlinville, Co. Macoupin, Illinois 16.9.1868, she being a month short of 15 years old. They had five children.

Mary Harlan Hedley 20.7.1869
Fenwick Yellowley Hedley 5.1.1871
Elijah Harlan Hedley 2.6.1872
Wilson Pattison Hedley 2.6.1872
Sarah Virginia Hedley 9.4.1877

There is a large web site for the Harlan family but there is so far no trace of any descendants from the five children. If you wish to have copies of archive material relating to the loss of the author's discharge papers and his subsequent letters when he was trying to obtain a pension please let me know. He had accidentally burnt his papers. He seems to have been in some way connected with The *Encylopedia of the History of Missouri,* published by the Southern History Company.

84 blood relatives attended a family reunion in 1998. They were all descendants on the author's uncle, my great grandfather.

Elizabeth Hutchings née Hedley Isle of Wight, England
Erratum. Inside flap of dust jacket. Read 1861 for 1860

Email elizabethh@bigwig.net www.bigwig.net/books
Tel 01983 740363

# MARCHING
# THROUGH GEORGIA

## FENWICK YELLOWLEY HEDLEY

Number _8 2_

First English Edition 1998
Limited Edition of 250

Copyright Elizabeth Hutchings 1998

Published by Hunnyhill Publications
Corner Cottage, Hunnyhill, Brighstone, Newport
Isle of Wight, PO30 4DU, England
Telephone: 01983 740363

Printed by Hobbs the Printers Ltd
Brunel Road, Totton, Hampshire, SO40 3WX, England

Bound by Cedric Chivers Ltd
9a/9b Aldermoor Way, Longwell Green, Bristol BS30 7DA, England

"Marching through Georgia."

# MARCHING THROUGH GEORGIA.

Bring the good old bugle, boys! we'll sing another song,
　　Sing it with a spirit that will move the world along—
Sing it as we used to sing it, fifty thousand strong,
　　While we were marching through Georgia.

CHORUS.—" Hurrah! Hurrah! we bring the Jubilee!
　　　　Hurrah! Hurrah! the flag that makes you free!"
　　　So we sang the chorus from Atlanta to the sea,
　　　　While we were marching through Georgia.

How the darkeys shouted when they heard the joyful sound!
　　How the turkeys gobbled which our commissary found!
How the sweet potatoes even started from the ground,
　　While we were marching through Georgia.

CHORUS.—" Hurrah! Hurrah! we bring the Jubilee," etc.

Yes and there were Union men who wept with joyful tears,
　　When they saw the honor'd flag they had not seen for years;
Neither could they be restrained from breaking forth in cheers,
　　While we were marching through Georgia.

CHORUS.—" Hurrah! Hurrah! we bring the Jubilee," etc.

" Sherman's dashing Yankee Boys will never reach the coast! "
　　So the saucy rebels said, and 'twas a handsome boast,
Had they not forgot, alas! to reckon with the host,
　　While we were marching through Georgia.

CHORUS.— " Hurrah! Hurrah! we bring the Jubilee," etc.

So we made a thoroughfare for Freedom and her train,
　　Sixty miles in latitude—three hundred to the main;
Treason fled before us, for resistance was in vain,
　　While we were marching through Georgia.

CHORUS.—' Hurrah! Hurrah! we bring the Jubilee," etc.

*—By Permission of S. Brainard's Sons. Cleveland.*

# MARCHING

# THROUGH GEORGIA.

---

## PEN-PICTURES OF EVERY-DAY LIFE

IN GENERAL SHERMAN'S ARMY, FROM THE BEGINNING OF THE ATLANTA
CAMPAIGN UNTIL THE CLOSE OF THE WAR

BY

## F. Y. HEDLEY,

ADJUTANT THIRTY-SECOND ILLINOIS INFANTRY, MEMBER OF SOCIETY OF THE ARMY OF
THE TENNESSEE.

---

*ILLUSTRATED BY F. L. STODDARD*

---

CHICAGO:

R. R. DONNELLEY & SONS, THE LAKESIDE PRESS.

1885.

# DEDICATION.

## TO MARY S. LOGAN,

WIFE OF MAJOR GENERAL JOHN A. LOGAN, HIMSELF A CONSPICUOUS REPRE-
SENTATIVE OF THE VOLUNTEER SOLDIERY OF THE NATION, AND THROUGH
HER TO THE NOBLE WIVES, MOTHERS AND SISTERS OF THE VOLUN-
TEER SOLDIERS, WHOSE GENEROUS DEEDS, WEARY ANXIETIES
AND TEARFUL MOURNINGS DURING THE GREAT STRUGGLE,
WERE THE MOST SACRED SACRIFICES MADE AT
THE ALTAR OF PATRIOTISM, THESE PAGES
ARE DEDICATED WITH AFFECTION AND
REVERENCE.

THE AUTHOR.

## ACCEPTANCE.

I thank you for the honor you do me in dedicating your book to me, and
through me to " The Noble Wives, Mothers and Sisters of our Volunteer Soldiers."
We have been drifting too rapidly from the memories of those terrible marches and
battles and anxieties, and I am glad that you have written as you have, for the
narrative will reawaken a spirit of gratitude to those who battled and suffered, and
stimulate patriotism in the breasts of those who have grown up since the days of war.

With great respect,

MARY S. LOGAN.

# PREFACE.

This volume does not pretend to be a tactical history of the campaigns of which it treats, and the grand movements of the Army are only mentioned in the most general way. Neither is it meant to extol the achievements of any particular individual or command.

It is intended to be, as its title indicates, a series of Pen-Pictures of the Every-Day Life of the Soldier during the campaigns beginning with the movement against Atlanta—how he lived, how he marched, and how he fought on skirmish line and in the line-of-battle. Its descriptions and incidents are drawn from the personal experiences of the author and those of his immediate comrades, and his recollection of events is freshened and confirmed by very complete diary entries, made at the time. They are from the standpoint of soldiers in the ranks, with whom the writer served as one of their number during a portion of the time covered by the narrative, and from whom he was never so far removed but that he was fully acquainted with their actions and sentiments.

These experiences, save in a very few instances, are such as were peculiar to no one soldier, but common to all, and any one of sixty thousand of "Sherman's Men" might say that his own history is contained in these pages. The incidents will prove at least suggestive enough to enable such a one to recall almost forgotten scenes. To his children they may not be uninteresting, telling as they do the story of what their father saw and did "While we were marching through Georgia;" and it may happen that some young man, who is hereafter to bear arms in the service of his country, will draw from the narrative an inspiration to unselfish and patriotic effort.

The author offers no apology for his style of writing. He has made no endeavor to meet the possible requirements of critics, but has written for those who by reason of experience or sympathy can enter into the spirit which actuated the Volunteer Soldier during the War for the Union. Many of these pages have been submitted to the criticism of one of the most prominent leaders of these men, and he has been pleased to say: "You write with great facility, and bring back to me, both in language and style, the occurrences of the war most vividly." With such commendation the author does not hesitate to place his work before his old comrades.

THE AUTHOR.

# CONTENTS.

## CHAPTER I.

The Drummer Boy. Rallying to the Defense of the Flag. The Drummer the Most
Conspicuous Figure in the Army. -    -    -    -    -    17

## CHAPTER II.

The School of the Soldier. How he was Educated. The Difference Made by Rank.
Heavy Marching Order. Surprised by the Paymaster. -    -    25

## CHAPTER III.

The First Dead. A Gunboat Expedition. The Tennessee River Opened Up. A
Gallant Fight. Death of a Noble Young Soldier. How a Company was
Reduced. -    -    -    -    -    -    -    -    32

## CHAPTER IV.

The Growth of a Regiment. A Nondescript Command. Forts Henry and Donelson. Battle of Shiloh. Siege of Corinth. Trouble on Account of Slave Emancipation. Siege of Vicksburg. -    -    -    -    -    42

## CHAPTER V.

The Army and its Personnel. Troops Gathering at Chattanooga. Their Glorious
Record. A Pen Picture of General Sherman. -    -    -    60

## CHAPTER VI.

Making Ready. Accumulating Supplies. Protecting the Railroad. The Railroad
Construction Corps. The Telegraph Corps. The Signal Service. Blazing its
Way. Georgia to be Overrun with the Bivouac. Wagons Lightened and Men
Loaded Down. Patent Coffee. -    -    -    -    -    69

## CHAPTER VII.

En Avant! The Advantages of Harmony. Grant Crosses the Rapidan, and Sherman Moves Out of Chattanooga. Engagement at Rocky Face Gap. The
Enemy Abandons Cassville. Allatoona Occupied by Sherman. -    82

## CHAPTER VIII.

An Incidental Campaign. A Severe Forced March. How Straggling was Punished.
The Amende Honorable. -    -    -    -    -    -    91

## CHAPTER IX.

View from Ackworth. A Grand Panorama. Kenesaw Mountain. The Troops in
Action at Big Shanty. A Railroad Engine Fired on by Artillery. Telegraph
Communication Restored. -    -    -    -    -    100

## CHAPTER X.

The Entire Union Army in Line. The Blue Line Crowding the Gray. The Soldier
on the Skirmish Line. Captor and Prisoner. An Independent Skirmisher.
Fighting for Apples. The Line of Battle. Under an Artillery Fire. Sports
behind the Works. -    -    -    -    -    -    106

## CHAPTER XI.

Before Kenesaw. Bishop-General Polk Killed. The Enemy Abandons Pine and
Lost Mountains. Privations of the Union Troops. A Desperate Assault upon
the Enemy's Lines. -    -    -    -    -    -    122

## CHAPTER XII.

Race for the Chattahoochee. A Horrible Night March. A Weird Spectacle. An
Army of Phantom Giants. Profanity in the Ranks. -    -    130

## CHAPTER XIII

The Lines on the Chattahoochee. A Long Flank March. Destruction of "French" Cotton Mills. Johnston's Masterly Retreat. He is Superseded by Hood. A Sharp Engagement. General Gresham Wounded. - - - 137

## CHAPTER XIV.

A Famous Division. Complimented by Sherman. Its Commanders: Hurlbut, Lauman, Crocker, Gresham, Giles A. Smith and Belknap. Personal Anecdotes. 145

## CHAPTER XV.

Dies Iræ. The Battle of July 22d. The Attack on Sherman's Left. His Troops Fighting on Both Sides of their Works. The Iowa Brigade Enveloped. Capture of both Union and Rebel Regiments. General Belknap Pulls a Rebel Colonel over the Works by his Coat-Collar. Hand to Hand Fighting. Death of McPherson. Logan Assumes Command. The Enemy Repulsed. Incidents of the Battle - - - - - - - 154

## CHAPTER XVI.

The Iowa Brigade. A Bitter Struggle. Capture of the 16th Iowa Regiment. Who were the Captors? The Flag of the 16th Iowa Restored Twenty Years Afterward, by the General who Captured it. - - - - 167

## CHAPTER XVII.

Logan Succeeded by Howard in the Command of the Army of the Tennessee. Bitter Feeling among the Troops. Sherman's Reasons. Who the "Bummer Generals" Were, and What they Did. - - - - 174

## CHAPTER XVIII.

Hammering Away! Another Flank March and Sharp Battle by the Army of the Tennessee. What Foreigners Said of the War. Trouble between Schofield and Palmer. Palmer Resigns. - - - - 179

## CHAPTER XIX.

The Old Chaplain. His Death. A Prophetic Address. How He Stood Up for "My Boys." A Noble Life. - - - - - - 189

## CHAPTER XX.

Important Movements. "Atlanta Ours and Fairly Won!" Importance of the Victory. Congratulations of President Lincoln and General Grant. The "Cracker-Line" Reopened. Blair and Logan Go Home to Take Part in the Presidential Contest. Sharp Correspondence between Generals Sherman and Hood. "We Must Have Peace, Not Only in Atlanta, but in All America!" - - - 195

## CHAPTER XXI.

A Breathing-Spell. Adventures of a Union Soldier in Returning to the Front. He Joins the Military Telegraph Corps. On the Track of Hood's Raid. - 207

## CHAPTER XXII.

Hood's Raid. Union Troops at Kenesaw and Big Shanty Dispersed. Allatoona Attacked. A Glorious Struggle. Sherman's Message and Corse's Answer. The Assault Repulsed. Verses by a Soldier Poet. General Sherman's Congratulatory Order. - - - - - 214

## CHAPTER XXIII.

A Family of Soldiers. A Hero at Allatoona. Patriotic Words from a Brother. The Soldier Father in Search of his Boy's Corpse. Meeting with General Grant. 234

## CHAPTER XXIV.

Hood Raiding the Railroad His Bloodthirsty Summons to Surrender. The Defiant Answer. Sherman in Pursuit. Death of General Ransom. - - 239

## CHAPTER XXV.

Sherman about to Move Southward. Reorganization of the Army. The Presidential Election in the Field. Orders for the March to the Sea. - - 245

## CHAPTER XXVI.

A Jolly Party of Soldiers. Their Amusement Interrupted by Sherman's Orders to March. The Departure of the Last Railroad Train Going North. Destruction of the Railroad. Atlanta Burned. A Suggestive Scene. - - 251

## CHAPTER XXVII.

On the March. Personal Characteristics of the Men. Their Endurance and Self-Confidence. How they Sheltered and Fed Themselves. Itinerary of the March. - - - - - - - 258

## CHAPTER XXVIII.

Genesis of the Bummer Orders for Foraging. The "Bummer" Searching for Provisions. His Politeness to Women and Affection for Children. His Efforts to Reach his Regiment with his Plunder. The Adventures of a Typical ' Bummer." A Sad Prank Played on a Staff Officer. - - 267

## CHAPTER XXIX.

The Events of a Day. The Army at Breakfast. The Troops on the March. The Skirmish Line in Advance. Personal Characteristics of the Men. Wading through Swamps. Building Corduroy Roads. Crossing a Stream. The Army in Ill Humor. Their Spirits Cheered by Martial Music. - - 278

## CHAPTER XXX.

A Real Camp Fire. Camp Songs. A Dead Enemy and his Picture. An Anecdote of Lincoln. Adventure at Vicksburg. A Cipher Dispatch. - - 289

## CHAPTER XXXI.

Crossing the Ocmulgee. Friendliness and Faith Shown by the Negroes. Passage of the Oconee. A Newspaper in Camp. Destruction of Provisions and Forage by the Citizens. The Army on the Point of Starvation. - - 310

## CHAPTER XXXII.

Tearing Up Railroad. Nearing Savannah. Within Sound of the Guns of the Fleet. A Sharp Skirmish on the Outskirts of Savannah. How a Shell Looks in Motion. A Severe Artillery Fire. Running Past the Enemy's Batteries. - 319

## CHAPTER XXXIII.

The Troops Starving. An Elaborate Meal. Fort McAllister Taken. Arrival of Supplies and Mail. The Boy who did not Live to Receive his Letter. Savannah Entered. - - - - - - 327

## CHAPTER XXXIV.

The Troops in High Clover at Savannah. A Staff Officer Finds Pleasant Acquaintance and Comfortable Quarters. Generous Hospitality of an Enemy. His Sad Death. A Genuine Poem. Alas, poor Yorick! - - - 337

## CHAPTER XXXV.

The Army Transferred to South Carolina. The Soldier on his Sea-Legs. An Uncomfortable Passage. Landing at Beaufort. Floundering in the Mud at Pocotaligo. - - - - - - - 343

## CHAPTER XXXVI.

Old Friends Heard From. Letters from Gunboat Officers and Others. An Incident in Mississippi. - - - - - - 349

## CHAPTER· XXXVII.

Wading the Salkehatchie. A Health-Wrecking Experience. Death's Bowling Alley. Occupation of Orangeburg. Marching Through a Blazing Pine Forest. 355

## CHAPTER XXXVIII.

Approach to Columbia. A White Horse Draws a Warm Fire. Passage of the Congaree River. General Belknap's Troops First to Enter Columbia. The Fifteenth Corps a Trifle Too Late. The 13th Iowa Regiment Loses its Flag. 365

## CHAPTER XXXIX.

Experiences of a Detachment of the 32d Illinois Regiment in Columbia. City Coun-
cilmen Anxious to Surrender. Burning Cotton in the Streets. Escaped Prisoners and Negroes Running a Muck. An Independent Skirmisher in the Tower
of the City Hall. A Jovial Party Meet in the Senate Chamber and Repeal the
Secession Ordinance. Curious Relics in the Arsenal. The City Fired. W.
Gilmore Simms Reviewed. Who was Responsible ?   -        -        -     375

## CHAPTER XL. ·

Revolutionary Battle-Grounds. Cheraw, South Carolina. Celebration of the Re-
Inauguration of President Lincoln. Skirmish at Fayetteville, North Carolina.
Arrival of a Dispatch Boat. A Curious Train of Refugees and Freedmen.
Nearing the End. To the Rescue! A Horrible Night March. A Sharp Skir-
mish A Remarkable Escape. Death of a Brave Conscript. The Last
Battle.        -        -        -        -        -        -     395

## CHAPTER XLI.

A Joyous Interlude. The Worst Brass Band in the Army. A Western Gunboat
Officer in New York. Interesting Interview with General Anderson, the Hero
of Fort Sumter. Lee Asking Terms of Grant. A Notable Scene in Wall
Street.   -        -        -        -        -        -     409

## CHAPTER XLII.

Beautiful Scene in Fortress Monroe Harbor. A Loyal Virginian. A Night Scene in
the Dismal Swamp. Assassination of Lincoln. Rage of the Troops and Terror
of the Citizens. The News Reaches the Army at Raleigh. Peace Negotiations
between Sherman and Johnston. Fears for the Safety of Sherman. The Crape-
Draped Sword.   -        -        -        -        -        -     421

## CHAPTER XLIII.

The Armies of Sherman and Johnston Confronting Each Other under Flag of Truce.
Sudden Appearance of General Grant. Surrender of Johnston. The Terms
Granted. Quarrel between Sherman and Stanton.   -        -        -     428

## CHAPTER XLIV.

Society of the Army of the Tennessee. Organized within the Sound of the Enemy's
Guns. A Brilliant Array of Presiding Officers. General Sherman in the
Chair.   -        -        -        -        -        -     438

## CHAPTER XLV.

On to Washington. "Yank" and "Johnny" on Good Terms. Richmond and Libby
Prison. Amusements of the Prisoners. Profane Psalm-Singing. Hanover
Court-House and Patrick Henry. The Battle-Ground at Fredericksburg.
Alexandria and Ellsworth.   -        -        -        -        -     448

## CHAPTER XLVI.

Arrival at the National Capital. The Grand Review. Meade's Army. The Soldiers
of the West. A Phantom Army. General Sherman's Farewell Order.     460

## CHAPTER XLVII.

Homeward Bound. Troops Shipwrecked on the Ohio River. The Army Sent Home.
General Logan's Farewell Order.   -        -        -        -     473

## CHAPTER XLVIII.

A Supplemental Campaign. Up the Missouri River. At Fort Leavenworth. On to
Utah! The Overland Stage and Pony Express. A Demoralized Command.
Remonstrances against the March. Arrival at Fort Kearney. Ordered Home
for Muster-Out.   -        -        -        -        -        -     479

## CHAPTER XLIX.

Arrival at Springfield. The Troops Discharged. A Reminiscent Picture. Vale!   487

# ILLUSTRATIONS.

| | |
|---|---|
| MARCHING THROUGH GEORGIA, - - - - | *Frontispiece.* |
| THE FIRST DEAD, - - - - - - | 35 |
| THE PEACH ORCHARD AT SHILOH, - - - - | 55 |
| ON THE SKIRMISH LINE, - - - - - | 75 |
| RESTORING COMMUNICATION, - - - - - | 95 |
| GEN. GRESHAM WOUNDED, - - - - - | 119 |
| MAP OF BATTLEFIELD, JULY 22, 1864, - - - | 143 |
| GEN. BELKNAP CAPTURING REBEL COLONEL, - - | 163 |
| A STRUGGLE FOR A FLAG, - - - - - | 183 |
| PORTRAITS OF COMMANDING OFFICERS, - - - | 203 |
| A DEMAND FOR SURRENDER, - - - - - | 219 |
| THE DEFIANCE, - - - - - - | 220 |
| GEN. CORSE AT ALLATOONA, - - - - - | 223 |
| UNION TROOPS DESTROYING RAILROAD, - - | 229 |
| ON THE MARCH, - - - - - - - | 243 |
| THE BUMMER, - - - - - - | 261 |
| MAKING CORDUROY ROAD, - - - - - | 279 |
| A REAL CAMP FIRE, - - - - - | 295 |
| AUTOGRAPH CIPHER DESPATCH, - - - - | 303 |
| A HUNGRY PARTY, - - - - - - | 315 |
| LAYING PONTOONS, - - - - - - | 335 |
| WADING THE SALKEHATCHIE, - - - - | 363 |
| BEFORE COLUMBIA, - - - - - - | 383 |
| REFUGEE TRAIN, - - - - - - | 403 |
| PORTRAIT AND AUTOGRAPH OF GEN. ANDERSON, - - | 417 |
| ACTION AT BENTONVILLE, - - - - - | 429 |
| HALT ON THE MARCH, - - - - - - | 451 |
| PORTRAITS OF DIVISION COMMANDERS, - - - | 467 |

2

Cherishes a true love for the men
who fought the Civil War to a
a successful Conclusion. and that I
wish them one and all the largest
measure of honor and happiness
on this Earth. I want all my old
Soldiers to retain the love they had
for "Uncle Billy"

Truly yrs.

W. T. Sherman

# Marching Through Georgia.

## CHAPTER I.

### THE DRUMMER-BOY.

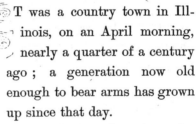

IT was a country town in Illinois, on an April morning,
nearly a quarter of a century
ago ; a generation now old
enough to bear arms has grown
up since that day.

Following close upon the
news of the firing on the
flag, a public meeting had
been held in the old brick
church, which also served as a school house ; and a
civil engineer, who had figured in the militia service,
delivered a lecture on " Fortifications," sketching upon
the blackboard the outlines of Fort Sumter, and noting
the position of the attacking batteries, as nearly as it
was possible to locate them by the published reports.
Newspapers were not so enterprising then, and dia-
grams and maps did not accompany their narratives.
The speaker was a quiet man, and his slow and meas-

ured speech, delivered with a foreign accent, and abounding in technical terms understood by but a few, fell upon the audience with depressing effect. The people cared nothing for science — their hearts were full of sentiment. They had expected an appeal to their patriotism, and a leader to direct them in the path of service for country, but they were disappointed and left in uncertainty. A day or two afterward, President Lincoln issued his proclamation calling for seventy-five thousand volunteers — how immense the number seemed then ! — and public sentiment began to crystallize.

R-r-r-r-r-r !

Right merrily the Drummer-Boy rattled away, as if his very life depended upon the effort. His little frame shook with excitement, and his eye sparkled as if his most ardent ambition were now realized. As he plied the drumsticks he kept up a running fire of remarks, addressed to the excited youths who stood about him, or in answer to questions, never losing a stroke or missing a beat the while.

" Yes, you bet I'm going ; an' so's Dan Messick, and Tom Johnson, and Watts Towse, and Johnny Rice, an' all the boys that's wuth shucks ! Why, we kin git up a whole company right here ; an' Palmer, he knows Lincoln, an' he kin git us them short rifles with swords on the end, like Major Burke brought home from Harper's Ferry. An' bein' volunteers, we kin drill as we please, and 'lect our own officers, and 't ain't like reg'ler soldierin' at all. Why, I seen Ellsworth's Zoo-zoos drill last summer, and you kin bet they do it nice ! That's the kind of drill we want ! And 't won't take so long to learn it, 'cause most of the boys was in the marching companies 'fore 'lection, and they got so's they could march good enough for anything, and they handled their torchsticks first-rate, but I reckon there's some difference between them and guns. But all you boys come up to the court-house to-night, and Palmer'll tell us all about it ! "

God bless the little Drummer-Boy ! The favorite design for soldiers' monuments throughout the country, seems to be the figure of the perfect soldier, fully armed and equipped, his whole bearing bespeaking the hardy veteran of many hard-fought battles and wearisome campaigns. More suggestive, and more completely typical of the aroused patriotism and enthusiasm of a people, and of their capability for putting sentiment into action, would be that of the Drummer-Boy.

When the flag was assailed, and all that it represents was put in jeopardy, the inspiring rat-a-tat-tat of his drum was heard in every village and at every cross-road ; and the young farmers from the fields, the apprentices from the shops, and the lads from the school-houses, fell in behind him and marched into

camp.   He was the youngest and smallest of them all,
but for the time he was the most conspicuous.   His
own rank was not high, but all rank sprang from him.
It took one hundred men to make a captain, a thousand
to make a colonel, and five thousand to make a general ; but the Drummer-Boy made them all.

In camp he had it all his own way, and he made the
most of his opportunities.   He began at five o'clock in
the morning, and the men were obliged to obey the
call, and appear in line in various stages of dress and
undress, to respond to roll-call.   Then he dragged
them out to the wearisome guard-mounting, and later
marked time for them at squad drill, company drill
and battalion drill.   Towards evening he summoned
them to the color-line for dress-parade, a perfunc-
tory ceremonial regarded with great contempt by
volunteers, as an amusement which should be left
entirely to holiday soldiers.   At nightfall he interrupted the seductive game of euchre, and dispersed
the gathering at the deceptive chuck-a-luck table, calling the men to their quarters to answer to another
roll-call.   Then, perhaps, in the middle of the night,
when all were wrapped in slumber, dreaming sweet
dreams of home, which they called, but not irrev-
erently, "God's Country," he would beat the long
roll, and bring them out into the darkness and storm,
sometimes to meet the enemy, but more frequently to
resist a charge of stampeded mules from the wagon

train. In all these persecutions he had firm allies in
the captain and colonel, who would put on extra duty,
or buck and gag, any who failed to respond to all
these irksome calls.

But there were occasions when the Drummer-Boy
performed a service in which all honored him. What
comrade does not remember the long marches, when
the soldier, overloaded with gun, knapsack, and what
all, with rations scant and water scarce, trudged along
the dreary road, until the limbs were weary and the
spirit broken; disgusted with the service, with his comrade and with himself; cursing the " Confederacy " and
his own government in one and the same breath. Then
it was that the Drummer-Boy, as weary and worn as
the soldier in the ranks, tightened up his snares, put
energy into his little tired frame, and rattled merrily
away. How the sound stirred the sluggish blood in
every vein! How it braced up every muscle! What a
mighty shout went up from the lips of the men, and
with what hearty determination did they push forward
on their way!

Then how all missed him during the long months
from Chattanooga to Atlanta, when the army was constantly in action, or seeking unsuspected points of
advantage by swift and secretive marches, and he was
forbidden to play lest his drum should give information to the enemy, and attract too much of their attention. And when the end of the campaign came at last,

and Sherman told the anxious friends at home, "Atlanta is ours, and fairly won!" and the drums and fifes and brass bands again broke the dreary stillness with their exultant strains, how all voices rose and swelled, and drowned out all other sounds! And again, when the men had exhausted themselves with shouting, how glorious was the harmony of martial music to their ears! What would have been the victory without it?

Recall that magnificent panorama in May of 1865, when, at the close of the war, two hundred thousand men of the Army of the Union marched in triumphal procession down Pennsylvania avenue, in the national capital. What would this have been without the drummer? A grand pantomime — a pageant without a soul—a picture without color—a flash of lightning without the thunder peal. It might have awakened admiration, but never enthusiasm. It might have dazzled the eye, but it could never have fired the heart.

Nor was the Drummer-Boy merely a musician. He was a soldier as well. Technically known as a noncombatant, he was seldom elsewhere than at the front; and he has given up his life, musket in hand, in the line of battle, or in the act of giving water to a wounded comrade under fire.

But what has been his reward?

Nearly a quarter of a century has gone by since

the vast Army of the Union sprang into being. A
generation has grown up since it fulfilled its mission,
and its returning heroes resumed the garb and duties
of every-day life. Year by year, old soldiers have
been wont to assemble to renew the friendships of
years agone. These gatherings have been prolific of
orators, and at each meeting eloquent addresses have
been made by speakers of all grades, from that of
Major General up to High Private—the latter rank
higher now, because, alas! there are so few of them!—
telling of scenes of battle and victory and death. The
exploits of all arms of the service, infantry, cavalry
and artillery, have been dwelt upon; and there have
been many descriptions of the achievements of some
individual command, to whose particular effort the
successful issue of the war has been shown to be due.
The mothers, wives, sisters and sweethearts of the
soldiers, have been lovingly remembered and grate-
fully eulogized for sending to their dear ones at the
front the delicacies they so often failed to receive
—no fault of the fair donors, God bless them! The
chaplains have received due recognition for lifting up
the voice of supplication on the right side of the question, and interpreting scripture to the confounding of
the enemy. Sometimes a quartermaster has distinguished himself by coming to the front—he was not
often credited with such performances in war-days
—in vindication of his own calling, and to whitewash

the character of that much misunderstood branch of the service, the government mule. Occasionally a sutler steps forward and lays claim to a little cheap credit—a commodity for which he charged the boys very high, when in the heyday of his glory; and in one instance an army surgeon has even been known to lay claim to honor for valuable assistance in putting down the rebellion, by putting down the throats of the soldiers a great deal of quinine mixed with a very little whisky (the panacea for every ill in the early days), and furnishing them unlimited quantities of blue ointment.

But amid all this jubilation, the most significant figure of war-days has been overlooked—the Drummer-Boy, the real recruiting sergeant for the Armies of the Union!

## CHAPTER II.

### THE SCHOOL OF THE SOLDIER.

OOK here, sonny! You'd just as well go right back home! Uncle Sam wants *soldiers*, he does, and has no use for *boys!* The mustering officer says recruits must be eighteen years old, five feet four inches high, weigh at least one hundred and twenty - five pounds, and be free from all physical defect. You are only seventeen; you are two inches too short, and you don't weigh enough by thirty pounds. Even if you were mustered in, you couldn't carry a knapsack, and your gun would be so long that you couldn't load it. You take good advice. Go home on the first train, sonny, and let *men* attend to this business!"

The speaker was the elder of a number of young men sitting on the bank of Clear Lake, near Springfield, Illinois. They had followed the Drummer-Boy into camp from the town before mentioned, and not yet

having been received into the service, were still clad in
the garb they had brought from home.   The majority
were young farmers; the speaker whose dogmatic utter-
ance is quoted, was a school teacher, and the one he
addressed so contemptuously was an undersized lad
who had but lately been promoted from the position of
printer's "devil" to that of compositor at the case.

About these men, gathered school, workshop and
farm companions, until the requisite number for a
company was made up, and all were presented to the
medical officer for examination.   Every man was
intensely patriotic, and it was with much misgiving
that he stripped himself, opened his mouth to show his
teeth, and passed under the measuring standard, fearing lest he should be rejected and sent home, there to
become the scorn and laughing-stock of his neighbors.
All but two passed the dreaded ordeal successfully, and
the company was mustered into the service of the
United States.   Among the successful candidates was
the printer-boy, but to preserve the truth of history it
is necessary to explain that he was obliged to muster
in as a musician, the regulations for the enlistment of
such being less proscriptive than for the ranks.   This,
however, was by private arrangement with the colonel;
and a few days afterward, the lad, who had never
handled either drum or fife, was, at his own request,
"reduced to the ranks," and took his place in the line,

at the tail-end of his company, the shortest man therein, or in the regiment, for that matter.

Now the education of the soldier began. As a sentinel on camp-guard he was armed with a club, there being a scarcity of arms ; and so solemnly was he impressed with the importance of his duties, and the penalty for any sin of omission, that when, as occasionally happened, he went to sleep on post, he felt as one risen from the dead, upon learning that he was not to be shot *this time*, but merely put in the guard-house, or bucked and gagged. He was carefully instructed in the salutes due to officers, and so religiously did he endeavor to discharge these important requirements, that on one occasion, when corporal of the guard, he turned out his entire force to present arms to a hospital steward, whose gaudy chevrons he, in his ignorance, took to be at least the insignia of a brigadier-general. He was drilled from the rising of the sun to the going down of the same, and when he moved himself clumsily he was relegated to the " awkward squad." This, perhaps, was in charge of a corporal who, at home, had been a green farm boy, and the butt of his boyish pranks ; and when he resented what he conceived to be the overbearing conduct of this petty officer, clothed with a little, so little, brief authority, and expressed himself, in language disallowed by polite society, and forbidden by the " articles of war," he learned how vast a difference had been built up between the two by a pair of worsted stripes. Perhaps the lesson was a difficult one to master, and the young soldier revolved it in his mind for a couple of days while engaged in the pleasant recreation of grubbing out an immense stump, with a guard standing over him, armed with musket and bayonet. At another time he would be tempted to mutiny and desertion, when, being detailed for "fatigue," he found that duty to be cleaning up in front of the tent of the captain, who, at home, was a carpenter or painter.

At a later day he struggled with the dreadful task of crowding into his knapsack a supply of clothing, and a general assortment of notions, almost sufficient to stock a cross-roads store. There were an extra pair of pants; two changes of under-clothing; several pairs of home-made socks ; a "house-wife" with its wealth of pins, needles, thread and buttons, put up by sister ; a Bible from his mother ; a portfolio with writing material ; a bottle of extract of ginger, or cholera cure, for use in case water  proved to be unwholesome ; a water-filter ; a patriotic song-book, and a " Manual for the Soldier;" a box of collars and a couple of cravats ; and finally, a "boiled shirt " or two. Then, more awful mystery yet, came the packing of the great-coat to the upper outside of the knapsack. To roll it so that it could be kept within reasonable compass, and not exceed the capacity of the straps which were to confine it, was an accomplishment but few mastered. However, it was not long before the poor fellow learned that he had no use for such an assortment of goods, or, at any rate, had not the disposition to transport them. So, little by little, the great packs were reduced ; the owner gazing ruefully upon the treasures with which he parted so reluctantly from time to time.

Then the soldier was overjoyed when the time came to draw arms. Heretofore there were in the camp but a few old-fashioned flint-lock muskets of the time of the Mexican war. These had been committed to the care of a few smart fellows who were members of militia companies before the war, and who, as " drill-masters," now displayed their dexterity in the manual of arms and bayonet drill, before gaping crowds of unarmed warriors on the parade-ground. But now the recruit had a gun of his own, and was at last a full-fledged soldier. It little mattered that the weapon was a clumsy old " Belgian," thrown away as useless by its petty crowned owner in Europe ; or an old government musket altered from a flint-lock ; it was a gun, and the soldier asked no questions. He learned to curse it before long, however, for he found that its destructive power was rather in his own direction than in that of the enemy.

The recruit was now completely armed and equipped, and he was ordered to take his place in the ranks for inspection and review. It was one of

the hottest days of midsummer, and, what with the
heat and the paraphernalia he carried, comprising all
the weapons and supplies drawn from the ordnance
officer and quartermaster, the ordeal was a severe one.
He was marched in column, by platoon and company front, at common time, quick time, and double
quick.   Finally, the pace was increased to a run,
which continued for nearly an hour, and the recruit,
all but exhausted, put forth his best efforts, fearing
that in case he failed in this final test, he would be
ignominiously discharged from service.

Perhaps the most astounding revelation of all to
the young soldier was the fact that he was actually to
be paid for his services.   Never to be forgotten is the
day when it was first announced that a real paymaster
would come into camp and count out to each man
twenty-two dollars for two months' time.   In his
ignorance and patriotic zeal, the recruit had never
anticipated anything of this nature.   To serve his
country was his sole ambition, and the approval of his
own conscience, and the plaudits of his friends, would
be an all-satisfying reward.   When he had been actually paid, he looked upon his money as something to
be gotten rid of as speedily as possible; he felt that to
hoard it would be to give opportunity for reflections
upon his patriotism.   Hence he at once sought out the
sutler, and soon exhausted his little fortune, paying a

dollar for a can of blackberries, twenty-five cents for a very ordinary cranberry-pie, and for other articles at the same rate. Thereafter he was frequently in debt to this despoiler, and pay-day never again came often enough.

# CHAPTER III.

### THE FIRST DEAD.

HORTLY after the capture of Fort Henry, General Grant ordered a reconnaissance up the Tennessee river, to develop the enemy's new line. The wooden gunboats "Tyler" and "Lexington" were dispatched for this duty, and upon the former was embarked the company referred to in the preceding chapter, while a companion company from the same regiment took passage on the latter.

It was a pleasurable excursion for men long accustomed to the irksome routine of camp duties, and wearisome marchings through swamps and brakes. The skies were bright, the atmosphere clear and invigorating. The shore on either side was putting on the verdant beauty of field and wood; and the fresh spring breezes were laden with the odors of fragrant flower and shrub. It was in the last days of February, and the surroundings were novel to those accustomed to the bleak winters of an Illinois prairie; so that, in spite of their loyalty to their own loved home, and their determination to see nothing admirable in Dixie, their spirits broke out with joyous exuberance, while their patriotism was stimulated by the cheers and benedictions of those, native to the soil, who flocked to the river's edge to look upon the flag of their country. A pathetic poem was printed in *Harper's Weekly* shortly afterward, depicting such a scene:

\* \* \* \* \* \* \* \*

> "And the south wind fondly lingers
>   'Mid the veteran's silvery hair;
> Still the bondsman, close beside him,
>   Stands behind the old arm-chair,
> With his dark hued hand uplifted,
>   Shading eyes, he bends to see
> Where the woodland, boldly jutting,
>   Turns aside the Tennessee.
>
> "Thus he watches cloud-born shadows
>   Glide from tree to mountain crest,
> Softly creeping, aye and ever,
>   To the river's yielding breast.
> Ha! above the foliage yonder,
>   Something flutters, wild and free!
> 'Massa! Massa! Hallelujah!
>   The flag's come back to Tennessee!'"

\* \* \* \* \* \* \* \*

Among those who came to the river's bank to greet the flag, were many young men seeking to escape the neighborhood sentiment, or practical conscription, which sought to drive them into the service of the "Confederacy." Several of these enlisted in Company "C"; and in one instance sixty patriotic young Tennesseeans, clad in their native butternut garb, and armed with their sporting shot-guns and rifles, came in a body, and were mustered into the national army.

The days passed merrily away, and where all were in the happiest mood, Dan Messick, orderly sergeant of Company "C," was the happiest and merriest of all. A compactly built young man of about nineteen years, with a full round face, and an eye which twinkled with humor, or if necessary flashed in command, he was one whom his comrades not only respected, but loved. But his career, begun with so much promise, was soon brought to a mournful end.

The vessels steamed up river, at times slowing their speed in order to examine the shores at points where an enemy might lurk. At Clifton they stopped to load a transport with wheat and flour from a mill operated for the Confederate army; and at Chickasaw Bluffs a midnight sally was made upon a party of rebel officers, who were merry-making at a farm-house near the river, and they were brought away as prisoners.

Having passed Savannah, the heights just north of Pittsburg Landing came into view about ten o'clock on the morning of March 1st. The troops were not aware that the commander of the gunboat had been

THE FIRST DEAD.

See page 39

informed by well-disposed citizens that the enemy was engaged in fortifying this position, with a view to again closing the stream so recently opened by the downfall of Fort Henry; and as field-glasses were not included in the equipment of private soldiers, they detected nothing suspicious. A few minutes later they had cause for wonderment when the engines slowed down, the wheels revolving just sufficiently to hold the vessel nearly motionless against the current. At the same moment the commander of the gunboat, Lieutenant-Commander Gwin, in complete uniform, with his sword by his side, appeared upon the bridge. His glass was fixed intently upon the heights, as if he expected trouble, and every eye followed the direction of his gaze, but without being any the wiser.

Presently a puff of smoke rose from the heights, then a heavy ball flew over the "Tyler" and splashed the water astern. The gunboat at once opened with her heaviest guns, 68-pounders, which were in her bow, firing shell at first, then grape-shot, steaming meanwhile nearer the battery. The "Lexington," somewhat farther down stream, opened fire a few minutes later. The enemy answered briskly, but without effect, for a short time, and then abandoned their guns.

Pittsburg Landing, which had been concealed behind the heavily wooded bluffs, now came into view, a mere landing place for steamboats, with a log-house upon the summit of the short and rather steep hill which rose from the water's edge. Infantry and cavalry were in sight. The latter were stampeded by a few well directed shots from a 24-pounder howitzer upon the "Tyler's" upper deck; but the infantry continued to deliver an effective fire, crippling three gunners, and leaving upon the vessel's sides, pilot-house and chimneys, marks which she bore to the close of the war.

The gunboats were well abreast of the landing, maintaining only sufficient headway to resist the current. Meanwhile, Messick counted off fifteen files from the right of Company "C," and they were ordered into the yawls, which by this time had been lowered to the water. Under cover of the fire of the gunboats, and of the muskets of the soldiers left aboard, the boats pushed off to the shore. The first to spring to land was Messick. A portion of Company "K," from the "Lexington," joined the party, and all advanced up the hill, the gunboats meanwhile being necessarily silent. Then the little band, not fifty men in all, reached the summit, and the enemy, occupying the timber which fringed the clearing on all but the river side, opened a fierce fire, which was handsomely returned. "Load as quick as you can, and give them the devil!" yelled the captain, himself a native Tennesseean, and the boys dashed past the log-house toward the timber, which secreted the enemy, firing as they went. The captain was partially disabled by a

bullet in his leg, but continued in command. Seeing
the folly of rushing upon a superior force, so well
posted, he ordered the men to fall back to the log-
house, from whose windows, and the spaces between
the logs, a fire could be maintained without great
exposure. Messick was some paces in advance of the
house, and presented a most conspicuous mark. He
wore his first sergeant's bright red sash, not around
his waist, as was usual, but over the shoulder and
across the breast, after the fashion of an officer-of-the-
day. He was seen to load his piece, take deliberate
aim and fire, and then turn partially about to reload,
when a ball struck him in the head, and he fell at full
length, dead. An effort was made by some of the men
to reach the body and drag it behind the house, but
the enemy's fire was too fierce to permit it. At this
moment it was discovered that the enemy's cavalry,
taking advantage of the silence of the gunboats, were
endeavoring to interpose between the little detachment
and the landing, and a retreat was ordered. One of
the men, while on the way to the boats, managed to
pick up a new Enfield rifle, lost by the enemy, a rare
weapon in those early days, when the Union troops
could boast nothing better than the old altered flint-
lock firing "buck and ball." Another made the
possession of a snare drum inscribed with the words,
" Captured from the Yankees at Manassas." A third,
descending the hill in great haste, unfortunately thrust

the point of his gun into the ground, and found himself propelled into the river, with no other injury than a thorough ducking. As the soldiers pulled off in their boats, the enemy followed them to the brow of the hill and poured down a fierce fire, to which the gunboats and troops aboard made hot reply.

March 2d and 3d, the gunboats, with the troops yet on board, passed and repassed the landing repeatedly, firing shell at intervals, but eliciting no reply. On the 4th, an officer and a party of soldiers landed under a flag of truce. They found that the enemy had withdrawn the guns from the earthworks commanding the river, and retired toward Corinth.

This was the first chapter of the campaign culminating in the fall of Corinth. The expedition had been eminently successful. It had prevented the fortifying of the bluffs at Pittsburg Landing, the most formidable defensive point on the river. Ten days later, General Grant's army arrived and made an unmolested landing.

March 15th, Company " C" found eighteen graves to certify to the skirmish fought two weeks earlier. The burials had been made so hastily that the toes of the dead protruded through the ground. Seventeen of the bodies were those of the enemy, the other was that of Messick. A sorrowful moment it was for the little company, mostly beardless youths, as they stood around the grave of their first dead, one whom they had loved so well, and for whose future they had cherished such lofty anticipations. He was a gallant soldier and a true comrade, born to command, with a spirit of dash and enthusiasm which inspired his fellows, and a boyish warm-heartedness which won the love and confidence of all. He was one who may be held up as a fit type of the American Volunteer whose shadowy image is honored and mourned in so many homes; and this weak tribute to his memory may be justly dedicated to the aged parents throughout the land, whose lives have never ceased to be embittered from such a death:

> " The old man desolate,
> Weeping and wailing sore
> For his son who is no more!"

# CHAPTER IV.

## THE GROWTH OF A REGIMENT.

HE company mentioned in the preceding chapter was part of a regiment which, in after days of battle and march, acquitted itself neither better nor worse than any one of a thousand others, drawn from the various States of the loyal North.

At the beginning, the regiment regarded itself as a most formidable organization, equal to almost any undertaking. If so required, it would undoubtedly have essayed the invasion of the seceded States, alone and unaided. But its colonel, who had held a subaltern's position in the Black-Hawk affair, which by a poetic license had been dignified with the title of "War," determined to make his command absolutely invincible; and he secured from the War Department special authority to recruit and add to it a battery of artillery, and a company of cavalry. These were secured, and, in the light of a later experience, it is comical to look back at that complex regiment on parade, with its ten companies of infantry, and artillery and cavalry on either flank, all making vain endeavors to obey the commands laid down in the blue-book for one arm of the service alone. The absurdity of the combination was soon apparent, and before entering upon active service the organization was broken up, the cavalry and artillery being sent to join appropriate bodies of their own kind, and the infantry put upon proper footing as an actual regiment.

The regiment lay at Bird's Point, Missouri, opposite Cairo, Illinois, during part of the winter of 1861–2. It was one of the few comprising General Grant's little Army of the Tennessee in the beginning, the force being divided between Cairo, Bird's Point, Missouri, and Fort Holt, Kentucky. Headquarters were at the first-named place, from which, before the coming of General Grant, emanated military orders with the somewhat pompous preamble, "Headquarters, Grand Cairo and Dependencies."

At a later day the regiment assisted in the investment of Fort Henry, and a portion of it took an unimportant and almost bloodless part at Fort Donelson, while other detachments made expeditions into the interior and up the Tennessee river.

Then came the ascent of the Tennessee river, already opened up by the engagement described in

the foregoing chapter. This was one of the finest
pageants of the war. The thirty-five thousand men
comprising the army of invasion were embarked upon
sixty transports, led by the gunboats. The fleet displayed bunting in profusion ; and with many of the
regiments were brass bands, whose music echoed from
shore to shore. Several of the boats were provided
with calliopes, and their patriotic melodies, softened
by distance, sounded enchantingly. As far as the eye
could reach, up stream and down, rounding bends and
threading their way among miniature islands, the long
line of vessels stretched away, a magnificent panorama
ever in motion.

March 16th, General Sherman's division disembarked at Pittsburg Landing, followed the next day
by General Hurlbut's. The regiment of which this
narrative treats, was a part of the latter command.
Original journal entries show that camp discipline was
rigidly enforced. Company and battalion drills and
dress-parades were invariably performed each day.
There was reason enough for this, not only in a military sense, but for the moral effect. Illness increased
rapidly among the troops, caused by unwholesome
water. For nearly all complaints the surgeons had one
sovereign panacea, whisky and quinine, prepared at the
hospital tent by the barrelful, and administered with a
tin cup. Unfortunately for those who had a taste for

the liquor, it was so unsparingly drugged that its use as a beverage was impossible.

March 29th, a new camp was laid out, one mile farther south. Camp-guards surrounded each regiment, and a picket was posted, but no works constructed. On the 31st, General Hurlbut reviewed his division for the first time, preparatory to a review by General Grant on April 2d. April 4th, a heavy rain began to fall, continuing all night and part of the 5th. About eight o'clock on the night of the former day, scattering firing was heard to the front, and the regiment, with others, was sent in that direction. A march of five miles was made, and the troops were ordered back to camp without encountering an enemy or learning the cause of the alarm. This was two days before the battle of Shiloh, and rebel prisoners taken in that engagement said that the Union forces that night marched inside their lines, and might have been captured, but for fear of causing an alarm.

Sunday morning, April 6th, a beautiful spring day, the troops were preparing breakfast, when sounds of conflict came from the right front. The battle of Shiloh had begun !

A few moments later, the long roll sounded, and the troops went into ranks on their color-line, and soon marched in the direction of the firing. At the side of the road they passed Colonel Pugh, of the 41st Illinois regiment, a gallant old white-haired man who had seen service in Mexico. There was a remarkable squeak in his voice, and no one who heard his words that morning will ever forget their forceful meaning or peculiar intonation : " Boys ! fill your canteens! Some of you 'll be in hell before night, and need water ! "

Farther up the road, the troops meet the stragglers from the front, some wounded, and all terror-stricken. Brave encouragement they give to men going into battle : " It's no use, boys ! We 're all cut to pieces ! "

On presses the column. At a turn in the road it changes direction to the right. In a fence-corner the surgeons have established their field hospital, and here are spread out their operating tables, and a glittering array of knives and saws, exposed to the sight of raw troops. It is horribly suggestive. No wonder many turn pale, or that the lad, who at home was an innocent Sabbath-school scholar, should take from his pocket a pack of playing cards and throw them away. He has perhaps a superstitious feeling that such property may bring him ill luck ; besides, if he is to be killed, he does not care to have his mother hear that he has fallen into habits she would not countenance.

Here is a gap in the rail-fence, and the column passes through, and forms in line of battle in an orchard of young peach trees. Other regiments connect with it, right and left. A battery of artillery gallops up on either flank and unlimbers. That on the left opens fire with great vigor upon the enemy, now plainly in sight; that on the right stampedes without firing a gun—the cannoneers cut the traces, mount their horses, and gallop wildly to the rear.

In front, and on the extreme edge of a field which lies beyond the orchard, is a dense forest, occupied by the enemy. The troops march bravely toward it. The colonel sees that he is not strong enough to carry the position, and he orders " About face." The men march rearward in line of battle. Here and there the line bulges; the men are gradually quickening their pace; there is every provocation for a stampede. The commander orders " Steady ! " and the gallant fellows set their teeth hard, and, with muskets at shoulder, regain the accustomed drill step. " Battalion, halt ! About face ! Lie down, and no firing without orders!" The regiment has not fired a gun, but it has received severe punishment. Its retrograde movement, under fire, is a magnificent exhibition of pluck for raw troops.

The enemy's batteries have now opened. They fire solid shot, which strike the ground a couple of hundred yards in advance, and reach the troops in ricochetting. Admirable range the gray-coated artillerists have ! A small tree near by, not thicker than a stovepipe, is bruised with the marks of five cannon-balls within the height of a man. A cannon shot knocks out the corner-post of a shed, letting fall the roof, and with it a squad of venturesome fellows who have climbed up to witness the panorama in front. Now the enemy fires shell and grape-shot. One of the iron missiles tears a cruel groove in the skull of a color-guard. Another knocks off the muzzle of a lad's gun as he is capping it for another shot. He completes the operation, and discharges his weapon, but when he brings it again to his side, he finds that he can not squeeze his cartridge-ball into the ragged muzzle. "Don't that beat the devil!" is his exclamation to his commander. The next moment he has another gun, which has been thrown away by a comrade, who flees in mortal terror, only to die in two days, not from a hurt, but from simple fright!

Now out of the forest in front marches the gray line of battle. On it comes, without a break in its ranks. The Union troops open upon it a terrific fire, each man loading and discharging his gun as rapidly as possible. The gray line cannot withstand the storm of leaden hail — it loses its pace, halts, and then recoils. Three times it attempts to pass over that dreadful field of death, and as often does it fall to pieces, and hasten back to shelter in broken fragments. More than a score of years afterward a rebel captain who was in the charge confessed to a soldier who opposed him that day, that the slaughter in the peach-orchard was the most horrible action in which he was engaged during the entire war.

Our regiment is now shifted to the left of the Corinth road, and engages the enemy at short pistol-range. The ground is broken and densely wooded—it is not far from the famous "Hornets' Nest." The fire on either side is horrible. The thick underbrush is literally mowed down by bullets. Men are shot in half-a-dozen places at once. The dead lie where they fall; the wounded drag themselves below the brow of the hill for protection from further harm. The ammunition is nearly exhausted. Where are the field-boxes of cartridges? Fatal blunder! there are none where they are most sorely needed. Here and there the soldiers drop behind the hill and take from the cartridge-boxes of the dead and wounded what ammunition is left, and resume their places in the line, only to repeat the act, again and again. So intent are they upon their errand, that one lad does not recognize the close friend and comrade whom he despoils. Twenty years afterward the two meet to talk of the battle, and the former learns, for the first time, whose form it was he bent over in that hour of desperate effort.

This is the key to the position of the Union army, and here the enemy makes his most heroic effort. A Tennessee brigade is broken under the terrible fire it encounters; one of its regiments rallies and advances three times, only to fall back again and again. Har-

4

ris, the Governor of Tennessee, appeals to his troops to make a final effort, and save the fair name of their State.   General Albert Sidney Johnston, the idol of the Confederates, now places himself at their head— leads them to the assault, and is mortally wounded.

In this valley of death the regiment loses more than one-half of the men who went into action.   Little wonder that, with a line so thinned out, in a dense wood, a young soldier, on his return to the front from a search for cartridges, thinks himself deserted, and takes his way to the rear.   At the head of the ravine the old colonel hails him :   " Where are you going ? "   " To find the regiment ! "   " Well, go to the front !   All that are left are there ! "   " All right, sir !   I thought they were all gone ! " and the lad again goes into action.

Every cartridge at last is gone !   "Fix bayonets!" is the command of the colonel.   But the left is crushed, and the enemy comes with a wild, surging charge from that flank, firing as they advance.   Every field officer is killed or disabled, the brave old colonel falling last of all, with a ball which he carries to this day.   There is little semblance of organization now, and the men seek the rear as best they can.   There are scores of regiments in the same plight, and the last hour of the day is given to seeking their own members, and reforming, to hold the lines that night, and prepare for a fresh struggle on the morrow.

The troops are without either food or water, and
their thirst is aggravated by the salty taste of the cartridges they have been biting all day.   Neither have
they tents nor blankets, for the enemy has possession of their camp.   Then the rain begins to fall, and
the men draw their gun-locks under their coat-skirts,
and sit up against the trees, seeking to shelter themselves as best they can.   All night long the earth shakes
with the concussion of the great guns on the gunboats,
and the explosion of their shells in the enemy's lines.
But neither army cares for a night engagement, and
the hostile lines confront each other in comparative
silence.   In the morning the Union troops advance
and sweep the enemy from the field, the fresh men of
Buell's army taking a glorious part in the victorious
onset.

For some days after the battle, this regiment was
firmly of the opinion that it had sustained the fiercest of
the enemy's assaults on that terrible Sunday; and that
the blunder of some other troops was the cause
of the temporary disaster.   But the men soon came to
learn the important truth, that in this, as in nearly all
conflicts between armed men, each portion of the line
has all it can attend to, and its best effort and most
fearful sacrifice, are equally necessary, no more and
no less, to a successful issue.

The siege of Corinth followed, a most wearisome
and exhausting campaign.   General Halleck was now

in command, and the troops were literally worn out with the excessive duty put upon them. Six weeks were consumed in passing over the thirty miles between Pittsburg Landing and Corinth. At every advance, earthworks, strong enough for permanent fortifications, were thrown up, with abattis in front. The discipline was more severe than ever before. No soldier was permitted to visit another regiment. The reveille sounded at five o'clock in the morning. From six to seven the troops were drilled at double-quick without arms. Squad and company drill lasted from ten to eleven; battalion drill from two to four; and dress-parade took place at four o'clock. By the casualties of the battle, the exposure, and labor during the siege, a company of ninety men, who left Illinois less than a year before, was reduced to twenty-three effectives, and this proportion probably existed throughout the army.

There was constant skirmishing, but no severe action, during the siege of Corinth, and the city fell into the hands of the Union troops, May 28th. The retreating enemy was followed a few miles, the army being then recalled and posted along the railroad between Corinth and Memphis, making frequent wearisome, and generally profitless, marches into Mississippi, pursuing or pursued. The battle of Hatchie River was an incident of this campaign. It was fought by General Hurlbut's division, which intercepted the forces of

Price and Van Dorn, after their repulse at Corinth in October, 1862.

The efficiency of the army had been greatly improved by the withdrawal of the old muskets. For these were substituted Enfield and Springfield rifled muskets, both admirable weapons. About the same time the complete "regulation" uniform was issued. This consisted of a ridiculous dress-coat of dark blue, with brass shoulder-scales; a tall, stiff felt hat, looped up on one side with a brass eagle, while in front was displayed a brass bugle. A feather and heavy blue cord completed the head-dress. The men had a great contempt for this assortment of military millinery, and exhibited a remarkable faculty for losing all the ornaments, which were not readily replaced; the hat crown they persisted in turning down to about one-third its normal height. The officers finally recognized the impossibility of maintaining such a uniform, and the troops soon took up with the comfortable blouse and fatigue cap, which were their distinguishing marks during the later years of the war.

During the marches in Tennessee and Mississippi, in the summer of 1862, large numbers of negroes flocked to the army. The Emancipation Proclamation had not yet been penned, and all these poor people were driven back to their masters, save a few able-bodied men (sixty to a regiment), whose use was permitted as teamsters and cooks. The slaves imagined that the coming of this army meant their liberation from bondage. Men, women and children followed the troops for miles, carrying knapsacks and bringing water for the weary soldiers. Their distress on being repulsed was pitiful to behold. At this time foraging was strictly forbidden, and severe punishment awaited the hungry soldier who entered a field for potatoes, or shot a pig. It was the day of the "rose-water war policy," so mercilessly ridiculed by Orpheus C. Kerr.

In September, 1862, the first great blow was struck against slavery, and the discipline of the army was put to its crucial test. President Lincoln had issued his cautionary proclamation, setting forth that, on the first day of January following, in the event of still existing rebellion, he would proclaim the freedom of the slaves. The majority of the troops were not in sympathy with this measure, and there was every prospect of wide-spread desertion. In many instances commissioned officers did not attempt to conceal from the men their own opposition, and expressed the intention of resigning. In this crisis, Colonel Logan, of the 32nd Illinois regiment, took a decided stand. He caused the proclamation to be read at the head of his command, and said that any officer tendering his resignation for this reason, or expressing disaffection, would be reported, with a recommendation for his dishonorable dismissal for insubordina-

THE PEACH ORCHARD AT SHILOH.

See page 47.

tion and disloyalty. The effect of this determined
action was most salutary. Not a resignation was
offered, and the brewing storm passed away. Other
commanders were equally patriotic, many in spite of
personal convictions ; there was no further open disaffection in the army.

In the winter, occurred the march through Mississippi, the intention being to reach the rear of Vicksburg. The campaign was brought to an abrupt close
by the disaster at Holly Springs. That important supply depot was yielded to the enemy, by its commander,
without firing a shot.

A few months later, the regiment was a part of
the army engaged in the operations against Vicksburg,
being under fire almost daily for three months. The
incidents of the siege would require a volume in
themselves. The bombardment at night by the gunboats and mortars was indescribably grand. The
labors of the army were arduous, but there was less
work with the spade than at Corinth. The troops
learned that slighter works were sufficient protection,
and they husbanded their strength for the skirmish
line. The Union army made some advance almost
every night, and frequent dashes by day. The end
came, July 4th, 1863, when the enemy displayed the
signal of surrender. It was not long before the
national colors were unfurled from many points in the
city ; and the fleet of gunboats steamed up to the

wharf, each vessel firing a national salute as she rounded to. The next day a large part of the Army of the Tennessee marched out to Jackson, and defeated General Joseph E. Johnston, who was threatening the Union rear, returning afterward to Vicksburg.

The remainder of the year was devoted to expeditions into Louisiana and the interior of Mississippi, which, while important in the general plans of the war, are not necessary to this narrative.

Now began preparations for the campaign against Atlanta. The army was in magnificent trim for the task. True, it had lost many a gallant soldier, who, if living, would have done yet greater service for his country, and won honorable distinction for himself. Alas, such are the fortunes of war ! Aside from this, campaigning had proved a severe school, and it yielded admirable results. It was a most thorough winnowing process. The sickly and infirm had been retired from service ; the half-hearted had dropped by the wayside ; the coward and camp-bully, generally synonymous terms, had deserted. The company mentioned in the opening chapter will serve to illustrate the casualties incident to these campaigns. Its ninety men at the outset had been reduced to thirty-five when the Atlanta campaign began. Anticipating the narrative, it may be mentioned that but twenty-six of the number marched out of Atlanta to the Sea. Only sixteen remained to the end, to be mustered out with the colors

at the close of the war ; and among these was the lad
who was bade go home, because he would never make
a soldier.  He participated in all the campaigns of
the Army of the Tennessee, from first to last, without
a wound, a day in hospital, or absence on sick leave.

Such was the history of one regiment.  Its experience was not peculiar ; with little exception, it
was that of most volunteer regiments in the field.

# CHAPTER V.

### THE ARMY AND ITS PERSONNEL.

HATTANOOGA, Tennessee, within the shadow of famous old Lookout Mountain, was the scene of extraordinary bustle and preparation during the month of April, 1864. Forces were being concentrated and equipped for what was destined to be one of the most brilliant and successful campaigns of the war, if, indeed, it did not surpass all others in brilliancy of conception, completeness of execution, and thoroughness of results. It was directed against Atlanta, and out of it grew the important, but frolicsome, march to Savannah, and the campaign of the Carolinas. So closely did these events succeed one another, and so intimately blended were their consequences, that the March to the Sea may be said to have begun at Chattanooga, and to have ended with General Joseph E. Johnston's surrender to General Sherman at Raleigh, North Carolina. These operations covered a period of twelve months, during which time almost every day was spent in marching or fighting, and frequently both. There were many severe battles, and at all times sharp skirmishing, sometimes here, sometimes there, and often along the entire line. But it was ever a grand " Forward ! " from first to last.

The troops selected for these important undertakings were the choicest of the nation, the veterans of the campaigns narrated. Many of them having nearly completed a three years' term of service, re-enlisted, and were designated by the War Department as " Veteran Volunteers," and authorized to wear the chevrons indicative of long and arduous service. They were just returning from home, after enjoying a brief furlough, granted in consideration of their re-enlistment. Every man was a seasoned veteran, toughened by exposure, and taught self-reliance through the workings of that first law of nature, self-preservation. His bearing proclaimed a high degree of pride in his soldierly record, a conscientious belief in his mission, and an unfaltering faith in the successful issue of his cause. He was not only a perfect soldier himself, but he was a schoolmaster to the raw recruits brought to the front from time to time to replace the fallen and disabled, who, taught by his example, learned the full duty of soldiers in vastly less time than he had acquired it, and became almost veterans by his side, before the campaign had fairly opened.

The largest body of troops was the Army of the Cumberland, the heroes of Stone River and other hard fought fields, commanded by Major-General George H. Thomas, a grand soldier, whose every feature proclaimed him to be as unyieldingly steadfast as the "Rock of Chickamauga," which name he bore. His own distinguishing characteristics were reproduced in his men, and their superb staying power, and capacity for giving and taking severe punishment, were appreciated by Sherman, who always sent them to hold an enemy while others sought his weak point. The Army of the Ohio, under Major-General Schofield, with many of the same traits, performed a similar mission in conjunction with it. Last, was the Army of the Tennessee, fresh from the victories of Vicksburg and Jackson, and the relief of the beleaguered garrison at Chattanooga—trained to long and rapid marches, swift in motion and as true to its mark as the arrow, which was the distinguishing badge of one of its corps. This command, as Sherman expressed it, was the "snapper to his whip-lash;" and it was thrown from flank to flank as necessity required, marching often by night to attack the enemy at an unexpected point by day. It was commanded by Major-General James B.

McPherson, one of the bravest who ever wore a sword, though as gentle and lovable as a woman.

Subordinate to these officers was a brilliant array of corps, division, and brigade commanders. Among the former were Logan, Blair, Dodge, Howard and Palmer; among the latter, Belknap, Gresham, the Smiths, Leggett, Mower, Force, Phillips, Rowett and others. Auxiliary to these forces, and principally engaged in protecting provision trains and covering the flanks of the army, but at times making rapid and destructive raids upon the enemy's communications, were large bodies of cavalry, commanded by Stoneman, Garrard and Kilpatrick.

In supreme command was Major-General William T. Sherman, the most unique figure of the war period. Spare of form, and careless in dress, he would have found difficulty in securing a position on a brigadier's staff in the early days of 1861, when gay trappings commanded a premium, and dress-parades and grand reviews passed for " war." But when he spoke he revealed his extraordinary mental powers and wealth of nervous energy. Whether ordering a movement of troops to meet an unexpected contingency, or listening to a report of disaster or success, he instantly comprehended the full import of the event; and, equal to any emergency, gave his commands with snappish promptness, and at the same time so explicitly that there could be no mistake as to his meaning. In some quarters he

had been censured for not being a "fighting general;"
he treated the sneer with a smile. " Fighting is the
least part of a general's work, the battle will fight itself," he said, on one occasion. To him the actual
conflict was an incident, which he knew could be trusted to the courage and ability of the officer actually
upon the spot. Not that he was wanting in the quali-
fications of a general ; he possessed them in the
highest degree, his mind constantly grappling with
great general plans. His men once in position, where
he wanted them, and there were those to direct the
battle, who had naught else to do.

General Sherman had won great renown as General
Grant's chief lieutenant at Vicksburg, and in relieving the Union army beleagured in Chattanooga.
History tells how competent he was for the chief
command in the great task now set before him ; but
no one, not with him, can realize how completely he was master of his forces and resources. Not a
detail was unknown to him. With wonderful direct-
ness and promptitude, he ordered the movements of
this vast army, at times separated into numerous
columns and detachments, all acting independently,
so far as they themselves knew, yet all co-oper-
ating in the grand plan of their chief. Like Grant,
he was a rare judge of men, and he was seldom
mistaken in his estimate. The weak points of this
brigade commander, the strong points of another, were

ever in his mind. He knew the various posts along
his railroad communications, hundreds of miles to the
rear, and their commanders. If the telegraph told
him that a block-house was attacked, he knew whether
the officer in charge would surrender to a cavalry dash,
or resist a division of infantry with artillery. He
knew, at all times during a campaign, just how many
rations and rounds of ammunition there were in his
wagon trains ; how his men were in health and spirit;
and the condition of the feet of his cavalry and artillery horses. With all this intimate knowledge of
officers, men and means, and an army having unbounded confidence in itself and in him, Sherman was
absolutely invincible.

Yet a little more than two years before this, he
had been semi-officially denounced as a " crank "
(although this precise term was not then in vogue),
and considered unfit for the command of more than a
brigade, because, at a moment in the first year of the
war, when some one high in authority prophesied
an end of the struggle " in sixty days," he insisted
that two hundred thousand men would be needed to
occupy Kentucky, and carry on offensive operations!
But this was not far from the number Fate had now
committed to his charge, to work out the greatest
problem of the day—the annihilation of the war-
supporting resources of the " Confederacy," and the

transfer of his army to the battle fields of the East, to co-operate with Grant in the destruction of Lee.

And more ! He was to write his own name high among those of the great masters of war ; and to plan campaigns that would be models for study by generations of soldiers yet unborn. His strategy was marvelous, and he found a worthy adversary in General Joseph E. Johnston, the opposing commander. Move succeeded move, like rook and pawn on the chess-board, one giving a check here, the other there. Sherman maneuvered so as to gain position after position with the minimum loss of men and material; Johnston retreated so skillfully before him that he scarcely lost a tin-cup. That the one should achieve victory where the other sought to withhold it, is high praise. No other such struggle of Titans was witnessed during the war.

As a writer, General Sherman was in many respects inimitable, and were he not a soldier he should have been an author. His orders, reports and letters, were often couched in homely but vigorous phrase, somewhat after the manner of Lincoln, emphasizing his points in such manner as to fasten them indelibly upon the mind. Once, while preparing for the great campaign, he said : " Beef and salt are all that is absolutely necessary to life, and parched corn once fed General Jackson's army on this very ground." Citizens, at various places along the line of his march, clamored to be fed; and the kind-hearted Lincoln urged Sherman to supply their necessities. He answered : " The railroad can not supply the army and the people too. One or the other must quit, and the army don't intend to do so, unless Jo. Johnston makes us. Let their friends relieve them by wagon, as they would before railroads were built." The enemy having endeavored to wreck railroad trains by planting torpedoes on the track, he wrote to a subordinate : " Order the point suspected to be tested by a car-load of prisoners or citizens implicated; of course an enemy can not complain of his own traps." Newspaper correspondents were a special abomination in his eyes, provoking him to great wrath, and spasmodic profanity of a highly original pattern. " They are," said he, " as a rule mischievous. They are the world's gossips ; they pick up and retail camp scandal, and gradually drift to the headquarters of some general who finds it easier to make reputation at home than with his troops. They are also tempted to prophesy events, and state facts, which reveal to an enemy a purpose in time to guard against it." The present editor of a great newspaper in the Mississippi valley, then a correspondent with the army, incurred the personal displeasure of the irascible General at, or immediately after, the battle of Shiloh, and was treated by him in such a manner as never to be forgiven ; even to this day the outraged scribe allows no opportunity to pass without giving the General a sharp rap in partial payment of the old score.

Since the war, if it be possible, General Sherman has grown even more completely into the affections of those he once commanded in the field; and his appearance at any of the numerous soldiers' reunions calls forth greater enthusiasm than that of any other general of the war period. This is largely due to his unaffected heartiness, when among those who wore the blue in the dark days of the Rebellion. He is the most approachable of men, as accessible to the private soldier as to the major-general; and his intercourse with all, whether in private, or upon public occasions, is such as to impress all with his entire honesty when he said, in a letter to the author of this narrative: "I cherish a real love for the men who fought the civil war to a successful conclusion, and I wish them, one and all, the largest measure of honor and happiness on this earth."

# CHAPTER VI.

## MAKING READY.

HE column about to move southward from Chattanooga was to consist of nearly one hundred thousand men, and the plan of campaign contemplated a frequent departure from the railroad, and dependence upon the wagon trains for subsistence. The army was to be re-clothed as far as possible, and these stores, together with food and ammunition for infantry, cavalry and artillery, and forage for animals, in sufficient quantities for a thirty days' supply, were all to be sent from Louisville, Kentucky, the base of supplies, nearly four hundred miles distant, over a single pair of rails traversing a hostile region. Although the road was guarded by several thousand men, posted along its length, in forts, stockades or block-houses, at towns, rivers, and water and wood stations, the enemy often made serious breaks, destroying scores of engines, hundreds of cars, and burning or carrying away vast quantities of stores, which were greatly needed at the front. At its ordinary capacity, when undisturbed, the railroad could do little more than provide for the necessities of the army.

To accumulate supplies for a forward movement, in the face of such difficulties, demanded close economy and extraordinary effort. All items of the army ration which could possibly be dispensed with, were stricken out, little being transported save hard bread, bacon, sugar, coffee and salt. Beef was driven from Louisville on the hoof. Only the most necessary articles of clothing were issued. Shoes and stockings, absolutely indispensable to the march, were provided in abundance ; little attention was given to supplying outer garments; the men were generally willing to wear the same coats and trousers they had brought with them from Vicksburg. True, in many cases, these dilapidated articles exposed more of the human anatomy than they concealed, but their wearers did not expect to see company which would be fastidious about such things. Many of the line officers were scarcely more presentable than their men, and with them partook of the same limited fare.

But supplies failed to accumulate. Cutting red tape with a stroke of his pen, Sherman ordered all railroad cars reaching Louisville, from whatever direction, to be loaded with supplies and sent to the front;

and in spite of the angry protests of railroad officials all over the country, his order was obeyed to the letter. Henceforth, trains on the "United States Military Railroad" were motley enough, and it may be said, without exaggeration, that in many of them there were not more than three cars belonging to any one road, and nearly all came from north of the Ohio river.

A few passenger cars were run as far south as Nashville, but none beyond that point; and an officer or soldier seeking his command at the front was obliged, on leaving Nashville, to find a place on the top of a freight car, as a member of the armed guard which accompanied each train. He was frequently fired at by guerrillas from behind trees and hills, and often his train was thrown from the track, by some obstruction or a displaced rail, and he was attacked at a great disadvantage by a considerable force of the enemy. But this route, rough as it was, was one of pure delight compared with the dirt-road assigned to most of those returning from home or hospital. The latter were organized into temporary companies or detachments, and obliged to drive and guard beef herds, or wagon trains, until they reached their destination.

Notwithstanding the difficulty of securing railroad transportation, and the urgent necessity requiring it entirely for military purposes, sanitary and christian commissions and volunteer philanthropists from every

State having a soldier in the field, sought the freedom of the road, only to be denied by the lynx-eyed Sherman. One of these well-meaning functionaries complained to his governor that the great general had treated him with discourtesy. The governor appealed to Stanton, Secretary of War, who lectured Sherman, whereupon the indignant general retorted in this characteristic way : "Even a single passenger is a small matter, but he is two hundred pounds avoirdupois, and his weight in bread and meat would feed one hundred men for a day. For mercy's sake allow us for the period of our brief campaign to have the exclusive use of our single track of rail, every foot of which we must guard, and every inch of which has cost us a precious life."

And this slender artery of life, upon which depended the very existence of a hundred thousand men, and perhaps that of the nation itself, was soon to be indefinitely extended, to keep pace with the army pressing southward, every additional mile costing more lives, adding to the risk of breakage by the enemy, and diminishing the moving column to the extent of the detachments left behind for its protection. Important bridges and strategic points were guarded by veteran troops, posted in earthworks with artillery; but for the greater part the defenses were block-houses and stockades, garrisoned by "short term" men enlisted for the purpose. It was a service of vast importance, but monotonous and inglorious, and the rudely painted sign displayed at each of these minor posts, addressed to passing trains, "Please throw us a paper!" told a pathetic story of loneliness and anxiety. In many cases these little garrisons were fiercely attacked and made gallant and successful resistance. The heroic defense of Allatoona, referred to hereafter at length, is almost as famous as the "Charge of the Light Brigade"—it was certainly far more momentous in its results.

The Railway Construction and Repair Corps, made up of civilians, was an all-important ally. Large detachments were stationed at suitable points, and dispatched to each break in the road as soon as one occurred. As a matter of fact, this corps was perpetually in motion. So thoroughly was it equipped, and so zealously did it push the work, that the enemy frequently heard the engine whistle at the front, within a few hours after they had inflicted damage which they believed could not be repaired in a week. Duplicates of bridges and important trestles were kept in reserve to replace those destroyed, each timber being numbered and fitted ready to put in place. Some of this work was almost marvelous. But the grandest achievement of the corps was the replacement of the bridges over the Chattahoochee, Etowah and Oostanaula, which had been destroyed by the retreating enemy. These structures, being within the enemy's lines, could not be dupli-

cated from the store-house, and most of the timber
had to be cut out of the forest, on either side of the
streams.   They were from six to twelve hundred feet
long, and from eighty to one hundred feet high, yet
they were replaced in two to five days.   The moral
effect was marvelous.   The Union troops were led
to believe that their communication with home could
never be interrupted, save for a few hours at a time ;
while the enemy was fully convinced that Sherman and his men were all but omnipotent, and that
destructive measures were of little avail to arrest their
progress.   Indeed, there was a story in those days to
the effect that Johnston had determined to blow up
an important railroad tunnel in order to stop the
invaders, whereupon one of his men remarked, " There
is n't no use in that, 'cause Sherman carries 'long
duplicates of all the tunnels ! "

Not less important was the service rendered by the
Telegraph Corps, also made up of civilians, and under
the charge of Colonel J. C. Van Duzer, who was designated "Superintendent of United States Military
Telegraphs."   Colonel Van Duzer was an operator
at Carlinville, Illinois, early in 1861, and, on that
dreadful April morning, gave to the people of that
place information of the first firing upon the flag at
Sumter.   He was accomplished in his profession ;
and a genial, whole-souled man.

At every fort and block-house was stationed one

ON THE SKIRMISH LINE.

See page 107.

or more of Colonel Van Duzer's corps. Each operator had for his equipment a navy revolver, and a miniature pocket "sounder," which frequently served a good purpose. At times, he was driven out of his office by a dash of rebel cavalry, or, perhaps, an infantry force seeking a lodgment upon the railroad. He usually made his escape, and the first thing he did, after bidding a hasty good-bye to his assailants, was to climb a telegraph pole, attach his pocket instrument, and notify General Sherman at the front, of the number and designs of the enemy, and the direction in which they had gone. Rarely did the rebels learn anything of importance from this trusty servant. He dealt in a cipher code, which was unintelligible save to the initiated, and even this was frequently changed.

Another important adjunct was the Signal Corps. Its members were chosen from officers and men of the army, with a special view to intelligence, daring and adaptability. Each detachment carried a white flag bearing a black square, colors recognizable at a great distance ; and signals were conveyed by certain movements to right and left, vertical and horizontal, indicating different letters of the alphabet. The letters signaled stood for other letters, so that a cipher code was necessary to the interpretation of a message, and the key was changed at frequent intervals. The officer in command of each detachment carried powerful field-glasses, and also a fine portable telescope, in order to distinguish signals at a great distance. The Signal Corps always sought the most conspicuous eminences, whence they could overlook a large scope of country, and detect the movements of the enemy; and frequently they erected a temporary observatory in the top of a tree, in full view, and within easy range, of the hostile riflemen. Some of their deeds were of momentous importance, as at Kenesaw Mountain, after the fall of Atlanta, when Sherman signalled to Allatoona, and encouraged its gallant little garrison to protract its resistance to Hood's desperate assault, until reinforcements could reach it. This service of the Signal Corps was fraught with great personal danger, as when, before Atlanta, on the memorable 22d of July, the observing officers held their position in a tree almost on the very line of battle.

With each column marched a Pioneer Corps, whose position was as near the advance as was safe, and which rendered invaluable service in repairing roads and bridges. As it traveled, it "blazed" its way on trees by the roadside, that troops following might make no mistake as to direction. Each army corps had its own peculiar "blaze," which was so familiar to all, that a straggler knew at a glance whether he was following Logan, or Blair, or Palmer, although there might not be a soldier or wagon in sight.

Each army corps had a distinguishing badge, the

color — red, white, blue, or yellow — indicating the
divisions. The badge was worn by the men upon coat
or hat ; and it was inscribed upon the wagons of the
supply and ammunition trains. Some of these emblems were peculiarly suggestive of the traits of the
commands to which they belonged ; as the " Arrow,"
worn by the Seventeenth Corps, noted for its rapid movements, and sureness in reaching a place when wanted ;
the " Cartridge-Box " of the Fifteenth Corps, famous
for its fighting qualities, and capacity for making
itself heard ; and the " Acorn " of the Fourteenth
Corps, which stood firm in action as the oak before the
storm. Less significant were the " Star " of the Twentieth Corps, the " Cross " of the Sixteenth, and others.

It was this complete system of organization, this
close attention to seemingly small matters, in very
many particulars peculiar to it alone, that raised this
army to so high a degree of efficiency, and gave to its
chief such a wonderful mastery over it. Well might
he say, as already quoted in these pages, " The least
part of a general's work is to fight a battle."

Napoleon once remarked that he had overrun
Europe with the bivouac. Sherman had caught the
same inspiration. Wagon trains were cut down to the
smallest possible number of wheels and animals.
Early in war days each company was provided with a
six-mule wagon, and three were considered necessary
for regimental headquarters. Even then, when a

movement was ordered, it became necessary to abandon much camp paraphernalia because of insufficient transportation. The cutting down process had been going on gradually, until now but one wagon was allowed to a regiment, and that for ammunition mainly, regimental officers being only permitted space enough for a tent-fly, a small mess-kit, and a few light valises; and this species of property was always the first to be abandoned, if it became necessary to lighten the load, on account of broken-down animals or unusually bad roads. A pack-mule for carrying cooking utensils was permitted to each company, but was often dispensed with.

Each army corps, of fifteen to twenty thousand men, had a commissary and ammunition train of about five hundred wagons. The various headquarters were provided with one or two tents each, to shelter the general and staff, Sherman himself setting the example. He was closely imitated, save by General Thomas, who took with him so large a headquarter train, that it went by the name of "Pap Thomas' Circus."

The "lightening of the army" involved a grim contradiction of terms. The number of animals was lessened, and their burdens decreased, but additional loads were put upon the troops. The endurance of the man surpassed that of the beast. General Sherman estimated that the soldiers of each *corps d'armee* carried upon their persons the equivalent of three hundred wagon loads; but this estimate includes arms and personal effects which would not be transported for the troops in any event. The men became almost pack-horses, and, encumbered as they were, their long and rapid marches were nothing short of marvelous. Each man carried his gun and accoutrements, forty rounds of ammunition in his cartridge-box, and one hundred and sixty more in his pockets, knapsack, or haversack. His blanket and light rubber blanket were made into a long roll, the ends tied together, so as to admit of being carried upon the shoulder. This roll generally contained an extra shirt, a pair of socks, and a half-section of a "dog-tent," or piece of light ducking, which, when buttoned to the half carried by a comrade, made a very fair shelter for two men. Occasionally a soldier carried an extra pair of pants or an overcoat, but this evidence of extravagance was regarded with contempt by most of the men. Knapsacks were often discarded entirely. The provision issued to the soldier was a much abridged ration, but it brought up the total weight of his burden to good thirty pounds, or more, no light load to carry for days at a time, in all weather, and over all kinds of road. He habitually had a three days' supply of hard bread and fat pork, and this was to last from seven to ten days in case of necessity.

But if Uncle Sam limited the boys as to their bread and meat, he more than made it good with his lavish

6

issues of sugar and coffee. And here let it be recorded, that coffee accomplished more toward suppressing the rebellion than any other one article, unless it be gunpowder itself. It was generous in quantity, beyond reproach as to quality, and "the boys" knew how to extract its subtlest virtues. Each one carried an old oyster can in which, after bruising the fragrant berry upon a stone, with the butt of his musket, he brewed the delicious beverage—the *summum bonum* of human comfort, the panacea for all ills. Black as the face of a plantation negro, "strong enough to float an iron wedge," and innocent of lacteal adulteration, it gave strength to the weary and heavy laden, and courage to the despondent and sick at heart. The withdrawal of the coffee ration would have moved the army homeward a great deal sooner than could Johnston or Hood. In fact, a dastardly experiment on the part of a soulless contractor almost provoked a great mutiny at one time.

It was when Halleck's army lay in front of Corinth, in 1862. For about two weeks there was issued to the troops, in lieu of the coffee berry, an extract which purported to be essence of coffee, compounded with sugar and milk. It came in half-gallon tin cans, and so much resembled patent wagon grease that it went by that name. A teaspoonful, stirred into a tin cup of hot water, was supposed to produce first-class home coffee, but taste and stomach revolted against the

villainous compound; and the pale air was streaked
with oaths of the most ornate and florid phraseology,
abounding in the most picturesque imagery of the
hadean future of the patentee and contractor, their
heirs, administrators and assigns forever. The commissary department never had the temerity to attempt
another issue of the vile stuff.

The troops were now ready to move out of Chattanooga. "The pomp and circumstance of glorious
war" were to be left behind with the sick, the
tents, and the surplus baggage. The army was at its
fighting weight, stripped to the buff, ready and
willing to give and take hard knocks. Henceforth,
for twelve months to come, until the end of the war,
there were to be no daily drills or parades, except for
a few days after the capture of Atlanta, and again at
Savannah. The drum and fife were seldom to be
heard, and the army marched and fought its way to
the Sea and to Grant, to the prompt and stirring summons of the bugle.

# CHAPTER VII.

## EN AVANT.

USING the language of General Grant, "heretofore the armies in the East and West had acted independently and without concert, like a balky team, no two ever pulling together."

General Grant had lately been transferred to the East as General-in-Chief, and General Sherman had succeeded to the supreme command in the West. Both were thorough soldiers; they were also intimate friends, rejoicing in each other's successes, and not only willing but glad to be so placed as to co-operate. They used the telegraph freely, and maintained a voluminous private correspondence, exchanging views with reference to the movements of the armies, East and West, suggesting means to this or that end, and each conforming his course to that of the other. In short, complete confidence and concert of action existed, and the war was carried on, from Chattanooga to Virginia, with a definite plan.

May 4th, 1864, General Grant crossed the Rapidan, moving toward Richmond; and, twelve hours later, General Sherman put his army in motion in the direction of Atlanta. Each was fully determined to furnish so much employment to the enemy in his front that no forces could be spared by either to confront the other.

Sherman's army numbered ninety-three thousand men for battle. Against him, Johnston had at the outset sixty thousand effectives, which number was shortly to be increased to seventy thousand. The latter army, being upon the defensive, and operating on interior lines, was by all rules of war more than equal to its assailant. This ratio was substantially maintained during the campaign ending with the fall of Atlanta; hence it will be seen that the federals had no material advantage over the enemy.

General Sherman's first step was the occupation of Dalton, naturally a strong point, and a railroad junction of great importance to the enemy. The direct route was impracticable. It lay through the pass known as Buzzard Roost, cleft by nature through Rocky Face, a formidable spur of the Alleghany range of mountains. The Army of the Cumberland, under General Thomas, occupied the northern entrance to the pass, supported by the Twenty-third Corps under General Schofield; while the Army of the Tennessee, under General McPherson, began that series of flanking movements for which it was soon to become famous. McPherson's line of march lay southward to Snake Creek Gap, which gave an easy access to Resaca, to the south of Dalton, occupied by the enemy under General Johnston. This movement was begun in excellent order, McPherson passing through Snake Creek Gap without difficulty, only meeting, at the farther end, a cavalry force, which was easily dispersed. On arriving in front of Resaca, however, he found the works so complete and well manned that he doubted his ability to take them by assault, and he fell back to Snake Creek Gap. Sherman was greatly disappointed, and used the only harsh language he ever uttered toward McPherson, who was, indeed, his most trusted lieutenant. He said: "Such an opportunity does not occur twice in a single life, but at the critical moment McPherson appears to have been a little timid. He could have captured half of Johnston's army, and all his artillery and wagons." At the same time he robbed his censure of much of its sharpness by saying that McPherson was perfectly justified by his orders.

Meanwhile, Thomas and Schofield fought Johnston hard at Rocky Face, until the failure of McPherson's movement upon Resaca was known, when Sherman ordered a concentration of his army upon the latter point. As soon as this became known to Johnston he abandoned Dalton, and both armies faced each other at Resaca.

The strength of the enemy's position here, and the nature of their works, proved to be all that McPherson had asserted, and the entire army found serious employment for some days. The enemy's line was developed May 14th, and the next day was a continuous engagement, more or less severe, along the entire line, the Army of the Tennessee taking the brunt of the work, and gaining a heavily fortified ridge from which it might reach, with its guns, the railroad bridge across the Oostanaula river. The enemy made repeated and desperate attempts to dislodge McPherson, but without success. That night Johnston abandoned Resaca.

From all over the South came a fierce howl of rage on account of this disaster, and Johnston was censured so severely that at a later day he thought proper to vindicate himself, in language which is a fine tribute to the army which opposed him. "My own operations," he said, "were determined by the relative forces of the armies, and a higher estimate of the Northern soldiers than our Southern editors and politicians were accustomed to express, or even the administration seemed to entertain. Observation of almost twenty years of service had impressed on my mind the belief that the soldiers of the regular army of the United States, almost all Northern men, were equal in fighting qualities to any that had been formed in the wars of Great Britain and France. General Sherman's troops, with whom we were contending, had received a longer training in war than any of those with whom I had served in former times.  It was not to be supposed that such troops, under a sagacious and resolute leader, and covered by entrenchments, were to be beaten by greatly inferior numbers."

Johnston, however, so far heeded the clamor as to issue a general order, promising to give battle at Cassville; and his troops, as was discerned from the utterances of prisoners, were constantly taught that they were not retreating because the fortune of war was going against them, but because their general was only drawing the enemy on to certain destruction.

On the 17th, General Johnston went into position at Adairsville, but the Army of the Cumberland pressed him closely in front, while the Army of the Tennessee threatened him seriously on one flank, and that of the Ohio on the other.  He therefore decided to retreat to Cassville, where he entrenched heavily, and issued to his troops orders for battle.  He failed to make a stand, however, and, on the 20th, retreated farther southward.

General Johnston always considered the abandonment of Cassville as suicidal, but fixed the responsibility upon Generals Hood and Polk, who maintained that their position would be enfiladed by the federal artillery, and that they would be unable to hold it. General Johnston says of this :  "Although the

position was the best we had occupied, I at last
yielded, in the belief that the confidence of the commanders of two of the three corps of the army, of their
inability to resist the enemy, would inevitably be com-
municated to their troops and produce that inability."
An angry discussion grew out of this affair, and many
statements have been made on either side, General
Hood in particular entering a bitter denial. In face
of these conflicting statements, it is extremely difficult
to arrive at the truth.

Upon abandoning Cassville, the enemy retreated
across the Etowah river, burning the railroad bridge
behind him, although immediately and hotly pursued.
Here Sherman halted his army for a brief time, for
much needed rest, as well as to enable the Construction
Corps to repair the railroad, and give opportunity for
reloading the provision trains, which were well nigh
exhausted.

Meanwhile, a division under General Jeff. C. Davis
made a rapid movement upon Rome, Georgia, somewhat to the right and rear, and entered that place after
a brisk engagement, in which he lost about one hundred and fifty men. This success not only relieved
the principal column from constant threat, but it also
made an easy pathway for General Frank P. Blair,
who was marching from the Tennessee river with two
divisions of the Seventeenth Corps, returning from
" veteran furlough."

Allatoona was the next obstruction, and a most formidable one. General Sherman determined to avoid it by a movement to the right, and on the 23d, General Thomas moved his command toward Dallas, taking twenty days' rations in haversack and wagon. He had approached near New Hope Church, when he found that the enemy had abandoned Allatoona and was again in his front. A sharp engagement ensued, in which the enemy was driven some little distance, to the vicinity of the church, where he entrenched, and Generals McPherson and Schofield were called to close up with the remainder of General Sherman's army, then in line. In this movement General McPherson was sharply attacked in the vicinity of Dallas, but his men, by brisk work, had succeeded in throwing up slight fortifications, and repulsed the enemy, inflicting considerable loss. Some days afterward General Sherman occupied Ackworth, again reaching the railroad, and the Construction Corps was set to work rebuilding the bridge over the Etowah.

During the month, since leaving Chattanooga, Sherman had driven the enemy nearly a hundred miles, fought six battles, captured twelve guns and two thousand prisoners, and killed and wounded fifteen thousand of the enemy. His own loss in killed and wounded was about ten thousand men.

## CHAPTER VIII.

### AN INCIDENTAL FORCED MARCH.

HE main army was joined at Ackworth by General Frank P. Blair, with the Third and Fourth divisions of the Seventeenth Corps. General Sherman had been loath to leave Chattanooga before the arrival of these troops, who had been home on the thirty days' veteran furlough granted to all soldiers re-enlisting for another term of three years. They could not be assembled in time, however, and he had been obliged to begin the campaign without them. They were now greatly needed to make up for the losses thus far; besides, General Sherman's intimate acquaintance with them, dating back to the early days on the Tennessee river, led him to depend upon them in an unusual degree.

General Blair's command had rendezvoused at Cairo, and was to be transported by boat to Clifton, on the Tennessee river, thence marching across the country by way of Huntsville, Alabama. There were some

curious incidents connected with this march. General
Blair, a gallant officer, was noted for strong self-
assertion, and a disposition to make this trait.quite
conspicuous when he happened to be in a position
where he could do so. Notwithstanding urgent and
repeated orders from General Sherman to hurry his
command to the front, he tarried at Cairo, taking
things quite easily. Possibly he had some excuse for
dilatoriness. The transports were under the control of
a high officer of the quartermaster-general's department, clothed with extraordinary powers by the Secretary of War, who was not disposed to regard the
emergency as sufficient to call for any unusual effort.
Nearly all the steamboats chartered by the government were engaged between Cairo and ports on the
lower Mississippi, and the diversion of any of them
to a trip up the Tennessee seemed to him too unimportant an undertaking to engage in.

At this juncture, Colonel John I. Rinaker, of the
122d Illinois Regiment, commanding the post of Cairo,
received telegrams from General Sherman, enquiring
as to the whereabouts of General Blair's command,
and directing him to take any measures necessary to
expedite its departure, if it had not already gone.
Colonel Rinaker at once issued orders for the seizure
of any boats coming into port, and it happened that
the first to arrive were fast side-wheel steamers,
engaged in general trade on the lower Mississippi.

The officers of the vessels entered loud objections, appealing to the quartermaster in charge of river transportation, who directed them to pay no attention to Colonel Rinaker's orders, suggesting that other and smaller boats would soon arrive, which would answer the purpose as well. Even this assurance was a great concession, but Rinaker refused to release the boats, and General Gresham, who was extremely anxious to reach the front, at once embarked his brigade and proceeded up river, closely followed by the remainder of General Crocker's division and that of General Leggett. General Gresham, in particular, was highly pleased with Colonel Rinaker's action, and expressed his obligations to him in warm terms.

The march from Clifton was an exceedingly unpleasant experience. Thirty days of high living at home, feasted by mothers, wives, and sisters, upon all the enervating delicacies to which they had so long been strangers, together with balls and late suppers, had softened the muscles of the men, while their pampered appetites rebelled against short rations of coarse food. But there was urgent necessity for these troops at the front, and delay was not to be tolerated. The men did not understand the requirements of the case as did General Blair, who had been goaded almost to desperation by the sharp and frequent messages of General Sherman, bidding him push forward in the shortest possible time, and they swore horribly at their commander for the rapid pace to which he continually pushed them. Sixteen miles a day was the shortest march expected; as a matter of fact, more frequently from eighteen to twenty miles was the distance actually accomplished. This was no small task, loaded down as the men were with rations and ammunition; besides, the weather was extremely hot. During the greater part of the march, the column was annoyed by Roddy's rebel cavalry, which, while not sufficiently strong to do any great damage, was numerous and alert enough to keep the blood warm and cause great watchfulness.

May 26th, the troops reached Decatur, Alabama, on the Tennessee river, one of the most picturesque situations visited by the army during the entire war. Later in the day, a pontoon bridge was laid and they crossed to the east side.

Before reaching Rome, much of the route lay over a very mountainous region. Sand Mountain, a spur from the southern continuation of the range of which the famous Lookout Mountain is the most conspicuous member, was particularly dangerous. This was not a single peak, as the name would imply, but a succession of mountains, of no great altitude, yet very precipitous. In the sides of these, immediately overlooking an almost perpendicular descent of hundreds of feet, a roadway had been cut, so narrow as to furnish room for only one team. A sudden pitch

RESTORING COMMUNICATION with WASHINGTON

See page 104.

sidewise, or a rough jolt against one of the many huge bowlders which lay in the roadway, was sufficient to upset a wagon and send it tearing down the mountain side, end over end. Several such accidents actually occurred, but fortunately no human life was lost, the teamsters being fortunate enough to leave their saddles and reach a place of safety before the crash came. The passage of the train necessarily put a great deal of arduous labor upon the troops, and it was by no means unusual to see a squad of soldiers bolstering up a wagon, in order to keep the center of gravity within the limit of safety.

Considerable straggling from ranks occurred during the march, and severe measures were taken to repress it. In one instance, by the personal order of General Blair, and under his own eye, one of the offenders was "spread-eagled" at the tail-board of a wagon, his arms being extended, and his hands tied to either end of the gate, his face to the wagon. Unable to see through the vehicle, or look down at the road, his punishment was painful enough in the passage over the mountain, as he was jerked violently from side to side, with every motion of the wagon. When night came, the wagon pulled in to the place selected for General Blair's headquarters; and the general, recognizing his victim, and appreciating the fact that the breach of discipline had been sufficiently punished, ordered him to be cast loose, and provided a good

7

supper and a canteen of "commissary;" then dismissed him, with an injunction to remain in the ranks thereafter. The soldier accepted the liquor, if not the advice, as the *amende honorable*, and bore no malice.

Near Warrenton, Alabama, a country post-office yielded a large mail sent out from the rebel army, under General Bragg, in the September previous. The letters had been held at this place on account of the impossibility of forwarding them to their destination, and were sealed as when the writers sent them out. The Yankees, having no respect for the sanctity of such communications, distributed and opened them, the contents in many instances provoking great merriment. The following extract from one of these letters gives an inside view of the feeling, not only in the enemy's ranks, but at their homes as well:

" MERIDIAN, Sept. 23d, 1863.

" DEAR MOLLIE:      *      *      As I know you will hear nothing at Natchez favorable to our cause, I will give you all the particulars known so far in regard to our great victory. On the 18th, after several unsuccessful attempts, Bragg forced Rosecrans to battle near Ringgold, Georgia, which has continued up to the present time, and is still raging. Bragg has gained a great, glorious and crushing victory. Rosecrans destroyed Chattanooga yesterday, crossed the Tennessee river, and is flying towards Nashville, hotly and vigorously pursued by Bragg, with the noble army of veterans who have already thrashed him soundly, taking over six thousand prisoners, fifty-two pieces of artillery, and innumerable small arms, etc. Bragg will make his victory still more disastrous to 'the best government the world ever saw.' It is his intention to drive the enemy across the Ohio river before he stops. Where are now the beautiful Misses ——, who cursed Jeff Davis and the Southern Confederacy when Vicksburg fell? Also, those cowardly

sneaks who have given up all hope; the men who have treated the Yankees with such favor, and entertained them at their houses? Their
shameful conduct will never be forgotten. * * Expect me home in
about fifteen days. I think by that time you will all be once more free.
* * With much love, as ever, WILL."

Rain fell almost without intermission during the
latter part of the march, but shortly before reaching
the Coosa river the sun again shone out, and dried the
men's clothing upon their persons. The river, already
greatly swollen, was rising rapidly; and, as the pontoon train was almost hopelessly anchored in mud, far
in the rear, the troops were ordered to ford the
stream. Being averse to again marching in water-
soaked clothing, they removed their shoes, socks and
trousers, and strapped them upon their knapsacks;
then, tucking their shirts under their arm-pits, plunged
in, dressing themselves on gaining the farther shore.
An elderly woman, connected with the Sanitary Commission, who swam her horse across in time to witness the passage of the strange procession, remarked
that she had never seen anything like it before.

June 8th, General Blair's command reached Kingston, Georgia, and opened communication with the
main body of the army, which was some miles farther
south.

## CHAPTER IX.

### KENESAW MOUNTAIN.

YE never gazed upon a grander scene than that spread before the vision from the summit of Ackworth's rugged hill that bright June .day, more than twenty years ago. To front and rear, the valleys stretched away in wide expanse of field, and orchard, and grove. The air was laden with the incense of flower and fruit. Fleecy clouds floated athwart the blue expanse above, intercepting here and there the bright sunshine, and mottling the landscape with alternate patches of light and shadow, which chased each other from field to field, across hillock and stream.

Through this fine setting passed a magnificent panorama. Following the meanderings of numerous roads, hither and thither, to right and to left, up hill and down dale, in sunshine and in shadow, long lines of blue, tipped with shining steel, threaded their way.

Here, borne by a mounted orderly, a yellow guidon, inscribed with the familiar devices belonging to general headquarters, spoke the presence of the supreme chief and his staff. At intervals, similar banners emblazoned with arrow, or cartridge-box, or acorn, designated the places of corps commanders; others with these emblems in red, white, or blue, told of the presence of division and brigade generals, enabling the practiced eye to recognize and name each command as far as the devices could be discerned. Between and among these, behind and in front, as far as the eye could reach, floated countless national colors, each marking a regimental organization. So far did they lie below the point of observation on Ackworth, that regiments seemed to be but companies, and no sound came up from the mighty host. In rear of each division followed the artillery, the bright brass of the Napoleons alternating with the dull color of the steel Rodmans. And then, away in the background, rising and falling with hill and valley, outlined against the bright green of field and wood, or the clear blue sky, the long wagon train stretched out, the white canvas covers seeming, in the distance, like the sails of ships at sea.

Far to the front, bounding the entire southern horizon, rose majestic Kenesaw, "the Twin Mountain," and its adjacent peaks, as if planted there to stay the steps of the onward pressing hosts, bidding

them go thus far and no farther. But already, almost
at their very base, white puffs of smoke rose in defiance from the rifles of the federal advance; while high
overhead, at Ackworth, waved the tell-tale flags that
bore the directions of the great war-chief to the
troops opening the conflict.

June 10th, the army reached Big Shanty, a railroad
station lying almost at the foot of Kenesaw Mountain. It was already famous, having been the scene
of a remarkable occurrence early in 1862. In order
to break the Atlanta railroad and prevent the rebels
from reinforcing their army, opposing General Grant
at Shiloh, General Mitchell sent twenty picked men to
this place, then far in the interior of the "Confederacy." They went disguised, pursuing different roads,
and in accordance with their prearranged plan came
together at Big Shanty, then a rebel camp. Watching
an opportunity, they stole a light freight train, while
the crew were at dinner, and made off at the utmost
speed in the direction of Chattanooga. Their intention was to burn various large bridges after passing
over them ; but hot pursuit was made by another
train, and they were unable to accomplish their purpose. They soon consumed all the wood and water
aboard the tender, and found the engine otherwise
becoming useless, the brass journals having actually
melted in the wild run ; and, when near Chattanooga,
the daring fellows found themselves obliged to jump

from the engine and seek concealment in the woods. The enemy hunted them down, however, and hung several of their number. A thrilling account of this remarkable adventure has been recently written by one of the survivors, now a Methodist minister.

Near by, and towering grandly upward, rose Kenesaw, a formidable range, nearly three miles long. Known as "the Twin Mountain," it might be better described as a single eminence with a slight break or depression about one-third the distance from its northern end. To the northwest lay Pine Mountain, and to the south, Lost Mountain, two almost conical peaks, connected with Kenesaw and each other by heavily timbered ridges. It was the most perfect natural fortification Sherman's army ever encountered, and the enemy made the most of the advantages it afforded. Their line from Kenesaw to Pine Mountain was generally semi-circular, the concavity being presented to the Union troops. From base to peak, these everlasting hills bristled with batteries and swarmed with men. Their elevation gave them a bird's-eye view of the federal skirmish and battle lines, and their flags could be seen waving from peak to peak, signaling every movement of their assailants. While everything transpiring in the Union army was distinctly noted by them, their own movements were concealed by the heavy timber which veiled their lines. A partial compensation for this

was found in the fact that the federal signal officers
had deciphered the enemy's code, and could read
their flags almost as readily as they themselves.   Indeed, it was by means of these signals that General
Sherman learned of the death of Polk, the rebel
Bishop-General, a few days later.   It is not improbable, however, that the enemy was equally quick-
witted, and acquired much valuable information in a
similar way.

The enemy's line was soon developed by the federal skirmishers, those of Blair's Seventeenth Corps
occupying the left, near the north flank of Kenesaw;
Logan's Fifteenth Corps and Dodge's Sixteenth Corps
joining them on the right.   Then came Thomas, with
the Army of the Cumberland, in front of Pine Mountain, and the interval between that and Kenesaw.
Schofield lay under Lost Mountain.

Before the close of the day, the skirmish line was
feeling the enemy along his entire front of nearly ten
miles, while here and there a battery threw a few
experimental shells.

The next morning, a sunless, cheerless, drizzling
day, General Sherman rode to the front, with a single
staff officer and an orderly.   Dismounting, he seated
himself upon a fallen log near the railroad track.
Colonel Van Duzer had just taken from his pocket a
light piece of wire, scarcely larger than a horse hair.
This he spliced to the telegraph wire which dangled

from a pole near by, and attached it to his pocket-instrument, not larger than an ordinary snuff-box. Seating himself beside the general, he began tapping the delicate little key, the general dictating. A half-hour later, Van Duzer's ear was closely bent to the miniature sounder, and his lips moved as he gave Sherman the answering message. The latter made a gesture, expressive of satisfaction, then mounted his horse and rode away. A few moments afterward, Van Duzer told the writer that the general had reported satisfactory progress to headquarters at Washington, receiving in return an answer, expressing great satisfaction, and conveying warm congratulations.

Later in the day, a daring federal engineer ran his locomotive up the railroad immediately under Kenesaw, and drew the fire of the rebel batteries. He blew his whistle defiantly, and then backed away without injury, while the vast Union army cheered and cheered, until the hills of Georgia rang with the sound. It was terribly exasperating to the enemy, and their skirmish line opened a spiteful fire, which was as viciously returned, night alone putting an end to the noisy but comparatively harmless conflict.

## CHAPTER X.

### ON THE LINES.

P to this time, the entire army had been engaged with the enemy at no one time, and the actual fighting had covered a small front. At Kenesaw, Johnston made his first decided stand, obliging Sherman to bring into use all the means at his disposal. Here the whole army went into line of battle, shoulder to shoulder, and from the 10th of June until the fall of Atlanta, in September, nearly three months later, there was scarcely a day but every division, brigade and regiment was under fire. The line was not far from ten miles long, and a picture of a single day's experience of any one regiment would be a faithful portraiture of what was transpiring along the entire front of the army each and every day of those three eventful months, except upon occasions when the grand skirmish rose to the dignity of a general action. Not that all the troops were engaged in similar degree. At times a part of the army was occupied in desultory skirmishing, while near neighbors were seriously employed. Again, these conditions would be reversed. On the whole, the experiences of the various commands may be regarded as balancing fairly at the end of the campaign, honors and losses being impartially divided.

And now the thin Line of Blue, deployed as skirmishers, pushed the Line of Gray steadily backward against Kenesaw. It was man against man — equally courageous, equally self-reliant, equally fervent in his endeavor. Rarely did either see more than a half-dozen of his enemy, more frequently but one, often none at all, sometimes only able to locate his position by the puff of smoke from his rifle. Yet, Blue and Gray were but short rifle-range apart, and a movement of the line-of-battle, constantly in easy supporting distance on either side, would have brought more than one hundred thousand men into an almost hand to hand conflict, and unloosed the throats of nearly half a thousand pieces of artillery!

At times, the soldier in Blue made a dash forward, gaining a score of yards of ground; but generally he crept warily from tree to tree, or crawled upon the ground, availing himself of every little hillock or inequality, to take advantage of his adversary, who, whether advancing or retreating, was as wary as himself. No matter what his position, his eyes were always to the front, and the slightest motion of the enemy was greeted with a shot from his ever ready Enfield. Loading his gun—it was a muzzle loader then, and he was obliged to bite his paper cartridge, and drive the charge home with his ramrod—was reduced to a science, which set at defiance all the minute and machine-like movements peculiar to the manual of arms. Behind a tree, without exposing a surplus inch of his anatomy, or prone on the ground, rolled upon his side or lying on his back, he drove his charge home, and was ready for instant action. He in Gray was equally quick and fertile of expedients. Not a foot of ground was lost or gained without a sharp struggle, and a list of killed and wounded on either side. A line was generally entrenched almost as soon as it was established, some of the men carrying spades, and others rails, against which they threw a little dirt. On level ground they sometimes dug a hole, in which to kneel down or stand up, so that they might peer over at their enemy. The best work in constructing these slight but valuable fortifications was often done by night, and the morning nearly always found the skirmish-line better prepared to inflict injury upon the enemy than it had been the night before. Frequently two or three men would occupy the same hole, and then all sorts of devices were used to circumvent the enemy, One would raise his cap on a ramrod to draw his fire, while a comrade took the opportune moment to spot the Gray who took the bait. Often the skirmishers were obliged to leave shelter before they had "warmed their holes," as they expressed it, to make a sudden dash upon the enemy, for the purpose of securing more ground, and sometimes it was their opponents who stirred them out in turn, and made them take a hurried trip to the rear. At times, having located their enemy's position during the day, they would make a midnight dash, noiselessly, without firing a gun, taking the Gray " in out of the wet," and bearing him back as a prisoner. Occasionally the Blue would keep his prisoner with him in his rifle-pit until he was relieved and could take him into camp. In such cases the two fraternized most heartily, the Yankee sharing his provisions with the " Johnny," and the latter dividing tobacco with his captor; both "swapping lies" the while, comparing notes as to where they had met before, and what they did upon that occasion, interspersing these reminiscences with highly imaginative prophecies of the outcome of the campaign; the Yankee meanwhile losing no opportunity to take a crack at his captive's relatives and friends. If the Blue line made itself particularly annoying to the Gray, and being the assailant, it generally did this daily, the enemy would sweep the ground with grape, canister, and shell, pro-

voking a warm return fire from the federal artillery.
This usually quieted both skirmish lines, and the
occupants of the rival rifle-pits would remain under
cover until the artillery duel was over, when they
would blaze away at each other with more spirit than
before. A storm had the same effect. No matter
how severe the skirmishing might be, it would
speedily die away under the effects of a rain; and as
soon as the sun shone out again, the firing would
re-commence with redoubled vigor, regardless of
provocation or possible result.

At nightfall, or just before, when the ground to be
occupied could be sufficiently discerned without attracting the attention of the enemy, the skirmishers
were relieved by others of their comrades. These
would bring provisions to last a day, and they in turn
would enter upon a round of experiences such as have
been described.

A figure on the skirmish line, familiar perhaps to
the entire army, was a vagabondish fellow, whose
regiment is not remembered. He conducted his part
of the campaign entirely after his own fashion.
Armed with a rifle having telescopic sights, and laden
with a spade, a couple of haversacks of provisions, and
a brace of canteens, he would find an eligible location,
dig a hole, and stay there until his rations or ammunition were exhausted, when he would go to the rear
for a fresh supply, only to return and resume his

murderous work. He was a dead shot, and the terror
of the enemy's artillerists, whose guns he had frequently silenced. Great effort had been made to kill
or capture him, but without success.

There were many comical incidents even where
death stared every man in the face. The skirmishers of Gresham's division of Blair's corps one
day found an apple orchard in their front. Their
mouths watered for the rare fruit, but it was certain
death to walk to the trees. Some of the men, by slow
and tedious effort, dragged themselves upon their
stomachs until they reached the much desired goal,
then flopped over upon their backs, and brought down
the apples by throwing sticks into the trees. The
enemy poured a hot fire through the orchard, and succeeded in killing one man and crippling others. At a
later day, Blue and Gray arranged a truce on their
own responsibility, and met here to enjoy the fruit
and exchange opinions with reference to the war. The
average Southern soldier could not by any means compare with the Northerner in intelligence or discern-
ment, for school houses and newspapers were too
unequally divided between the two sections. Some of
the ideas of the Southerner were extremely crude.
The typical Gray—he of the "poor white trash," who
made up the great majority of Georgian and Carolina
troops, "Corncrackers" and "Tar Heels," as they were
known—saw only one cause for the conflict: "What

did you'uns come down here to steal we'un's niggers
for?"

It was a remarkable fact that the bitterness of
the Southerner increased as he had less interest in
negro property, by reason of his utter poverty, which
absolutely forbade his owning even one "nigger."
His views on the conduct of the war were equally
comical. One whom the author recalls to mind,
expressed a sentiment frequently heard from his
fellows, that "Sherman didn't fight f'ar," that Johnston had offered to fight him at a dozen different
places, but "Sherman darsn't take it up, and only
flanked him." But "Sherman would soon git to whar
he couldn't flank no mo', and then he'd have to fight,
and Johnston'd lick him." Strange as it may appear,
the same ideas were expressed, but in better language,
by the Atlanta papers, which frequently fell into
federal hands. One of these, by the way, was an old
friend with a new face—the *Memphis Appeal*, which,
on the occupation of that city by the federals, in 1862,
was moved, and became the *Grenada Appeal*. Like
the Wandering Jew, it was obliged to "on," and after
three or four more removals finally brought up at
Atlanta, as the *Atlanta Appeal*. The boys in Blue,
who were always alive to an opportunity for a joke,
had long before dubbed it the "Moving Appeal,"
which it was, in spirit and in fact.

So went life on the skirmish line. And death, too!

For each night, when the new line went out, it found that some of those who had gone forth a few hours before, to battle for country, had been "relieved from duty" by that dread commander, whose army is the grim and silent majority, and whose decrees are inexorable.

And others of the gallant skirmish line crawled painfully back, or were borne tenderly by comrades, pierced by bullet or bruised by shell, to drag out a maimed existence, or perish miserably in hospital.

The line of battle was habitually from one to five hundred yards in rear of the skirmish line, the distance depending greatly upon the conformation of the ground, and always strongly entrenched. The men were as expert in the use of the spade and the ax as with the rifle, and two hours' work made a very fair protection. Earth was thrown up to the height of two or three feet, sometimes higher. Frequently head-logs were placed upon the parapet, the ends resting upon skids leaning inwardly, and to the ground. The space between the head-log and the parapet permitted the troops to aim their rifles at the enemy with little exposure of themselves, while the skids provided a way for the head-log to reach the ground without doing injury to the men, in the event of its being dislodged by a cannon ball. Immediately behind these works the troops erected their shelter tents. They were not allowed to leave their quarters, but were kept

8

continually on the ground, ready to move forward at
any moment to support the skirmish line, make an
onslaught upon the enemy, or to resist an attack. No
music was permitted, and frequently fires were forbidden. The latter regulation was, however, a dead
letter, except in very rare cases, where the men themselves could actually see its necessity by immediate
danger. Coffee was their staff of life, and they must
have it, no matter what risk attended. The most
disheartening event that could happen a soldier was
to be called into line just as his coffee pot was beginning to bubble.

At night, the men in the line of battle rested
lightly, with their arms at their sides, and seldom
undressed. Firing on the skirmish line, more or less
noisy, continued all night, and frequently some unusual stir on the part of the enemy, real or fancied,
provoked a lively fusilade, causing the troops on the
main line to fall into ranks, ready for such emergency
as might arise, at times remaining under arms until
after daylight.

Even when in repose, the casualties in the line of
battle, hidden perhaps from sight of the enemy, were
often as numerous as on the skirmish line, for it
caught nearly all the bullets that overshot the skirmishers. David Kimball, now superintendent of
newspaper distribution in the Chicago post-office, will
long remember his own experience. He was seated

just within a light barricade of logs, built to protect
his field-desk, with his back to the enemy, when a
rifle-ball flew over and nipped a piece of skin from
his neck.  It was amusing to see him throw his hand
upon the injured spot, and hear him express himself
in language not authorized by the Book of Common
Prayer!

But when the enemy opened with his batteries it
was really hot!  The shells burst at the most awkward moments, while the solid shot whistled through
the trees, tearing off huge branches, and making
it generally uncomfortable.  Eccentric enough these
missiles were, and their ways past finding out.  In one
case an elongated shot—a "lamp-post," as that sort
of a projectile was called—struck the root of a tree
in front of a staff tent, belonging to General Giles A.
Smith's headquarters.  The shot glanced, and followed the trunk twenty feet upward, tearing off the
bark, and finally cutting away a large limb which, in
its fall, nearly wrecked tent, and occupants as well.
The next shot cut down a tree which fell upon a "fly"
adjoining, spraining the leg of an ordnance officer,
and breaking one for his orderly.

These slight drawbacks did not disturb the spirits
of the men.  They gathered in knots near their
color-line, playing the "little game" of euchre
or seven-up, discussing the campaign, and prophesying as to the next movement.  In every regiment

was someone who had seen somebody, who had heard
somebody from headquarters say, etc., etc., and then
he would relate the news.  There was no newspaper,
no intelligence whatever from the outside world, but
surmise and imagination amply supplied the defi-
ciency.  Canards, more or less plausible, were set
afloat, seemingly without any foundation, but they had
the rare merit of being innocent lies, that injured
no one.  If it were a tale of disaster, it had happened
to Grant, or had occurred out in Missouri, or down in
Texas—it was never at home.  It is highly suggestive
of the unbounded self-confidence of this army, that
there was never bad news from any part of itself.
Palmer, away over on the right, or Schofield as far to
the left, might have had a severe battle; he might have
lost two or three thousand men; yet the story was passed
over as unimportant.  It would not affect the general
result, and the corps which had come to grief, would
make up for it to-morrow or the day after.  But after
every story, probable and improbable, had been told,
and commented upon; and after the men had exhausted
their ideas with reference to the immediate future, all
would agree that nobody knew anything about it,
except "Uncle Billy," and that he was a "long-headed
cuss" who "would work it out all right."  Fertile subjects for discussion at these veritable camp-fires were
the occurrences on the skirmish-line, the men who had
just come in, leading off, narrating with remarkable

vividness, and more vigor of expression than could be permitted in these pages, every incident of the day.

"Between deals" the good and the bad traits of those who had "turned up their toes," as the boys expressed it, were discussed with remarkable freedom, and the old adage, "*de mortuis nil nisi bonum*," was set at utter defiance. If, as sometimes happened, a soldier had been killed near the skirmish-line while looking on, it was unanimously voted that he was "a —— fool," and "it served him right,"—there were opportunities enough for a man to be killed while in the strict line of duty, without poking around where he had no business. Not that these men were heartless, but they regarded death as a necessary and familiar incident to soldiering, and they had grown into the habit of putting the best face upon their surroundings. It would have been a spiritless army if the troops had gone into mourning over every comrade lost.

At intervals, in the line of battle, on little spurs, were redoubts occupied by the field batteries. These were favorite resorts of the general officers, presenting favorable opportunities for reconnoitering the enemy's lines. Often a corps commander with his staff, and the division and brigade commanders, came to such places on this errand, and their presence invariably attracted a considerable number of soldiers, curious to know the meaning of such a gathering. Such an unusual throng could not fail to attract the attention of the enemy, and his batteries would open a fierce fire, driving all but the gunners to shelter. A laughable circumstance occurred at one such time in the vicinity of Spear's Fifteenth Ohio Battery. A wagon loaded with intrenching tools belonging to the Pioneer Corps, was covered with darkies, curiously looking on, when a solid shot plumped into the vehicle, and there was an irruption of picks, spades and "Contrabands," as if they had been vomited out of a volcano. The darkies reached solid ground almost before the tools had ceased to fly, and "lit out for tall timber" at an astonishing gait.

Artillery duels were of daily occurrence, and some splendid practice was done. Clayton's First Minnesota Battery of Rodman guns was particularly efficient, having gunners whose fire was as true to the mark, as that of a good rifleman. The range of these splendid guns was marvelous. In a trial between this battery and one of Parrott guns, belonging to Osterhaus' division of Logan's Corps, the former pitched shells entirely over Kenesaw Mountain, while the latter barely reached the summit.

A well known figure during these events was that of Mr. Davis, the skillful artist of *Harper's Weekly*, who was on the ground making sketches for that journal. He was frequently under fire, but his work at such times bore little resemblance to the actual scenes

GEN. GRESHAM WOUNDED.

See page 141.

he intended to depict. He merely outlined the ground and positions, and then filled in guns and troops from memory, when and where he could work with less strain upon the nerves.

## CHAPTER XI.

### BEFORE KENESAW.

AIN fell daily for almost two weeks from the time the army went into line near Big Shanty. The roads became quagmires, and the movement of artillery and supply trains was all but impossible. The effect upon the men, almost shelterless, and subsisting on short rations of hard tack, pork and coffee, was most depressing; yet operations were not suffered to lag, and there was continuous skirmishing. As a matter of fact, the excitement of the conflict was a necessity from a sanitary standpoint. Suffering from inclement weather, and illy provisioned, as the men were, inaction would have begotten disease and death; action was health and vigor.

June 14th, an unusual gathering was seen upon the summit of Pine Mountain. The Union forces, supposing it to be a party reconnoitering their lines, opened a sharp artillery fire, dispersing the group on the instant. A few minutes later, the enemy's signal flags were unusually active, and one of Sherman's signal officers, who had deciphered their code, read their message, which said that General Polk had been killed during the cannonading. Polk was a corps commander, and also a bishop in the Protestant Episcopal Church. It was charged by the enemy at the time, that the fatal missile was discharged from a gun aimed by General Sherman in person, with a full knowledge of his identity. It was an absurd statement to make, and manifestly false. There was much controversy between various batteries, which claimed to have caused his death, among them being Spear's Fifteenth Ohio Battery, attached to Gresham's division of the Seventeenth Corps. The point at issue was never definitely settled, but General Sherman expressed an opinion favorable to the claims of a battery belonging to General Howard's Fourth Corps.

The next day, June 15th, was one of great activity all along the entire front of the army, General Sherman having ordered a general advance, with the intention of breaking the enemy's lines at any point where a weak spot might be discovered.

At nine o'clock in the morning, the Union artillery opened a fierce fire, eliciting no reply until two hours later, when answering volleys were returned. The shells from the rebel batteries rendered the headquarters of Gresham's division uninhabitable, so tents were struck and the wagons sent to the rear, while the general and staff made their quarters for the time in a redoubt occupied by Spear's Fifteenth Ohio Battery. This location was not more comfortable, but one from which all the movements in front might be viewed. Artillery firing and sharp skirmishing were kept up by both lines, and at one time a gallant charge was made by Gresham's division, and two lines of the enemy's rifle pits were taken.

To the left of Gresham's division was Leggett's, which was the extreme left of the army. The latter command overlapped the enemy's front, and Force's brigade made a splendid charge, gaining the rebel rear, capturing an Alabama regiment entire, and compelling the enemy to re-arrange his lines with considerable loss of ground. Thomas and Schofield were equally successful on the right; and, as another result of the operations during the day, the enemy was obliged to abandon Pine Mountain, drawing in his forces to Lost Mountain. This, with Kenesaw and the connecting heavily timbered ridge, became his new line, which was semi-circular, its concavity being presented to the Union army.

The next day, June 16th, a further advance was made; and, as a consequence, the enemy was obliged to abandon Lost Mountain. His position was now Kenesaw Mountain, and its heavily timbered flanks;

but this effectually covered the town of Marietta, pro-
tected the railroad behind the mountain, and covered
all avenues to the Chattahoochee river.

June 17th and 18th, the rain again descended in
torrents, flooding the country, rendering the roads
worse than before, if it were possible, and drenching
the illy-sheltered troops to the skin. Notwithstanding these discouragements, the Union lines were
pushed up closer against Kenesaw, a little each day,
Blair's Seventeenth Corps and Logan's Fifteenth
Corps making the greater progress.

Skirmishing continued in a desultory way, the
monotony being at times relieved by artillery duel-
ing, until June 27th, when a determined assault was
made upon the enemy's lines. This was the severest
engagement thus far in the campaign. To the Army
of the Tennessee was assigned the task of gaining a
foothold at the break in the mountain—the point
which marked the distinction between "Little Kenesaw" and "Big Kenesaw"—and the brunt of this
attack fell upon Morgan L. Smith's division of the
Fifteenth Corps. The remainder of this command
and Blair's Seventeenth Corps supported the movement.

Early after breakfast, the troops were formed for
the attack, concealed as much as possible by the
timber. At eight o'clock, three guns, upon an eminence near the center, gave the signal for the advance,

and Smith's assaulting column dashed from under
cover. As soon as the troops emerged from their
shelter, the enemy's batteries opened upon them with
grape and canister, and over their heads the Union
gunners poured answering volleys. The very ground
shook with the tremendous concussions, and every
known missile of death hurtled through the air. On
went the Blue lines at a keen run, passing beyond the
rifle pits of their own skirmishers, and entering upon
the border land of the valley of the shadow of death.
Still on they pressed, at a rapid pace, firing scarcely a
shot, reserving all their energies for the supreme
effort. They ran over the rifle pits of the enemy's
skirmishers without a thought of the fleeing occupants. Their goal was five hundred yards farther on.
And then, from the light red line of earth, which held
a concealed foe, came a storm of lead, which, united
with the volleys of artillery on either flank, bore down
countless scores. At every pace of their magnificent
advance, men dropped, mangled or dead. None
stopped to see who had fallen—looking neither to the
right or left, they instinctively sought each other's
side, closing up the gaps, and continually shortening
the line, but resolutely pressing on. The only instinct
left alive was that of destruction. And now they came
upon the abattis in front of the enemy's position,
reaching up the steep ascent of the foothill of Kenesaw Mountain. No line could be preserved here. The

obstructions were more fatal to military formation than iron or lead. The men tore through, climbing over or under the entangling tree-tops and twisted vines as best they could. It was slow and painful work. And now from front and flanks came a fire of musketry, tenfold fiercer than before, and every missile that artillery could throw. The lines were irretrievably crushed, and the men sought such shelter as the ground afforded, afterward falling back and occupying the enemy's late skirmish line.

Assaults were also made by Thomas and Schofield, and all failed. The result was another chapter in the lesson of war which the army, from general to private, was learning. The direct assault upon heavily fortified lines was to become almost a memory of the past. It was founded upon the old traditions of warfare in the days of rude short-range arms, when a dense charging column might advance with impunity near to an enemy, and bear him down by sheer force of numbers and momentum, before he could deliver an effective fire. Improved small arms of long range, and well served artillery, firing shell, grape, and canister, rendered obsolete such columns of attack.

General Sherman, however, successfully defended the experiment. "All looked to me," he said, "to 'outflank.' An army, to be efficient, must not settle down to one single mode of offense, but must be prepared to execute any plan which promises success."

He feared that such constant fighting behind entrenchments, even frail as they were, would beget a timidity that would cause the troops to fail him at some critical moment when a decisive aggressive movement was necessary; he also hoped that the assault might be successful, arguing that strength of position sometimes made defenders negligent, and an easy prey to a determined onset.

The Union loss in this engagement was two thousand five hundred men. The enemy, fighting from behind cover, lost not more than one-third as many. The operations for the month practically closed here. Sherman had lost seven thousand five hundred men, and Johnston nearly six thousand.

The Union troops suffered great privations during this time. The weather was horrible, heavy rains being of almost daily occurrence, making the movement of wagon-trains extremely difficult. This of itself was a sufficient obstacle to feeding the army; but the difficulty of procuring supplies was aggravated by the raids made by rebel cavalry upon the railroad to the north. A journal kept by the author, notes that "the railroad has been broken so much of late that, with the utmost endeavor, it is only able to supply bread, meat, coffee, and ammunition. The men are even cautioned to be sparing of cartridges. No soap is to be had; the men have no clothing except that upon their persons, and there is great suffering on account of vermin." June 30th was a red-letter day, the journal for that date noting that " an issue of soap was made, and the troops had an opportunity to wash their clothes." The scarcity of tobacco was a serious hardship to many; some experimented, in a persistent but unsatisfactory way, with dried coffee-grounds smoked in pipes as a substitute. One ardent lover of the weed considered himself highly favored in securing a one pound bale of smoking tobacco in return for a five dollar bill.

It was during the closing days of the month that newspapers from the North found their way into camp, an unusual incident, for there were no news-venders with this army. These papers contained information of the renomination of President Lincoln, an event which the troops hailed with great satisfaction, as being an emphatic rebuke to the so-called peace-proposition policy strongly urged at the North, and a full assurance of the vigorous prosecution of the war to a successful issue; while the Illinois soldiers were doubly joyful to learn of the nomination of General Richard J. Oglesby for Governor. He was a gallant soldier, who had been severely wounded at Corinth; and, besides, a plain man of the people, whom all loved.

Notwithstanding the great hardships of the campaign, the end of June found the troops in excellent spirits, and in every way well prepared for farther hard service.

9

## CHAPTER XII.

### THE RACE FOR THE CHATTAHOOCHEE.

ND now Sherman, convinced of the futility of attempting such an impregnable position as Kenesaw in front, again called into requisition his peculiar talent for " flanking ; " which, in other words, was accomplishing successfully by means of brains, ends which many a commander would have failed to reach with much loss of life. Not that Sherman's maneuvers were bloodless, but he reduced the loss of life to a minimum.

He determined again to leave his railroad communications for the time, and make a detour, placing himself on the Chattahoochee river between Atlanta and Kenesaw, thus compelling his adversary to abandon his works, in order to avoid being cut off from the Confederacy. The wagon trains were filled with hard bread, meat, coffee and ammunition; while the rations issued were reduced to the lowest limit, to guard against absolute starvation, in the event of pending operations being protracted beyond the time hoped for.

The Army of the Tennessee, under General Mc-Pherson, occupied the extreme left, and was to march first, having the greatest distance to travel. Pending its movement, its trenches were occupied by dismounted cavalry, armed with seven-shooters, and able to make as much noise as the infantry, which had ordinarily occupied these lines. Every precaution was taken to order the movement so that no intimation of it could be gained by the enemy occupying the overhanging mountain. The march was to begin July 2d; the day previous, the enemy displayed a white flag and proposed a truce, to permit the burial of the dead on either side, who had already lain upon the field for forty-eight hours. But even this was refused, lest in some manner the plan might be exposed. At ten o'clock of the night designated the grand movement was begun.

Who that made that night march will ever forget the weirdness of the spectacle, the strangeness of his sensations? Without note of bugle or roll of drum the sleeping army was roused from its slumbers. Secresy was the watchword of the hour. Artillery and wagons moved with muffled wheels. Then out

into intense darkness advanced the silent hosts. From
the side of the road the moving column might be felt,
but it could not be seen. The army literally walked
by faith, each man following in the steps of one he
believed to be in advance of him. The ground,
sodden with heavy rains, gave no sound of foot or
hoof, and feet and wheels rapidly converted the roadway into a sea of mud.

Now the troops "string out" in the darkness until
they reach over three times their ordinary ground,
even in marching order. The ranks are not compact
and well dressed; each man goes as he pleases.
The head of column halts on account of some obstacle,
and those in the rear, not knowing what has occurred,
"close up" on their comrades in front, and collide in
the darkness. Then is heard angry dialogue, the men
being forgetful of all injunctions to silence. "Why
the —— don't you keep up?" "What the —— are
you running over me for?" "Hold up your —— gun,
and keep it out of my eye!" "—— your eye!" and
so on, with countless variations. Then one finds himself anchored to the ground by the depth and consistency of the mud; and, while endeavoring to extricate
himself, those hurrying on from behind stumble over
him in the darkness, until a score or more of men are
piled on top of one another, before the word "ease
up" can be passed back.

Oh! the profanity of that night march! The

objurgatory division of the mother-tongue stood revealed in all its elaborateness and comprehensiveness; and yet, reinforced as it was by copious selections from foreign languages, it proved utterly inadequate for such an emergency. Oaths of the most intricate construction and far-reaching meaning were thrown upon the midnight air, with a vehemence which left no doubt as to the sincerity of the swearer. He damned all things, visible and invisible, known, unknown and unknowable. The United States and the "Confederacy" were alike relegated, side by side, to the grim sulphurous shades of the forever cursed; then the swearer wished that Sherman and Johnston were both in hadean regions "to fight it out themselves;" and further expressed the conviction that it would be comparative bliss to be there himself. Nor was the swearing spasmodic and occasional, but persistent and unanimous.

Shortly after midnight, a great blaze of light burst from Kenesaw, and then it was known that the enemy was also in motion toward the Chattahoochee! Sherman had found as wily a strategist as himself. Johnston knew by intuition what the movement of his antagonist would be—it was the step he himself would have taken if similarly situated, and he hastened to anticipate it.

There was no longer reason for concealment; nor was it even attempted; and now, at intervals along the column of Union troops, blue lights were burned to guide their quickening steps. The scene thus revealed can scarcely be imagined, and but faintly described. Victor Hugo would have revelled in the spectacle. Doré might have sketched it, and called it "A Night in Hell!"

In relief, against the awful black background of mountain and forest, stood revealed, in an instant, hosts of moving men in tattered and travel-worn uniforms; not marching with precision as if on parade or review, but plodding along irregularly, each man as best he could. They carried their arms in every possible position. Their countenances were ghastly in the unnatural glare. Here were faces of dogged determination, of uncomplaining patience, of hopeless weariness. Many wore patches and bandages about the head to cover wounds, and others limped painfully. At intervals, from unusual elevations, the glare of light threw the distorted and exaggerated images of the moving host in bold relief against a leaden sky—an army of phantom giants marching in air!

Plodding wearily, yet rapidly along, passing by the Twentieth, Fourteenth and Fourth Corps, the Army of the Tennessee reached Schofield's corps, the extreme right of the army. It was now early morning of the 3d. Halting only long enough to make coffee, the troops again pressed on to Nickajack creek, six miles from where it empties into the Chattahoochee river, and sixteen miles from Atlanta. The night's march had been upward of twenty miles. Here the progress of the troops was arrested, and the skirmish line was again deployed. The enemy was immediately in front.

Sherman had hoped to deliver a blow while his enemy was crossing the Chattahoochee river; and he confessed to a feeling of disappointment on discovering that Johnston had previously prepared works on the north side of that stream, and along the Nickajack, and now occupied them in force, with every appearance of making a stand.

The Army of the Tennessee held the right flank of the Union army, extending along Nickajack creek. Gallant charges were made at various times, and considerable ground gained, by Logan's, Dodge's and Blair's corps. In the movement by Gresham's division, the latter command was led by Colonel Logan's 32d Illinois Regiment, under the eye of the division commander. In this affair the regiment suffered severely; among its dead was Private Doty, who was killed by the concussion of an exploding shell. Not a bruise was found on his body, nor was a drop of blood started.

July 8th, the enemy made a vigorous but unsuccessful assault, endeavoring to regain the works of which they had been dispossessed.

The only information received by the troops from
the outer world, during these operations, was through
the medium of Atlanta papers, and these contained
very little of what might be really called news. The
fire-eating class of editors was not yet extinct, and
little was to be found in their journals except boasting
of the achievements of their own troops, and slanders
at the expense of their enemy. One issue of *The Appeal* spoke contemptuously of "Sherman and his great
raiding party," attributing their spirit in battle to
plentiful potations of whisky, and prophesying that
their "Dutch courage" would ooze out when
Wheeler's cavalry should succeed, as they surely
would, in breaking the railroad to the North, thus
cutting off the liquor supply. The abandonment of
Kenesaw Mountain, by Johnston, was referred to as a
fine exhibition of "strategy," which would lead Sherman to certain destruction. The Union troops were
accused of unusual inhumanity. *The Appeal* said
that, on one occasion, when a flag of truce was displayed by them after a severe skirmish, the question
was asked by a confederate officer: "What do you
want? To bury the dead?" To which the reply
was: "Dead be —— ! We want to trade for
tobacco!" The news from the North was very
meagre, the Southern journals being only able to
reprint from such Northern papers as fell into their
hands in the East, or were occasionally brought within
their lines by citizens from Memphis and Vicksburg.

## CHAPTER XIII.

### BEFORE ATLANTA.

YING on opposite banks of the Chattahoochee river, Blue and Gray again confronted each other. The Army of the Tennessee had worked its way down Nickajack creek to its mouth, and was exchanging shots with the enemy across the stream, while Cox's command had made a lodgment on the river farther to the left; meanwhile Johnston had crossed his army to the Atlanta side of the Chattahoochee. The tactical history of the campaign by which Sherman forced his adversary to again retreat, is not necessary to this narrative. The next problem was to force a passage of the stream.

After several days had been spent in demonstrating upon Turner's Ferry, the Army of the Tennessee was assigned to its old familiar task of passing from one flank to the other. At two o'clock on the morning of the 16th it marched northward, and at dawn halted at Marietta, behind Kenesaw Mountain, nearly twenty

miles north from Turner's Ferry, whence it started.
On the 18th, the command reached Roswell, on the
Chattahoochee river, twenty miles northeast from
Marietta. Here had been located large cotton mills,
managed by persons who claimed the protection of the
French flag, which was displayed with great assurance. It was notorious, however, that the establish-
ment was conducted in the interests of the "Confederacy," manufacturing cloth for the rebel army; and a
cavalry force under General Garrard had, a few days
before, destroyed the property in spite of the remonstrances of the ostensible foreign proprietors. General Garrard made a very full report of the affair,
enclosing with it the owners' protest and claim for
French protection, whereupon General Sherman wrote
him : "Your report is most acceptable. I will see as
to any man in America hoisting the French flag, then
devoting his labor and capital to supplying armies in
open hostility to our government, claiming the benefit
of his neutral flag. Should you, under the impulse of
anger, natural at contemplating such perfidy, hang the
wretch, I approve the act beforehand." A large number of the female operatives gladly availed themselves
of an offer to be sent North, where "white wheat
bread and a dollar a day" were to be had. Most of
them eventually arrived in Indiana, and found employment in factories.

On the 19th, the Army of the Tennessee crossed

the river at Roswell, and established itself firmly on the south bank. The next day it passed through Decatur, marching directly toward Atlanta. At this place were found several hundred pikes—iron blades mounted on poles about nine feet long—with which the enemy had promised to do great execution at close quarters. These remarkable weapons were never seen in action, being as useless implements of war as the magnified bowie-knives ("corn-cutters," as they were called,) of Fort Donelson days.

Here the Union forces learned that the Confederate government had retired Johnston, appointing Hood to command of the army which had so long opposed them. Johnston was a fine strategist, and had so conducted his retreat as practically to lose nothing from Chattanooga to Atlanta, except the territory he had been obliged to abandon, and the men killed, wounded, or captured in action; he had scarcely lost a straggler, or so much of his equipage as a tin-plate. But he had not succeeded in checking the much dreaded Sherman and his vandal cohorts. The "Confederacy" wanted "a soldier who would fight." There was a camp story to the effect that, on receiving the news of Hood superseding Johnston, General Sherman called a council of officers, who had known the new Confederate commander personally, in order to learn something of his character. Several officers, who had been classmates with General Hood at West Point, ex-

pressed themselves in various ways, pertinent and
otherwise; but the climax was reached when an old
Kentucky colonel remarked that he "Seed Hood bet
twenty-five hundred dollars, with nary a p'ar in his
hand!" This anecdote convinced all that such an
exhibition of nerve was good evidence of the fighting
qualities of the new commander. However this may
be, General Sherman was satisfied that the change of
commanders betokened more vigorous measures, and
made his dispositions accordingly, sending notice of
the fact to every part of the army, and notifying his
subordinates to be prepared, at all times, for sharp
and unexpected battle. The troops grasped the import of Hood's appointment with as quick intelligence
as the officers, and expressed great satisfaction with
the assignment, regarding Hood as a hot-headed
fellow, who would butt his brains out against their
entrenchments, thus shortening the campaign and the
war.

July 20th, the Union army pressed on toward
Atlanta, the Army of the Tennessee occupying the left
flank on the line of the Augusta railroad. The enemy
was driven handsomely for two miles, without great
resistance. The attack was resumed next day, and
two lines of rifle-pits taken, almost at the point of the
bayonet. In these operations, Gresham's division of
Blair's Seventeenth Corps lost five hundred and

twenty-five killed and wounded—an extremely large proportion of its strength.

It was on the first of these two days, July 20th, that General Gresham received a serious wound, which not only retired him from active service altogether, but deprived him of the opportunity of winning great personal distinction ; besides, it was indirectly the cause of immense loss to the Union army. Had he not been wounded, in all human probability Atlanta would have fallen into his hands that day; the bloody battle which was fought on that very ground two days later, would have no place in history, and McPherson might have been spared a glorious but needless death.

General Gresham's division, holding the extreme left of the army, advanced in splendid order, driving before it a strong cavalry force. The General had left his horse at the foot of a slight hill, and ascended the slope, occupied by his skirmishers, to reconnoiter the enemy's lines, which were posted on an eminence now known in history as Leggett's Hill, the key to the position of the Union army during the battle of July 22nd. It was evident to him that he was well on the enemy's flank, and he was making his dispositions to take advantage of the opportunity, when the rebel skirmishers opened a sharp fire. His aide, Captain Duncan, received a score of bullets through his clothes, but escaped injury; the General fell, pierced in the thigh by a rifle-ball, and was at once removed to the rear. During the confusion incident to this untoward disaster, and the assignment of another officer to the command, a strong division of Hood's infantry was hurried to Leggett's Hill, and the magnificent opportunity was lost.

General Gresham's injury was so serious that he had hard work to save his leg from the surgeons, who seemed determined to saw it off; but he was full of pluck, and stoutly insisted that this should not be done. Some days later he was sent to his home at New Albany, Indiana, and thus ended his service in the field.

DRAWN BY ENGINEER OFFICER, JULY 23d, 1864.

By Permission of Sergt. A. M. Barker.

See page 155.

## CHAPTER XIV.

### A FAMOUS DIVISION.

ENTION made of the Fourth Division of the Seventeenth Corps, in the preceding chapter, recalls somewhat more of its phenomenal history, and the unusual career of its commanders. Of the six generals who led it from first to last, two became members of the President's cabinet, one of this number holding, at different times, the portfolios of the Post-Office and Treasury Department, and becoming recognized at a later day as a probable candidate for the Presidency. Another was an assistant to a cabinet minister, while a fourth held an important appointment in the diplomatic service. The remaining two died before the war ended. Of the entire number, the two ex-cabinet members alone survive.

This command, under General Stephen A. Hurlbut, was the Fourth Division of the original Army of the Tennessee, as that body was constituted at Shiloh, where it first went into line in its entirety. In that

10

desperate action it sustained a glorious part, and its list of killed and wounded was one-fifth of the casualties of the entire army, six divisions in all. It bore a full share in the siege of Corinth, which followed. At a later day, it fought and won the battle of the Hatchie, which General Hurlbut made the occasion for issuing a congratulatory order, wherein he said: "The title of 'Fighting Fourth,' won at Shiloh, has been burnished with additional splendor."

Shortly before this, the Fifth Division, which had been an elbow-to-elbow companion from the outset, was sent to duty in another field, and its commander, General William T. Sherman, wrote the following letter, which is quoted as showing the estimation in which he held General Hurlbut's command:

HEADQUARTERS, 5TH DIV., ARMY OF THE TENNESSEE.
MEMPHIS, TENN., SEPT. 6, 1862.

Brig. Gen. S. A. HURLBUT, Commanding Fourth Division, Army of the Tennessee :

DEAR SIR : Permit me through you to convey to the officers and men of your division an expression of my deep regret that the necessities of the public service, should at this time separate our commands. Our divisions were the first to disembark at Pittsburg Landing in the early part of March, and through storm and sunshine, adverse and prosperous times, we have been side by side. Not only have social ties arisen between us, but the habit of acting together has made us as one command, and I feel at parting with you as if my own division was divided. I need not express to you the assurance of my high personal and official respect, for I hope I have evinced it on many and all occasions. For Generals Lauman and Veatch, I must say that no officers could have been more zealous, close, and attentive to their important duties than they have ever been. I can not recall an instance of their having been away from their posts for even an hour. To them I predict an honorable and brilliant future. Indeed, with very few exceptions, your division is composed of a class of steady, good men, who by their behavior in camp, on guard, on the march, and in battle, reflect honor and credit on themselves and their country. Be pleased to convey to all my hearty thanks, and assure them that I will hail the change in events that will bring us again together.

With sentiments of high respect, your friend and servant,

W. T. SHERMAN,

Major General.

Hurlbut's division was a part of the army with which General Grant marched into Mississippi, in his effort to reach the rear of Vicksburg, in the winter of 1862, returning soon afterward to the line of the Memphis and Charleston railroad. Upon the organization of *corps d'armee*, this division became the Fourth of the Sixteenth Corps, and General J. G. Lauman was assigned to the command, General Hurlbut having been made a major general and corps commander. It participated in the siege of Vicksburg, and, the next day after the surrender of that famous stronghold, marched with other troops to attack General Johnston at Jackson. In the action at that place it made a brilliant but disastrous charge, and sustained great loss. The responsibility was charged upon General Lauman, and he was relieved of his command. He returned to his home in Iowa, and died shortly afterward of a broken heart, if ever man so died. He was an officer of tried courage, and a man of fine personal traits.

General Lauman was succeeded by General Marcellus M. Crocker, of Iowa, and the division became a part of the Seventeenth Corps, retaining the same numerical designation. Some time afterward, sev-

eral of the old regiments were transferred to other
commands, and their place was taken by the "Iowa
Brigade," a magnificent body of men, formerly com-
manded by the same officer who now became their
division general. These troops, with the 32d Illinois
Regiment, which had belonged to the old Fourth
Division from the beginning, now constituted the
Third Brigade.

General Crocker was an officer of superior ability,
great personal courage and determination, and a
man of irascible temper. It is due to his memory
to say that his irritability was, in large measure, due
to his physical condition, for he was a great sufferer
from asthma; while his anger was rarely bestowed un-
deservedly. But his rage, when once aroused, was
something frightful. Upon one occasion he called a
careless regimental commander to account. The
latter answered in an insolent way, whereupon the
general threatened him with ball and chain, and a
passage from Natchez to Cairo in the hold of a steam-
boat. He would doubtless have experienced this treatment had he not hastened to tender proper apologies,
and made profuse promises of future good behavior.
In another instance, a wealthy planter, living in the
vicinity of Natchez, came to General Crocker, then
commanding the district, and applied for a permit
to ship a large quantity of cotton to the North.
This commodity then commanded an extravagant

price, and there were officers of no small rank who stood accused of conniving with rebel owners to place it on the market, and divide the proceeds. General Crocker was a man of mean fortune, but of incorruptible integrity.

"You can ship your cotton, sir," said he, addressing the citizen, "under the regulations of the Treasury Department. You must furnish proof of loyalty, and subscribe to the oath of allegiance."

"But, General," was the response," I can not take the oath. My government—"

"What government, sir?" angrily asked Crocker.

"The Confederate—"

The enraged general allowed the rebel to proceed no further.

"You infamous —— —— scoundrel! You come here to ask favors of me, and talk about *your* government! Get out of my office, and be thankful you get out alive!"

"But, General, I can make it to your advantage—"

This was the last irritant. The enraged general had the fellow speedily ejected, but the end was not yet. General Crocker sent for his engineer officer.

"Captain," said he, when that officer had appeared, "that —— —— rebel, ——, has been here talking about his loyalty to *his* government, and offering me money to let him ship his cotton North. We can't hold this place without works, and I want you to lay out a line, and plant a fort on the very foundations of his house ! ''

Forty-eight hours later, the home of the indiscreet rebel, just at the outskirts of the city, was razed to the ground, and a battery of artillery planted on the ruins of what, shortly before, was one of the handsomest residences in the South.

Early in 1864, General Crocker's division took its veteran furlough, and then rendezvoused at Cairo, preliminary to taking part in the Atlanta campaign. Soon after the movement began, the general's health failed utterly, and he returned to his home in Iowa, where he died not long afterward.

General Walter Q. Gresham, who had commanded a brigade under Crocker, succeeded to the vacant command. One anecdote always leads to another, and mention of the latter officer recalls one of the former.

At Natchez, in October of 1863, General Gresham was post-commander. He was detached from his brigade, and had only a handful of troops for provost guard duty, making necessary, when an emergency arose calling for additional force, a requisition upon General Crocker, the district commander, who had a large division in the outskirts of the city. One bright Sunday morning, a barge loaded with forage came from up the river, and required immediate unloading; whereupon the following correspondence took place, the originals of which are now in the hands of the writer of these pages:

> POST HEADQUARTERS,
> NATCHEZ, Miss., Oct. 11, 1863.
>
> GENERAL : I have to ask a detail of one commissioned officer and fifty enlisted men, to report at these headquarters immediately, for fatigue duty. Very respectfully,
>
> W. Q. GRESHAM,
> Brig. Gen. Comdg.
>
> Brig. Gen. M. M. Crocker, Comdg. District.

To which the following answer was returned:

> HEADQUARTERS, DISTRICT OF NATCHEZ,
> NATCHEZ, Miss., Oct. 11, 1863.
>
> GENERAL : I have to acknowledge the receipt of your requisition for one commissioned officer and fifty men for fatigue duty to-day. Is the detail absolutely necessary ? See order from Executive Mansion [forbidding labor by troops on the Sabbath, except in case of imperative necessity—AUTHOR] of November 16, 1862 ; also one of the Ten Commandments. Very respectfully,
>
> C. CADLE, Jr., A. A. G.
>
> Brig. Gen. W. Q. Gresham

To which General Gresham made the following reply:

> POST HEADQUARTERS,
> NATCHEZ, Miss., Oct. 11, 1863.
>
> SIR : The order from Executive Mansion of Nov. 12, 1862, has been repeatedly read and duly admired, and will be faithfully observed whenever practicable. The "Commandments" referred to are not on file in this office. Very respectfully,
>
> W. Q. GRESHAM,
> Brig. Gen'l.

General Gresham's march from Clifton to Ackworth, and his wounding before Atlanta, have been

narrated in previous chapters. He was a gentleman
of fine mind, and of those gentle and winning ways
which made every soldier his friend. He had been
with the division ever since the days of Shiloh, where
he was a field officer in an Indiana regiment; and the
entire command deplored the sad event which unfitted
him for further service. When General Grant became
President, General Gresham was appointed a United
States district judge, from which position he was called
by President Arthur to become Postmaster General.
He acted in that capacity but a few months, when he
was appointed to the Treasury Department. Shortly
afterward he was recalled to the bench, a position
much more agreeable to him.

General Gresham was succeeded in command by
General Giles A. Smith, a gallant officer, who had
received a severe wound at Missionary Ridge. When
the war had practically ended, General Smith was
assigned to a command on the Rio Grande, where a
large force had been gathered in anticipation of
possible foreign complications, growing out of Napoleon's Mexican policy. He served as Second Assistant Postmaster General under President Grant, and
died a few years ago in California, whither he went
seeking renewed health.

The latest commander of the division was General
William W. Belknap. He was a man of commanding
appearance, stoutly and compactly built, and so

admirably proportioned that neither his height nor
weight left any unpleasant impression; of fair complexion, with blue eyes beaming with sympathy and
good nature; wearing a full long beard, somewhat
inclined to reddishness, he was a magnificent specimen of the ideal Anglo-Saxon type. He was a man of
indomitable resolution and great personal courage.
In the saddle, directing the movements of his command, or in his office, dispatching routine business, he
could be decided, severe, even exacting; but he knew
also how to be affable, and in a social way was a most
admirable gentleman. He was originally major of the
15th Iowa Regiment, and rose to the colonelcy. In
the engagement at Nickajack creek, July 5th, he
attracted special attention by his wise dispositions
and personal courage; and again, in the battle of
July 22d, he distinguished himself in a marked manner. The recommendation for his promotion to the
grade of brigadier general was made by General Sherman, by telegraph. The appointment was made by
the President immediately; and it seemed as if all
joined with their great captain in the verdict that "no
promotion was ever more fairly made, nor more hon-
estly earned."

Upon General Grant's election to the Presidency,
at the close of the war, General Belknap was appointed Secretary of War. He resigned after a time,
and is now practicing law before the federal courts in
Washington.

## CHAPTER XV.

DIES IRÆ.

ULY 22d was a day of dis-
aster and sorrow. The
disaster was retrieved.
The sorrow will endure
as long as patriotism and
heroism are honored.

History has told how Hood
made his brilliant sally—how
he twisted up the federal left
wing—how the gallant McPherson fell, early in the
battle, and how Logan's inspiring presence gave assurance of final victory ; but it is only from narratives such as this, however imperfect, from the pen
of eye - witnesses and participants, that the actual
events, and the personal heroism of individuals, may
be known.

After the action of July 21st, the Army of the
Tennessee was moved farther to the left, in order to
keep pace with the enemy's lines, which were being
extended in that direction. The Fourth Division of

the Seventeenth Corps, commanded by General Giles
A. Smith, held the extreme left of the Union army.
The troops worked hard that night, entrenching their
position, and so urgent was the necessity for every
man, that the flank and rear were picketed in part by
the headquarters guard, who were among the very
first upon whom fell the enemy's attack the next
morning.

Early on the morning of July 22d, General
Smith's front line was advanced a considerable distance, meeting with little opposition; and, inasmuch as
the enemy was said to be abandoning his position in
General Thomas' front, General Sherman concluded
that Atlanta was to be yielded to him without further
struggle. He was speedily undeceived. . Hood had
merely shifted his army in order to make a desperate
and almost successful attack from a quarter whence
danger was scarcely expected.

About eleven o'clock, sharp firing in the rear of
the hospital, near Smith's headquarters, gave warning
of what was to occur. By great effort, the ambu-
lances containing the wounded and sick, about four
hundred in number, were driven to the safest place to
be found, the right and front, just behind the general
line of battle. The headquarters wagons followed,
their movement being hastened by the advance of the
enemy's skirmishers, closely supported by a full line
of battle, moving over the ground just vacated, en-

veloping Smith's flank and rear, and reaching as far as Dodge's Sixteenth Corps. As a matter of fact, by reason of the inclination of the assaulting line, Dodge's command sustained the first attack. His troops were marching down the road in column, to connect with the Seventeenth Corps. They at once halted, faced the foe, and delivered a fire which checked the onset almost on the instant.

General Smith was poorly prepared to meet the assault, his rear being presented to the enemy; and the attack fell upon him with dreadful force. He was fortunate, however, in having on the left of his line the brigade of Iowans formerly commanded by Crocker, noted for its thorough discipline and incomparable *esprit de corps.* These troops, already under fire, were ordered to the reverse of their works, to occupy the side heretofore presented to the enemy. This movement was successfully accomplished, except by the 16th Iowa Regiment, which, with a two-gun battery, was captured, after an heroic struggle.

The Iowans were assailed in front, as well as rear, and upon the flank, and portions of the command repeatedly moved over their own works, from side to side, to repel attack. So rapid were the movements, and so much was crowded into a few hours, that it is impossible to gain an entirely correct idea of the sequence of events. Cool-headed men, who were upon the ground, vary as much as two hours in timing signal circumstances with which they were personally concerned; but discrepancies of this nature are by no means peculiar to this battle.

The works of the Iowans were charged by three separate brigades, in succession. Govan's, the first, was driven off, taking away with it, however, as prisoners, the 16th Iowa Regiment, as before mentioned. Lowry's brigade followed, in a magnificent charge, which led to the most desperate fighting of the day, but was finally repulsed. The last attack, likewise unsuccessful, was made by Smith's brigade, and is not particularly noticeable as compared with Lowry's.

Lowry's assault was courageous and persistent in the highest degree. His troops actually reached the works of the Iowans, but were unable to surmount them. The contending lines were only separated by thin earthworks, less than shoulder high, and the fighting became desperate and promiscuous. Musket clashed against musket, and color-bearers flaunted their standards in face of each other.

As the 15th Iowa Regiment, Colonel (afterward General) Belknap commanding, sprang to the reverse of their works, they were confronted by the 45th Alabama Regiment, whose commander, Colonel Lampley, waved his light felt hat, as he led the charge. Colonel Belknap, taking the act to be a signal of surrender, ordered his men to cease firing (a command heard only by few, owing to the tumult

of battle), and, at the same time, beckoned the rebel
officer to come in.   A young soldier by Lampley's side,
and by his direction, as was plainly to be seen, fired
three shots at Belknap, but without effect.   Meanwhile the Alabamians advanced nearer and nearer,
and Belknap discovered that, instead of thinking of
surrender, they meant fight in bitter earnest.   Three
color-bearers of this one rebel regiment were shot
down in rapid succession.   When the last fell, the
contending lines were at such close quarters that the
flag was torn from his dying grasp by a member of
the 11th Iowa.   The trophy was afterward claimed
by the 15th Iowa soldier who shot down its bearer,
and it was delivered to him.   The Alabamians were
now at the very foot of the Union works, and to
deliver a fire upon them it was necessary for the
Iowans to hold their muskets over the works, almost
perpendicularly.   Belknap jumped upon the parapet
and again beckoned Lampley to come in.   The
latter shook his head, and urged his men to make
a final dash.   He came nearer, until he was fairly
against the works.   Then Belknap, watching his opportunity, leaned over the parapet, fastened his grasp
upon Lampley's coat-collar, and, with the aid of a
corporal near by, dragged him inside.   Within a few
minutes, every Alabamian who was not killed, or lying
wounded upon the field, was a prisoner.   Colonel
Lampley was found to be wounded, but the injury was

so slight that his own men ascribed his death, which occurred a few days later, to depression at the misfortune of being captured, rather than to the wound.

Meanwhile, the battle raged elsewhere on the lines of the Iowa brigade with scarcely less fury. At one time the colors of four rebel regiments were displayed within a stone's throw of the 11th Iowa. The 32d Mississippi Regiment all but reached the works, losing in the attempt one-third their number from a single volley of musketry. A soldier of the 11th Iowa and a rebel died together in a desperate struggle on the top of the defences. Sergeant-Major Safely, of the same regiment, with a few comrades, made a sally and captured a colonel, captain, and more than their own number of privates. An Iowan jumped upon the works, swinging his gun over his head, singing "The Battle Cry of Freedom," and died, with the unfinished words upon his lips. Colonel Jones, commanding the 53d Indiana, of the right brigade of the same division, was wounded, and, while being carried from the field on a litter, was killed by a shell. Chaplain Bennett, of the 32d Ohio Regiment, also of the same division, fought through the battle. He was a crack shot, and kept a wounded soldier busy loading guns for him. The poor fellow was killed at his side. A gallant signal officer, in his station in the top of a tree overlooking Atlanta, was forced to make a precipitate retreat, his observatory being demolished by a shell.

The opening of this onset by the enemy was the occasion of the death of the brave and beloved McPherson.

Between ten and eleven o'clock that fatal morning, General McPherson visited a hospital tent, where were a number of officers and men of the 16th Iowa Regiment, who had been wounded in a charge the day before. Among them was Captain McArthur (subsequently of General Belknap's staff), to whom he spoke encouragingly, complimenting him and his comrades upon their good conduct the day previous. Shortly afterward, the General was seen making some dispositions in the vicinity of General Dodge's corps. Thence he passed, in full view of many of the troops, in the direction of General Blair's position. A man of fine personal appearance, always with a most amiable expression of countenance, he never looked to better advantage. His entire staff had been dispatched on one urgent errand or another, and he was attended by a single orderly. Passing along a blind road, he disappeared in the dense forest. Hundreds of soldiers saw him at the moment, but no one attached any concern to the incident, for the lines were supposed to be well connected.

A few moments later, a volley of musketry was heard in the direction he had taken, and his well-known horse, wounded and riderless, dashed rapidly to the rear, giving the first intimation of the dreadful event; and the news that General McPherson was killed, or a prisoner, spread rapidly among the troops, causing great dismay.

At a later hour, it was learned that, upon entering the forest which was the scene of his death, General McPherson suddenly encountered the enemy's skirmishers. In response to the summons to surrender, he touched his hat in soldierly salute, and at the same time pulled his rein to ride to the rear. A volley of musketry was discharged, killing his orderly, and he himself fell from his horse, mortally wounded. The enemy's line was soon pushed back, and a private soldier of the 15th Iowa Regiment, George Reynolds, found his dying general prostrate upon the ground, and moistened his clammy lips with water from his canteen. When assistance came, life was extinct. The body was sent to the rear, whence it was conveyed to the old family home in Ohio. The estimation in which he was held was suitably voiced by General Sherman, who, in his report to the Secretary of War, said:

"General McPherson fell in battle, booted and spurred, as the gallant and heroic gentleman should wish. Not his ,the loss, but the country's; and the army will mourn his death, and cherish his memory, as that of one who, though comparatively young, had risen, by his merit and ability, to the command of one of the best armies which the nation had called into existence to vindicate her honor and integrity. History tells of but few who so blended the grace and gentleness of the friend with the dignity, courage, faith and manliness of the soldier. His public enemies, even the men who directed the fatal shot, never spoke or wrote of him without expressions of marked respect. Those whom he commanded loved him even to idolatry, and I, his associate and commander, fail in words adequate to express my opinion of his great worth. I feel assured that every patriot in America, on hearing this sad news, will feel a sense of personal loss, and the country generally will realize that we have lost, not only an able military leader, but a man who, had he survived, was qualified to heal the national strife which had been raised by designing and ambitious men."

A scene of dramatic power occurred when Logan, the next in rank, succeeded McPherson in command. At all times a man of unusually fine soldierly appearance, he now became a picture for an artist. Bareheaded, flushed with rage, and an instinct to avenge the death of his commander and friend, he spurred his high-strung black charger to its utmost speed, and dashed along the lines of his troops, somewhat disordered in places, restoring confidence everywhere by his gallant bearing and sharp, assuring words. Whether or not he shrieked the words which some have attributed to him, "McPherson and Revenge!" is not material; his action spoke them, had his lips been silent. What Sheridan was at Winchester, that was Logan at Atlanta. His presence itself was an

GEN. BELKNAP CAPTURING A REBEL COLONEL.

See page 158

assurance of the triumph shortly to be wrenched from a foe who already believed himself the victor.

Meantime the gap in the Union lines between the Sixteenth and Seventeenth Corps, into which the gallant McPherson rode, meeting his death, had been occupied, the first troops to arrive being the 64th Illinois Regiment. This command was fortunately armed with the Henry rifle, a sixteen-shooter, and it opened a rapid and murderous fire. As it delivered the first volley, the enemy's line bent forward, almost halting, as if to avoid the deadly discharge, and then rushed forward with redoubled speed, seeking to reach and bear down the Union troops before they could reload their pieces. But, rapidly as lever could be moved and trigger drawn, the men of the gallant 64th fired volley after volley, and the Gray line staggered, halted, and then fell back, leaving behind them their battle-flag and a number of prisoners. The placing of this regiment was in obedience to the last orders General McPherson ever gave ; but their execution came too late to save the life of the gallant soldier. From this moment, on to the end, although the lines swayed backward in places, and the troops at times found it necessary to fight from both sides of their works, the general position was assured, and the possibility of any overwhelming disaster averted.

The battle raged fiercely throughout the day in front of the Seventeenth and Fifteenth Corps. How

Smith's division fared has been already told. Leggett's division, of the same corps, had a no less serious time. They occupied the hill which was the key to the Union position, and only held it by the most desperate courage. At times they were all but cut off from the remainder of the army. General Force, one of the brigade commanders, was shot through the face, and reported as dead, but he recovered in time to engage in the "March to the Sea." A large portion of the Fifteenth Corps was dislodged from its position, but made a gallant charge and regained its ground.

At nightfall the enemy drew off, crushed and dispirited. His loss during the day, according to the best authorities, was not less than ten thousand, killed, wounded, and prisoners. Smith's division of the Seventeenth Corps took three hundred and twenty-six prisoners, including the 45th Alabama regiment, with its field and company officers, and five stands of colors. Sherman's loss was three thousand five hundred and twenty-one men, and of this number Smith's division lost one thousand and forty-two men, and the Iowa brigade alone lost six hundred and sixty-four.

## CHAPTER XVI.

### THE HISTORY OF A FLAG.

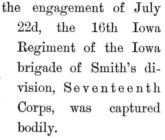

N the engagement of July 22d, the 16th Iowa Regiment of the Iowa brigade of Smith's division, Seventeenth Corps, was captured bodily.

The skirmishers of this regiment were driven in about one o'clock in the afternoon. The regiment itself, occupying the trenches, was ordered by the colonel, Ad. H. Sanders, to withhold fire until the word of command. The enemy's columns charged forward, until they had nearly approached the works. Colonel Sanders said they came within fifty yards — the rebel commander said the distance was thirty yards. Then the Iowans opened a murderous fire, and the assaulting force staggered back, seemingly annihilated. A second charge was as successfully repulsed, and this time a large part of their force advanced so near that the men could neither go farther nor retreat ; they hugged the ground, giving and taking a severe fire, which continued for nearly a half-hour.    They then displayed a white flag and asked to be permitted to surrender.    This was agreed to, and they were ordered to lay down their arms and come inside the works as prisoners.    The demand was complied with, and the captives were found to be the 2d and 8th Arkansas regiments, with a small body of Texans, perhaps seventy-five men.

Colonel Sanders now held in his rifle-pits, as prisoners, nearly twice the number of his own command. He had employment for his entire force, making it difficult to spare men to take the prisoners away. Before he was able to dispose of them, the enemy had gained the rear of his line, and he was attacked from that direction as well as from the front.    In order to protect the rear, some of Sanders' men fixed bayonets and stood guard over their prisoners, compelling them to stand between themselves and the enemy, thus silencing the fire from that quarter, while the Iowans continued the battle.    At this juncture, many of the prisoners, who still retained their arms, finding them-selves to outnumber their captors, and further emboldened by the persistence of their own troops in front, again began to show fight.    Colonel Sanders disarmed two of them, when he was surrounded by rebels, who pointed their guns at him, demanding his surrender. He saw that the works to his rear were in possession of the enemy, whereupon he determined to call upon his men to move by the flank and cut their way out. The battle then became a *melee*. A rebel captain seized a gun from one of his men, and fired at Colonel Sanders, the ball passing between his legs. Color-Sergeant Lucas, who had planted his colors in the ground, shot the captain on the moment. Lucas again took up his colors, and two rebels attempted to snatch them away from him, but he held them with a firm grasp. A moment later, a rebel struck Lucas over the head with his gun, prostrating him upon the works, and securing his flag. Meanwhile, a free fight with clubbed guns and bayonets raged on all sides.

The 16th Iowa was now entirely surrounded, and with it two companies of the 13th Iowa, who had been sent to its assistance. The ammunition of the little command was utterly exhausted, and to surrender was the only way to escape annihilation. Yielding themselves prisoners, the 16th Iowa were marched within the enemy's lines, their captors being, in part, the very prisoners they had themselves taken but an hour before.

Nearly twenty years afterward a thrilling scene, one without precedent, and a most fitting sequel to the deadly struggle before Atlanta, was witnessed at Cedar Rapids, Iowa. It was upon the occasion of the reunion of the survivors of Crocker's Iowa Brigade.

While Secretary of War, General Belknap (who had fought in the Iowa Brigade during the bitter struggle which has been described, and a few days later wore the star of a brigadier, and succeeded to the command,) received from General Govan, commander of the assaulting forces on that day, a letter in which he stated that the flag of the 16th Iowa Regiment had come into his possession. He expressed his desire to return it to the former owners, who, he said, "bore it with such conspicuous courage and gallantry in my presence on that memorable occasion, and only parted with it when to retain it longer was impossible, after having done all that could be expected of human courage and valor to defend it." General Govan added, that when the flag came into his possession, a fragment had been torn from it by the storm of bullets, and the portion wanting had been replaced by a part of his own Confederate battle-flag, sewed therein by the hands of his wife. In reply, General Belknap returned heartfelt thanks to General Govan for his magnanimity and soldierly courtesy, and extended to him a cordial invitation to attend the reunion of the Iowa Brigade, to be held at Cedar Rapids, Iowa, September 26th, 1883, and return the captured flag in person.

The invitation was accepted in the same friendly spirit in which it was given; and, in the presence of several hundred survivors of the Iowa Brigade,

and a large concourse of interested spectators, General
Belknap unrolled the old flag and waved it over his
head, while all present rose to their feet, and in
great excitement cheered and cheered until they were
fairly exhausted; while the veterans who had followed
the starry symbol so long and through such stirring
scenes, sobbed and wept with very joy.

Then, in response to repeated and urgent calls,
General Govan was invited to the stage, and in a
voice trembling with emotion, said :

" *Veterans of Crocker's Iowa Brigade :* I am
unable to find words to express the feelings of
pleasure and satisfaction that I feel in standing before
you. I feel it a compliment, not only to myself, but
to every Confederate soldier who served in the war,
that I am permitted to participate in this reunion.
They will feel grateful for this honor, and will respond and return it whenever an opportunity offers.
I have testified heretofore to the valor of your Iowa
soldiers in their heroic resistance at Atlanta. And if
I had said nothing, the long roll of the killed and
wounded of my command would bear mute but irre-
sistible testimony of your courage and valor on that
occasion. In behalf of our ex-soldiers, I beg leave to
return to you the flag won from you on that memorable occasion. I trust you will bear it as honorably
as you did then; and I assure you, should it ever
again be assailed, the men who opposed you that day
will stand by you in the future, and vie with you in
its defense. I hope that flag may float as long as

the everlasting hills endure, over a free, prosperous, happy and united people, as long as the waters flow to the great ocean."

As soon as the applause which greeted this address had died away, Colonel Ad. H. Sanders, the commander of the 16th Iowa Regiment, came forward, and, with a voice husky with emotion, said :

"The old flag! Lost, captured, but never disgraced. Let those who in solid line, and line massed on line, as brave soldiers, Confederates though they were, as ever did a soldier's duty, charged and charged again on the 16th Iowa, July 22d, 1864, till enemies dead and wounded numbered half as many as our men in the rifle-pits, and prisoners from their ranks nearly doubled our whole number; let them say, whether in the final capture of this flag, they thought in the hour of their triumph it had been disgraced by our defense, or their victory. They know, because they were there, and it was a sad and awful place for brave men to be, whether thirsting for glory or hungering for that flag. Only the day before, sixty-five men of the 16th Iowa fell in a charge on rebel works, with these same colors waving at their front. Was the old flag, with all its record of victories, and never a defeat, the very next day to be trailed in the dust, without a struggle such as men fight to the last drop of their hearts' blood, when honor more than life is at stake ? The old flag ! In many a battle, eyes have glazed in death looking at its loved folds. Men, with gaping wounds, and suppressed cries of agony, broke from the field, having turned their last gaze at the old colors, still fluttering mid smoke and shot. But never was so much blood shed for the defense of this flag as was spilled like rain for its capture, on that 22d day of July. Ask those who won it and wore it, and now, as gallantly as they fought for the prize, restore it to the brave hands that once so proudly upheld it. In the presence of the brave and chivalrous officer who, with so many complimentary expressions accompanying the gift, has restored this flag to the regiment from which his command once wrenched it, I can not find heart or voice at this hour to disparage the cause which secured such defenders as General Govan and his brigade. The flag of the Union, represented by these colors, still waves, vindicated, triumphant. Its friends and foes of two decades ago, are now as one, equally ready and equally brave, to defend the old flag, and all it represents, whether danger threatens from abroad or at home. Now, in the name, and as representative on this occasion, of the survivors of the 16th Iowa Infantry, I receive again our old loved colors—and, in the name of these comrades, I return thanks for the generous, chivalrous kindness which has enabled us this night to rejoice with even greater joy than those other comrades of the Iowa Brigade, who never lost a flag!"

Addresses were also made by Generals Gresham and Belknap; and letters were read from Generals Grant, Sherman, and Logan. Altogether, the event was a most notable one, and stands among the unusual incidents growing out of the Rebellion.

## CHAPTER XVII.

"THE BUMMER GENERALS."

FEW days after the battle of July
22d, the Army of the Tennessee
was greatly disturbed on learning that General O. O. Howard
had been assigned as their commander, sending General Logan
back to his corps. Howard was a
gallant officer, but a stranger to this
army, and he was devoid of that personal magnetism which gave Logan
so firm a hold upon the confidence
and affection of his troops. Logan
had made a brilliant record as regimental, brigade,
division, and corps commander ; he had been severely
wounded; and the men of the Army of the Tennessee
looked upon him as the most conspicuous representative of the genuine volunteer soldier. Besides,
whether rightly or not, they were disposed to blame
the "regulars" for endeavoring to monopolize more
of the honors of the war than their numbers or services entitled them to, and to feel that his being set

aside was in some way a reflection upon themselves and their achievements. General Sherman himself was evidently uneasy as to the outcome of General Howard's appointment, for he said in his "Memoirs," published since the war, referring to the battle of July 29th:

"This was the first fight in which General Howard had commanded the Army of the Tennessee, and he evidently aimed to reconcile General Logan in his disappointment, and to gain the heart of that army to which he was a stranger. He very properly left General Logan to fight his own corps, but exposed himself freely; and afterward walked the lines, the men gathering about him in the most affectionate way. To this fact at the time I attached much importance, for it put me at ease as to the future conduct of this most important army."

But much harm was done General Logan personally; General Sherman's criticisms being enlarged and made much of by those bitter partisans who were not in sympathy with General Logan's political views. General Sherman had said in his "Memoirs:"

"I did not consider him (Logan) equal to the command of three corps. Between him and General Blair there existed a natural rivalry. Both were men of great courage and talent, but were politicians by nature and experience, and it may be that for this reason they were mistrusted by the regular officers. . . I regarded Logan and Blair as 'volunteers,' that looked to personal fame and glory as auxiliary and secondary to their political ambition."

These expressions were eagerly caught up by newspapers which had been known during the war as "fire-in-the-rear" sheets. One of these printed a long and bitter screed entitled "The Bummer Generals," taking for a text the paragraph quoted above. Such articles excited great indignation among the men who had served in the Army of the Tennessee; and many angry replications found their way into print. An article by the author of this volume contained the following, which acquired a wide publicity:

"The effect of such assaults is great injustice to noble men who deserve better treatment. In the early days of the war, when well-known 'regulars' tried their best 'to keep out of the current,' as they themselves expressed it, Frank Blair, 'the bummer general,' with a handful of Home Guards, principally Germans, was overthrowing a rebel camp in the suburbs of St. Louis, and by the act held Missouri faithful to the Union. . . . Logan, Oglesby, Palmer, Hurlbut, the Smiths, Crocker, Belknap, McArthur, and scores of others who became 'bummer generals,' were holding public meetings, and bringing squads, companies, and regiments to the support of the government."

Referring to the battle of July 22d, the same article said:

"    .  .    When it was known that McPherson

had been killed, portions of the line wavered and broke. It was then that General Logan assumed command, and by his courage, and that personal magnetism which gave him so much power with his troops, succeeded in restoring confidence, and saved the day, and perhaps the army. In this, he was nobly seconded by General Frank P. Blair. Yet, notwithstanding all this, General Logan, and after him, General Blair, were not deemed fit to succeed McPherson. Although they were the commanders of western troops, which they had largely assisted in enlisting, and with whom they had been identified from the beginning of the war; yet the command was given to Howard, a perfect stranger to them, of whom they knew nothing. General Howard was never a favorite with the Army of the Tennessee; and we are satisfied, brave and honest man as he was, that had he been in command on the 22d of July, the result might have been far different."

The same article continued, referring to General Sherman's complaint, that General Logan and others went North at the close of the Atlanta campaign in 1864, to engage in the presidential campaign:

"We believe the honest sentiment of the country will admit that they did the cause a better service than had they remained at the front. The campaign was over, and the army was resting, with nothing to do but hold its ground until prepared for another movement. But at the North, 'peace conventions' had declared the war a failure, and many earnest Union men had almost lost heart. President Lincoln needed their influence at the polls ; and it was such men as Logan, and Blair, and Oglesby, wounded and victorious heroes, who kept up the faith of the people toward their government, and largely aided to make a successful issue at the last."

General Logan never did a nobler act in his life than when, after the action of July 22d, he testified to his own honesty of purpose, and stern ideas of soldierly duty, by returning uncomplainingly to the command of his corps, on being supplanted in the command of the Army of the Tennessee by one who was not guilty of the atrocious crime of being a civilian, or "bummer" general. True, Logan was not a professional soldier, but he was such a soldier as might well be held up as a fit exemplar for soldiers the world over. He was one of the bravest among the brave ; among the true, he was one of the truest. Where duty commanded him to go, he went ; where it called him to stay, there he remained. He was of such stuff as the men of the Light Brigade, who made that glorious charge at Balaklava ; as the men of the " Cumberland," who fired their guns at the enemy as their ship went down beneath the waves.

There are wars to be fought hereafter, and the sons of men now living may possibly fight them. God grant that they learn their lessons of a soldier's duty from a "bummer general" such as John A. Logan, rather than from a "professional soldier," such as Fitz-John Porter !

## CHAPTER XVIII.

### HAMMERING AWAY.

UPON the close of the engagement of July 22d the enemy drew back into his entrenchments at Atlanta. The next day a truce was declared, to admit of either army burying its dead. For ten days thereafter a great part of the army was engaged in burning the ties and twisting the rails of the Georgia and Virginia railroad, reaching east. This task was preliminary to a movement by the right flank to reach the only railroad remaining open out of Atlanta, that running south. As usual, the rapid march, which was the main incident of the plan, fell to the lot of the Army of the Tennessee.

As soon as it was sufficiently dark, on the night of July 26th this command silently moved out of its works, and marched north and west around Atlanta,

thence south to Ezra Church, which lay almost due
west from the point of departure. The movement consumed almost the entire night, and the distance covered was about twenty miles.

Immediately upon taking up the new line the troops
entrenched. It was remarkable how quickly this kind
of work was performed. Frequently a brigade would
pick up a rail-fence so clean that nothing was left to
mark where it had been, and carry the rails half-a-
mile, throwing them down to serve as a protection,
when they had advanced as far as possible. Often the
same rails sufficed for half-a-dozen different lines,
being carried forward whenever an advance was
made.

The Army of the Tennessee found itself in trouble
at early dawn on the 27th, and sharp skirmishing
continued throughout the day, at times almost rising
to the dignity of a regular engagement. The next
day was one of serious fighting, Logan's Fifteenth
Corps taking the brunt of the work, and successfully
withstanding six vigorous charges. General Logan
lost upward of five hundred men, and Blair and Dodge,
who sent reinforcements at a critical moment, sustained some loss. The casualties of the enemy were
not less than five thousand.

General Howard said of this engagement : " I
wish to express my high gratification with the conduct
of the troops engaged. I never saw better in battle.

The general commanding the Fifteenth Corps, though ill and much worn out, was indefatigable ; and the success of the day is as much attributable to him as to any one man."

This practically closed the campaign for July. Sherman had lost nine thousand seven hundred men; the enemy, ten thousand eight hundred and forty-one. Hood had forced the fighting at fearful cost to himself, and was already falling into disfavor. An Atlanta paper said : "If Mr. Hood keeps on in this way of fighting, his army will be wiped out in ten days, and the Yankees will still have a few men to go to Mobile left." But the Unionists had also lost severely, although better able to afford it. Another paper printed the following : "Some one asked a Frenchman if the American war was over. 'No,' said he, 'I still see a few inhabitants !'" This piece of humor was credited to a French paper — a familiar expedient with newspaper men when they concoct a lie, and do not desire to be held responsible for it.

Sharp skirmishing and fierce artillery duels were of daily occurrence until August 4th, when an unsuccessful attempt was made upon the enemy's left. The Twenty-third Corps (Schofield's) was the assaulting column, and the Seventeenth Corps advanced its lines in support. The latter command moved promptly at the moment designated ; but Schofield's either failed to move, or did so with such little spirit, that the Seventeenth Corps was subjected to a severe enfilading fire, compelling it to retire. The attack was repeated the next day, and was again repulsed. The affair resulted in General Palmer resigning the command of the Fourteenth Corps, an event of great moment, inasmuch as it was the first and only serious disagreement between the general-in-chief and a subordinate, during the entire campaign.

It may be premised that, at the time of this unfortunate occurrence, the understanding in the Army of the Tennessee was, that the responsibility for the difficulty rested upon General Palmer. The writer was in a position to know the feeling in the highest places in that portion of the army, and his journal says, under date of July 5th :

"General Schofield was to reach and hold the railroad (south of Atlanta). General Palmer was under orders to report to Schofield, but Palmer raised many objections. While the two generals were quarreling, our skirmish line (Seventeenth Corps) was stoutly resisted and compelled to retire."

This was the statement made at the time in the Seventeenth Corps. The details have since been ascertained.

General Sherman, in his report of the campaign, says :

"I ordered General Schofield to make a bold at-

A STRUGGLE FOR A FLAG.

See page 169.

tack upon the railroad, and ordered General Palmer to
report to him for duty. He at once denied General
Schofield's right to command him. . . I wrote to
General Palmer :

"'From the statements made by yourself and General Schofield to-day, my decision is that he ranks you
as a major-general. The movements of to-morrow are
so important that the orders of the superior on that
flank must be regarded as military orders, and not in
the nature of coöperation. I did hope that there
would be no necessity for my making this decision;
but it is better for all that no question of rank should
occur in actual battle. The Sandtown road, and the
railroad, if possible, must be gained to-morrow if it
costs half your command. I regard the loss of time
this afternoon as equal to the loss of two thousand
men.'"

The same day, General Sherman wrote to General
Thomas, General Palmer's immediate superior :

"Yesterday General Palmer raised the question of
rank with General Schofield. I went in person, and
found that General Schofield ranked General Palmer,
and so decided. . . General Palmer asked to be
relieved of his command. I declined, and ordered
him to go on to-day and execute the plan prescribed
for yesterday, in connection with and under the command of General Schofield."

To this General Thomas answered :

"I regret that Palmer has taken the course he has,
and, as I know he intends to offer his resignation as

soon as he can properly do so, I recommend that his application be granted."

General Sherman sent the purport of this note to General Palmer, and said :

"If you resign because you measure your number of men as greater than his (Schofield's), and your services in battle as giving you greater right to command, you commit the mistake of substituting your own individual opinion over law and military usage. The special assignment of General Schofield to the command of a separate army and department, shows that he enjoys the confidence of the President even above his mere lineal rank. If you want to resign, wait a few days, and allege some other reason, one that will stand the test of time. Your future is too valuable to be staked on a mistake. . . I again ask you not to disregard the friendly advice of such men as General Thomas and myself, for you can not misconstrue our friendly feelings toward you."

General Palmer persisted, however, and was relieved, and shortly afterward was assigned to the command of the Department of Kentucky, with headquarters at Louisville, in which position he acquitted himself with full satisfaction to the government. His retirement from active service was greatly regretted by his troops, who felt much as did the Army of the Tennessee when Logan was set aside to make way for Howard; but the remainder of the army almost unanimously sided with Sherman.

At a later day, General Palmer authorized the following statement, but it was not put into such form as to secure widespread circulation :

"He (Palmer) was ordered to take a position in the rear of the Army of the Ohio, and support General Schofield. A question of rank arose. Palmer said that rank made no difference to him in the operations then pending; that he was there to support the Army of the Ohio by order of General Thomas, and as Schofield was in charge of the movement, he held himself subject to his orders. General Sherman met General Palmer soon after, and said to him that he thought he was wrong. Palmer replied that he had waived all questions of rank, for the purposes of the contemplated movement, and was awaiting orders from Schofield. General Sherman rode on to Schofield's headquarters. On that night he sent a letter to General Palmer, saying that his voluntary consent to obey Schofield's order was not enough; that he must acknowledge his inferiority of rank. General Palmer asked to be relieved. Sherman replied that he could not properly ask to be relieved in the presence of an enemy. By the advice of General Thomas, Palmer concluded to waive the question of rank until the end of the campaign. It was supposed that would settle the matter; but, on the following night, to his complete astonishment, he received a letter from Sherman, saying that he (Sherman) understood from Thomas that he (Palmer) intended to offer his resignation at the end of the campaign. If so, he might fairly say that the campaign was already closed, and resign. Palmer answered in effect : 'Yesterday, when I asked to be relieved on a question of rank, you wrote that I could not honorably do so in the presence of the enemy. Now, you write otherwise. On this plain evidence of your unfriendliness, I conclude that I can be of no service under your command, and respectfully ask to be relieved.' "

## CHAPTER XIX.

### THE OLD CHAPLAIN.

H I L E the operations about Atlanta were yet continuing, the author was called to Marietta, twenty miles rearward. Here he found, in the hospital, "Father" M'Millan, the chaplain of his regiment, prostrated with disease. The venerable man was already at death's door, and could converse only with great difficulty. It was a sorrowful meeting. The two were warmly attached, having known each other for many years, and both realized that in life they could not meet again. A day or two later the old man breathed his last.

The writer can not halt his pen without paying a feeble tribute to the memory of this noble soldier of the cross. He was of such stuff as the martyrs and saints of old, who illumine the dark pages of history with gleams of brightness. Born in Tennessee, he inherited from his Scotch-Presbyterian ancestors stern ideas of right, and unflinching devotion to duty as it came to him. Although reared amid the corrupting influences of slavery, he conceived the "institution" not only to be a foul blot upon our civilization, but a sin against God ; and, unwilling that his children, all sons, should be subjected to the demoralizing influences of this " sum of all villainies," he abandoned a fine position, as the head of a leading educational institution, and high family connection, to educate them in a land of freedom. He removed to Illinois, and assumed the pastorate of a Presbyterian church in a growing town in the interior of the state. Here he won the love of all by his unaffected sincerity and genial warm-heartedness. The reason for his removal from his native state was soon known throughout the community, but his opposition to slavery did not lead him into any excesses of speech. He denounced the system as a moral crime and a political wrong ; but, like many of the old-school Whigs, believed it to be so hedged about by the sacred constitutional compact, that none could rightfully seek its overthrow, except by moral agitation. He discerned, however, the true impórt of the storm already rising. He had lived through and listened to the angry threats of the Southern nullificationists, and had heard disunionism preached in his native state. John Brown had made his crazy raid

upon Harper's Ferry ; extreme Southerners had said
that the election of an " abolition " President would be
just cause for secession ; and Lincoln, then opposing
Douglas for Congress, had startled the country with
the vehement declaration, not born of fanaticism, but
founded upon the inexorable logic of God's decrees,
" This nation can not permanently endure, half slave
and half free. 'A house divided against itself can not
stand.' " Never to be forgotten by any one of his
hearers, was a sermon delivered by the venerable clergyman just before the war-cloud burst. He plead for
conservatism and brotherly toleration, and a settle-
ment of the question at issue through the development
of ideas, rather than a resort to passion and blows.
His peroration was a masterly piece of rhetoric. He
said : " Before me I see two mighty armed hosts.
One bears the banner, ' God and Slavery !' the other,
' God and Freedom !' There are my brothers, my
friends ; here am I and mine own ! Shall I raise my
arm against them ? Will they discharge their fatal
volleys into their brother's breast? Forbid it, Almighty
God, if may be ; but if not, work out Thy mighty decrees with us, Thy feeble instruments, even though
our blood be spilt in expiation of the crime of the
nation ! "

At a later day, in Tennessee, his own state, while
the war was in progress, and he wore the uniform of
his chaplaincy, when the question of emancipation was

just coming to be discussed, he wrote resolutions advo-
cating that policy, purely as a war measure. These
resolutions were adopted by his regiment in mass
meeting, without a dissenting voice ; and so dispas-
sionate and convincing were they, that they attained a
wide publicity. The New York *Times* referred to
them as the most logical and convincing statement of
the case that had yet been presented. Their salient
points, showing the spirit of that day, curiously blend-
ing radical war-aggressiveness with conservative political ideas, are here given :

1. The integrity of our blood-bought Union, "one and indi-
visible." "It must and shall be maintained."

2. A prosecution of the war commensurate with all the resources
of the nation, till the last vestige of the rebellion is obliterated, and the
majesty of law vindicated and fully established.

3. Settle the question whether we shall have a government to
administer, before we divert public attention from the great matter in
hand, to the question what political party shall administer it.

4. While the South remained loyal to the Union, we were ever
ready to protect all her constitutional rights ; and when she returns to
her allegiance we pledge her the same. But since she has forced war
upon us, by whipping and hanging, without form of trial, and viciously
mobbing those who, by the constitution, were entitled to all the immu-
nities and privileges of citizens ; by wantonly seizing the property and
funds of the nation ; by confiscating just debts, property and funds of
loyal citizens ; by refusing to allow the evacuation of Fort Sumter
unless it was surrendered ; by bombarding and reducing it when the surrender was refused ; by publicly declaring her purpose, by force of arms,
to take the capital of the nation, with its archives ; and by setting up a
government of her own within the territorial limits of the United States ;
we are now for giving her war until she is subdued to her proper
allegiance. We are for weakening her by cutting off her resources, confiscating her property, slaves not excepted ; and by every means known
to civilized warfare, reducing her to her proper loyalty.

5. As the rebels have employed slaves, first in making their forts,

and more recently under arms (?), we approve the policy of arming slaves to meet slaves in battle. *Nor do we fight to free the slaves, but free the slaves to stop the fight.*

But this is anticipating. Soon after the organization of the regiment mentioned, he was called to the chaplaincy, and joyfully accepted the charge, regarding it not only a sacred duty, but a high privilege, to be enabled to go where he might "watch over my boys," as he put it, meaning the sons of many of his old neighbors and parishioners. Many of the army chaplains fell into disrepute during the war, drifting into the general tide of demoralization; and, if not positively vicious, losing sight of almost everything but their own comfort. Chaplain M'Millan never lost an iota of his dignity of character, his sense of duty, or his kindly affection for those about him. His care for "my boys" was solicitous and touching. More than once he personally rebuked officers of high rank for using towards soldiers, language that would not be tolerated elsewhere than in the field. In camp, he visited the hospital and the tent of the private, writing letters for those unable to do so themselves; and cheering the down-hearted, and admonishing the erring. On the march he was ever watchful for the crippled and infirm, and daily left his saddle to allow such a one to ride for a time. The exposures of campaigning told severely upon his aged frame, and he finally succumbed to disease, breathing his last, far

13

from kindred and home, within hearing of the conflict he had so graphically portrayed in advance of its opening. The epitaph of such a man might well be the noble words uttered by Paul :

"I have fought a good fight, I have finished my course, I have kept the faith. Henceforth there is laid up for me a crown of righteousness which the Lord, the righteous judge, shall give me at that day."

## CHAPTER XX.

### "ATLANTA IS OURS, AND FAIRLY WON!"

HE remainder of August was marked with unceasing activity. Under date of the 7th, the writer's diary notes, "Our lines were shelled fiercely to-day. This division lost many men." On the 10th: "Enemy's artillery much more active than in the early days of the campaign. We endured four hours' shelling to-day. The enemy having heavier guns than ours, has it pretty much all his own way." 17th: "The enemy has raided the railroad again, and orders have been issued limiting rations, and instructing the men to be saving of ammunition. Demonstrated heavily on the enemy's lines to-day to aid Schofield, who is on the right." 19th: "Demonstrated again to-day. Schofield does not seem to be able to reach the railroad." 20th: "Late last night the firing on the skirmish line was suddenly quieted by a tremendous rain. As soon as it ceased, the lines opened a brisk fire again." An entry the same day, summarizes the losses of the division (Giles A. Smith's) thus : "June 10th, at Big Shanty, this division numbered five thousand men. To this date, we have lost one hundred and seventy-five killed, eight hundred and fifty wounded, seven hundred and sixty missing—in all, one thousand seven hundred and eighty-five men."

August 26th, the army commenced a movement against the West Point railroad. All artillery and wagon trains that could be moved without attracting attention, were sent early in the day in the direction to be pursued; and, as soon as night fell, the guns from the front followed with muffled wheels. A slight skirmish line was left in the pits, with instructions to keep up sufficient firing to induce the belief that the ordinary force was present, and all other troops silently left their works. The march was continued until daybreak, which found them thirteen miles to the south and west. Coffee was hastily made, as hastily swallowed, and another six miles added to the distance. The remainder of the day was given to rest, which was sadly needed.

Next day, August 28th, the troops marched eight miles, and found the enemy at Red Oak Station. They were driven without great effort, and a footing on the railroad gained, when the army went to work with a will to destroy it, burning the ties and twisting the rails to such an extent as to utterly preclude the possibility of their use again.

The following day, August 29th, a further march of twelve miles was made, and early next morning the enemy was again encountered on Flint river, near Jonesboro. They assaulted the Union lines, evidently hoping to catch them before they could get well straightened out for action, but were repulsed.

September 1st, a stout engagement was fought, resulting in the defeat of the enemy. His loss was severe; and among the prisoners taken was General Govan, who captured the 16th Iowa Regiment on the 22d of July, as narrated in a preceding chapter, and the greater part of his brigade.

That night, heavy explosions were heard in the direction of Atlanta, twenty miles distant, leading to the conclusion that General Slocum was making an attack; but, the next morning, prisoners brought in by the cavalry, reported that the noise was caused by Hood blowing up some of his ammunition trains; and, in consequence of the raid upon his railroad, he had abandoned the city.

Then it was that General Sherman sent to Washington his announcement of the victory, which contained the famous sentence : "Atlanta is ours, and fairly won !" Referring to it, General Sherman says in his "Memoirs" :

"This victory was most opportune. Mr. Lincoln

told me afterward that even he had felt in doubt. . . .
A presidential election then agitated the North.   Mr.
Lincoln represented the national cause, and General
McClellan had accepted the nomination of the Demo-
cratic party, whose platform was that the war was a
failure, and that it was better to allow the South to go,
free to establish a separate government, whose corner-
stone should be slavery.   Success to our arms at that
time was a political necessity.   The brilliant success
at Atlanta filled the requirement, and made the election of Mr  Lincoln certain."

Immediately upon the occupation of Atlanta, General Sherman issued orders proclaiming the end of the
campaign, and ordering the army into camp "for rest,
and reorganization for a fine winter's campaign."   The
Army of the Cumberland was to be grouped in and
about Atlanta ; the Army of the Tennessee at East
Point, and the Army of the Ohio at Decatur.   This
movement began September 5th, and proved to be a
remarkable conclusion to an eventful campaign.   It
rather resembled the retreat of a defeated army, than a
victorious march by conquerors.

As the head of the column turned toward Atlanta,
Hood's army was but a little distance behind it, and
his cavalry was particularly active.   It was necessary,
therefore, that the artillery and supply wagons should
precede the troops.   A heavy rain had been falling all
day, and, what with the unmeasurable mud in the
roads, and the unserviceable condition of the animals,

consequent upon long service and ill-feeding, it was nine o'clock at night before the long train was straightened out, and the troops began to move. The march was spasmodic and painful. For a few minutes at a time, the men plodded along as well as was possible in the intense darkness and blinding rain ; then a halt would occur, sometimes for five minutes, sometimes for a half-hour, caused by a portion of the wagon-train stalling or breaking down. Occasionally a wagon, irretrievably wrecked, or its team utterly worn out, was thrown to one side of the road, and burned. At one moment, startled by such a conflagration, the writer's horse made a sudden leap, and the rider, asleep in the saddle through sheer exhaustion, was awakened by falling into the mud. After a march of six miles, consuming twelve hours' time, a halt was called, and the wearied troops prepared such food and took such rest as the weather would permit. During the day a further hard march of six miles was accomplished, and camp established near East Point.

That evening, general orders were read to the troops, communicating the following historic papers :

EXECUTIVE MANSION,
WASHINGTON, Sept. 3, 1864.

The national thanks are rendered by the President to Major General W. T. Sherman and the gallant officers and soldiers of his command, before Atlanta, for the distinguished ability and perseverance displayed in the campaign in Georgia, which, under Divine favor, has resulted in the capture of Atlanta. The marches, battles, sieges, and other military operations that have signalized the campaign, must render it famous in the annals of war, and have entitled those who have participated therein to the applause and thanks of the nation.

ABRAHAM LINCOLN,
President of the United States.

CITY POINT, VA., Sept. 4.

MAJ. GEN. SHERMAN : I have just received your dispatch announcing the capture of Atlanta. In honor of your great victory, I have ordered a salute to be fired, with shotted guns, from every battery bearing upon the enemy. The salute will be fired within an hour, amid great rejoicing.      U. S. GRANT,
Lieutenant General.

And now that the troops fully recognized the import of their brilliant but wearisome and bloody three months' campaigning, and learned with what joy the news was received at home, they gave way to a protracted jubilee. The brass and martial bands, which had been silent all the long way from Chattanooga to Atlanta, now played their most exultant airs ; and the men vied with the instruments in making noise expressive of great joy. All were happy and smiling, from the commander-in-chief to the humblest private in the ranks, and even the bray of the half-starved government mule seemed mellow and melodious, as it added to the din.

Better yet, "the cracker-line," as the railroad was called, was again in repair, after having been greatly disturbed by the enemy ; and presently the troops enjoyed the novel experience of abundant rations and frequent mails.

At this time, by the urgent request of President

Lincoln, Generals Blair and Logan went North to speak during the presidential contest, then at its height. Blair returned in time to accompany his corps in its march to the sea. Logan, however, when just on the eve of return to the front, was cut off by Sherman's departure from Atlanta. He at once went to Washington, and was ordered to Nashville to relieve General Thomas, who rested under the imputation of want of enterprise. On reaching Louisville, however, Logan was so fully convinced of Thomas' ability and determination to stop Hood at Nashville, that he went no farther, but telegraphed General Grant that it would be neither just nor expedient to relieve Thomas when he was doing so well. Accordingly, Thomas retained his command, while Logan remained at the North until Sherman reached the sea, where he rejoined the army, and resumed command of his old corps.

While the army was resting in the vicinity of Atlanta, General Sherman busied himself in preparing for another campaign; and, as a necessary incident to the success of his plans, he demanded that the entire population of Atlanta should be removed, the people being given the privilege of going North or South, as they might prefer. To those electing to go North, he proffered rations, and transportation for themselves and their effects; those preferring the South he would remove, with their goods, to Rough and Ready, twenty miles distant, and place them under the protection of the Confederate military authorities. Negroes in the employ or keeping of these people, were to be free to go South with their masters if they so desired.

The determination to depopulate Atlanta provoked an angry correspondence between Generals Sherman and Hood, in course of which the latter dealt in much florid rhetoric, and exposed himself to the most cruel thrusts of Sherman's caustic pen. Hood protested "in the name of God and humanity," and declared that " the unprecedented measure transcends, in studied and ingenious cruelty, all acts ever before brought to my attention in the dark history of war." He added : "We will fight you to the death ! Better die a thousand deaths than submit to live under you or your government, and your negro allies."

In reply, General Sherman defended his course, and suggested it as "unnecessary to appeal to the dark ages of the history of war, when recent and modern examples are so handy;" and instanced numerous cases, adding, "You defended Atlanta on a line so close to town that every cannon-shot, and many musket shots, that overshot their mark, went into the habitations of women and children." He continued : "Appeal not to a just God in such a sacrilegious manner—you who, in the midst of peace and prosperity, have plunged a nation into a dark and cruel war."

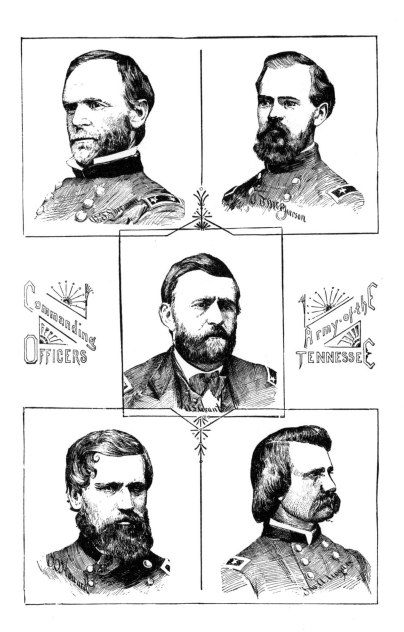

Commanding Officers

Army of the Tennessee

The civil authorities of Atlanta also sought to secure a revocation of the order, and instanced some pitiable cases of real distress which would follow its enforcement. To them General Sherman replied in pregnant terms : " My order was not designed to meet the humanities of the case, but to prepare for the future struggle in which millions of good people outside of Atlanta have a deep interest. We must have peace, not only in Atlanta, but in all America. To secure this, we must stop the war. To stop war, we must defeat the rebel armies. . . When peace does come, you may call on me for anything. Then will I share with you the last cracker, and watch with you to shield your homes and families against danger from every quarter."

Even while General Sherman's brain was busy with these matters, and his plans for a new campaign, he found time to give kindly thought to the unfortunate men of his own and of other Union armies, who had fallen into the hands of the enemy. A flag of truce station was established at Rough and Ready, and such of the rebel prisoners as had not been sent North were delivered to General Hood, in exchange for an equal number of Union prisoners. But General Sherman's kindness of heart found its most eloquent expression in the consideration he gave to alleviating the distress of the unhappy wretches held in the Andersonville prison pens. He had learned their condition from the few captives who were so fortunate as to escape, and asked permission from General Hood to send within the rebel lines a train-load of clothing and other necessaries to relieve their immediate wants. The request was granted, and the Western Sanitary Commission, through its agent, Mr. James E. Yeatman, of St. Louis, upon General Sherman's request, forwarded a large quantity of under-clothing, soap, scissors, and fine-combs—articles for which there was the utmost need. The well-meant effort was unproductive of good, however, for before the supplies could reach Andersonville, the prisoners were removed to keep them from falling into the hands of Sherman's army, which, by that time, was sweeping through the "Confederacy," making

> " A thoroughfare for Freedom and her train,
> Sixty miles in latitude, three hundred to the main."

# CHAPTER XXI.

## A CHAPTER OF INCIDENTS.

URING the breathing spell which followed the end of the Atlanta campaign, the adjutant was granted a brief leave, accompanied with a hint from Colonel Cadle, General Blair's adjutant general, to "get back in a hurry, or you will lose some fun." His journey was marked with so many incidents of an unusual nature, that the narrative is given, although it obtrudes somewhat more of the personality of the actor than he had intended at the outset.

A part of the adjutant's mission at the North was to procure commissions for a number of meritorious non-commissioned officers, for whose promotion the casualties of the campaign had made opportunity. Visiting the office of the Adjutant-General, he made known his errand, and presented the necessary recommendations; but those in charge did not receive him with great cordiality, apparently resenting the irregular method of dealing with the department, instead of observing the usual red tape channels prescribed by military etiquette. In this strait, the adjutant called upon Governor Yates, and presented his case; whereupon that great-hearted man, ever a warm friend of the soldier, and now doubly glad to have an opportunity for rewarding in some measure well deserving men of that army which had rendered such distinguished service, made the crooked path straight, and ordered the immediate issuance of the commissions so much desired.

Reaching Louisville, October 1st, on his return to the front, the adjutant learned that the railroad was a forbidden way to soldiers, peremptory orders requiring them to go forward, if at all, in marching detachments, all rolling stock being absolutely necessary for the transportation of army supplies. He was so fortunate, however, as to have a personal acquaintance with the commander of the district, and that officer kindly provided him with a railroad pass to Nashville, which was as far as his authority extended.

The next day, the adjutant reached Nashville, and was greatly disconcerted to learn that no soldiers were allowed to pass south of that city under any pretext whatever ; and that all transient officers and men were required to report to the local military authorities for assignment to provisional commands, then being organized for the defense of the post. No particulars were given of the emergency calling for these unusual dispositions, and the wildest rumors prevailed.

Sorely out of patience, the adjutant wandered about the city disconsolately, delaying compliance with the printed orders which stared him in the face wherever he turned, and hoping to find some way out of the difficulty. No experience is so hard for the soldier, as to find himself far away from his own command, and obliged to do duty with strange troops, especially when the latter are of a hap-hazard, made-up-for-the-occasion character ; and his memory reverted to his experiences when, as a private, he was so situated at Memphis, and made to do duty with a spade, in the trenches of Fort Pickering.

While his mind was thus occupied with painful reminiscences of the past, and doubtful misgivings as to the future, the adjutant's eye fell upon a building with a sign-board inscribed, " U. S. Military Telegraph : J. C. Van Duzer, Supt." He hailed the name with glad surprise, for it was that of his old friend, the telegraph operator " at home," before the war began. Colonel Van Duzer was fortunately present, and, in answer to anxious inquiry, gave a startling account of affairs at the front. Hood had interposed his army between that of Sherman, at Atlanta, and Chattanooga, and was marching down the railroad, wrecking it completely. How near he had approached

14

to Chattanooga, or what course Sherman was taking to stop him in his all-devastating career, could not be ascertained.  However, none but construction trains were running south from Nashville, and they with fear and trembling ;  while all soldiers reaching that city from the North, were being held and organized for local defense, or to be dispatched to such point on the road as might require their services.

Colonel Van Duzer then gave the adjutant assurances that he would assist him to rejoin his command at the earliest possible opportunity, and, in the meantime, guarantee him immunity from draft for local military duty.  It would be necessary, however, for him to lay aside his uniform, and masquerade for the time as a member of the Telegraph Repair Corps.  To this the adjutant readily consented; and, what with the friendly offices of Colonel Van Duzer, and the companionship of two *bona fide* members of the corps, who had been school-day and workshop companions with him, in former years, he found himself much more pleasantly situated than he had expected.

At length came a day of release from all uncertainty.  At noon on the 4th of October, the adjutant mounted the top of a box-car loaded with artillery ammunition bound for Chattanooga.  He wore a cap bearing the initials, " U. S. M. T." (United States Military Telegraph) ; and in his pocket bore a pass under the hand of Colonel Van Duzer, certifying to his connection with that corps, and ordering all trains to transport him at pleasure. The train ran but slowly, and darkness came before half the distance had been accomplished. Then fell a torrent of rain, continuing all night, thoroughly drenching the unhappy traveler. In places the track ran through tunnels, and long cuts in the solid rock, where the water came down from the mountain sides in floods, making necessary a firm grip upon the brakeman's footway, to avoid being swept away.

On the 7th, by virtue of his pass, the adjutant boarded a repair train and ran to the Oostanaula river. The bridge there had been destroyed by the rebels, and with a companion, a genuine telegraph repairer, he crossed the stream in a scow. On the other side another engine was found, which conveyed them to the Etowah. Here, again, the bridge was gone, and again a scow was brought into requisition. On the other side were found an engine and tender which had been cut off by the rebel raid. The engineer was alone, his fireman having deserted ; and his joy was great at finding blue-coated friends, with something in their canteens and haversacks, instead of gray-jacketed enemies seeking his life. His engine was cold, and almost out of wood, but there was fortunately some water in the tank. The U. S. M. T. orders were produced, and the engineer readily consented to go anywhere, if the necessary fuel could be had; whereupon the three chopped up sufficient fence-rails and fallen timber to fill the tender, then got up steam, and started south.

On the evening of October 8th, the party reached Allatoona. Hood's attack had been made but three days before, and everything was in confusion. All the red tape belonging to the subsistence and ordnance departments had gone down in the general wreck, and the adjutant found it necessary to issue, without the formality of a requisition, food, arms and ammunition, to a squad of fifteen men belonging to commands farther down the road, who attached themselves to him on learning his destination. The party followed the railroad south, marching on foot. Night overtook them about midway between Allatoona and Big Shanty, where they went into bivouac, posting pickets, and refraining from making fires, lest the enemy might be lurking about. In the morning the journey was resumed, and in due time all reached their various regiments.

The railroad between Allatoona and Big Shanty, a distance of fifteen miles, had been entirely destroyed by the enemy. Every tie was burned, and every rail twisted; the cuts in the road were filled with heavy trees felled from the side of the road, and the wrecks of many engines and cars, given to the flames after their supplies had been removed to the enemy's wagon trains.

At Allatoona, the adjutant met some of his friends of the 7th Illinois, and other regiments, among whom was Captain M. R. Flint, General Corse's aide, from whom he derived a vivid narrative of the bloody battle which had been so lately fought.

## CHAPTER XXII.

### ALLATOONA.

THE enemy had passed around Atlanta with the intention of destroying the railroad in Sherman's rear, hoping to compel him to retreat northward.

The first blow was struck at Big Shanty, on the morning of October 4th. This post was garrisoned by a portion of the consolidated Fourteenth and Fifteenth Illinois Veteran Battalions, of the Fourth Division, Seventeenth Corps. The little command made a vigorous resistance, but the enemy was in strong force, and captured it almost bodily.

Somewhat farther south, guarding the water-tank, a short distance from the base of Kenesaw Mountain, was posted the 32d Illinois Regiment, of the same division. The commander of this regiment, Major Davidson, on hearing the first scattering shots of the enemy's advance upon Big Shanty, formed his line, threw out skirmishers, and pushed forward to learn what the noise meant. He advanced within half a mile of Big Shanty, when a heavy attack was made upon his flank by a greatly superior force, dispersing his men after a sharp conflict. Several of the skirmishers were captured; among them Sergeant John M. Rice, a young man of unusual intelligence. Rice was taken at once before General Jackson, and sharply questioned respecting the position and character of the troops farther up the road ; and, using his own language, he " had hard work inventing lies fast enough to answer the questions, and keep from self-contradiction." The General assured Rice that his personal effects should be respected, but within ten minutes after leaving the presence of that officer, he was robbed of all the clothing he wore, receiving a motley assortment of villainous " butternut," in exchange. With other prisoners from his own regiment, and those of the Fourteenth and Fifteenth Illinois Battalions, Rice was sent to Andersonville, and did not regain his liberty until the close of the war.

From Big Shanty the enemy pressed northward, and only halted when he arrived in front of Allatoona. At that point were stored vast supplies of subsistence and ammunition, indispensable to the existence of the Union army. To Sherman the loss of this post meant a disastrous ending to a hitherto successful campaign. To Hood, its acquisition promised means for prosecuting offensive operations, and held out a hope for the absolute ruin of his enemy.

Neither the movement nor its purpose escaped the shrewd and ever-watchful Sherman ; he saw the one, and divined the other. Hastening to Vining's Station, from whose summit he could convey messages to Kenesaw, and thence to Allatoona, by the flags of his signal corps, he instructed the commanding officer at the latter place to call General Corse from Rome to his assistance. He also said : " If he (Hood) moves up toward Allatoona, I will surely come in force." By a poetic license, some verse-maker twisted this message, making it read, " Hold the fort, for I am coming ! " and wrote the hymn which goes by that title. Unlike most popular songs, this one has never been followed by an " answer." Possibly the response of Corse, after the battle, " I am short a cheek-bone and an ear, but am able to whip all hell yet ! " was not considered an appropriate text.

The garrison at Allatoona was a brigade of three small regiments, and a battery of field artillery, all commanded by Lieutenant-Colonel Tourtelotte, of the 4th Minnesota Regiment. General Corse arrived from Rome, during the night of October 4th, bringing with him Colonel Dick Rowett's brigade of three fragmentary veteran regiments, which increased the number of the garrison to nearly two thousand men. The 7th Illinois, of Rowett's brigade (his own regiment) was

so important an acquisition to the defensive power of
the garrison, that its services can not be overestimated.
It was armed with the Henry rifle, a sixteen-shot magazine gun ; and the rapidity and effectiveness of its fire
told fearfully upon the charging columns of the enemy
at various times during the action which followed.
Indeed, it is questionable whether the comparatively
slow fire of muzzle-loading guns would have been able
to cope with the dense masses of the enemy in their
desperate assaults.  The moral influence of this fire-
arm was probably as great as its destructive power.
The enemy held it in great dread, speaking of it as
" a gun the Yanks loaded up on Sunday, and fired off
all the rest of the week." · The 7th had received these
arms only a few days before the battle, the men supplying themselves, out of their own means, at a cost of
fifty-one dollars a gun, more than three months' pay.

Rowett's brigade might have been readily intercepted by the enemy.  The troops came by railroad,
in freight-cars; and their safe arrival at Allatoona was
only due to the fact that so few men were visible, that
the enemy supposed the train to be loaded with supplies, and, confident of their ability to capture the
post, permitted it to run into the depot under the
protection of the forts.  The train bearing the second
brigade of Corse's division ran off the track soon after
leaving Rome, and did not reach Allatoona until after
the battle.

General Corse's command left the cars about two o'clock in the morning, and at once formed line. The enemy was even then within easy rifle range, and kept up a spattering fire. Captain M. R. Flint, of General Corse's staff, annoyed by the incessant zip-zip of the bullets, and anxious to be employed, asked his chief whether it would not be advisable to carry the ammunition from the train into the fort. The General was not apprehensive of serious trouble, and did not think it necessary, but left the matter to the discretion of his aide. Captain Flint at once detailed a sufficient number of men, and carried out his suggestion. The act was providential—it was but a few hours before the ammunition was sorely needed; its absence might have caused a great disaster and changed the entire campaign.

Shortly after sunrise, on the morning of the memorable 5th of October, General Sherman stood upon the summit of Kenesaw Mountain, anxious for tidings from Allatoona.

At the same moment General Corse and staff stood at the signal station on Allatoona. By his side was the signal officer, transmitting the message of his commander. The flag fluttered to right and left, slowly spelled out the words: " Corse is—— "

At this moment, the enemy occupying the valley below and to the south, discharged a battery of artillery. A shell cut away the flag-staff in the hands of

Around Allatoona
Oct: 5th 8.15 Am 1864

Commanding officer
U.S. forces Allatoona

Sir.

I have placed the forces
under my command in such positions
that you are surrounded, and to avoid
a needless effusion of blood I call on
you to surrender your forces at once and
unconditionally – Five minutes will be
allowed you to decide.
Should you accede to this, you will
be treated in the most honorable
manner as prisoners of war.

I have the honor to be
very respectfully yours
S. G. French
Maj Genl
Comdg Forces.
C. S.

Head Quarters 4th Div
15th Army Corps
8:30 A.M. Oct 5/64

Maj Genl S. G. French
C. S. Acc

Your
communication demanding
surrender of my command
I acknowledge receipt of
and respectfully reply that
we are prepared for the
"needless effusion of blood"
whenever it is agreeable
to you

I am very respectfully
Your Obt Servt
John M. Corse
Brig Genl
Commanding Forces U.S.

its bearer, and the message was not completed. Before a new flag could be procured, the mist, and smoke rising from the enemy's batteries, spread an impenetrable veil between Kenesaw and Allatoona. What must have been Sherman's anxiety at Kenesaw! " Corse is ——!" What should have been the remainder of the message? Was Corse at Allatoona, or was he not? Was he living, or dead?

Allatoona Pass is a lofty hill cleft by the railroad. The summit on either side was crowned with fort and rifle-pits. Colonel Tourtelotte's brigade occupied that on the east, General Corse's that on the west. At the foot of the hill lay the warehouses with their immense stores of supplies, upon which so much depended.

About eight o'clock, a flag of truce came in, bearing the following letter:

AROUND ALLATOONA, Oct. 5th, 8.15 A.M., 1864.

*Commanding Officer, U. S. Forces, Allatoona:*

Sir : I have placed the forces under my command in such positions that you are surrounded, and, to avoid a needless effusion of blood, I call upon you to surrender your forces at once, and unconditionally. Five minutes will be allowed you to decide.

Should you accede to this, you will be treated in the most honorable manner as prisoners of war.

I have the honor to be, very respectfully yours,

S. G. FRENCH,
Major-General Commanding Forces C. S.

At this moment the enemy, not less than five thousand in number, surrounded the little garrison on three sides. Their columns, all prepared for the charge, were in plain sight on the west; a strong force was moving up the hill from the north; and the batteries in the valley to the south were in position.

Corse was a man of small stature, but his every pound of flesh and blood was that of a hero. His eye flashed as if lighted with a Promethean spark; and his chest swelled with angry defiance to the hideous threat implied in the summons to surrender.

"Captain Flint," said he, "answer this!"

Drawing from his pocket a small order-book, Captain Flint seated himself upon a tree-stump, and wrote as follows, General Corse at once dictating, and directing the placing of his forces:

HEADQUARTERS FOURTH DIVISION, FIFTEENTH ARMY CORPS,
8.30 A.M. Oct. 5th, 1864.

*Major-Gen. S. G. French, C. S. A., etc.*

Your communication demanding surrender of my command, I acknowledge receipt of, and respectfully reply that we are prepared for " *the needless effusion of blood*," whenever it is agreeable to you.

I am, very respectfully, your Obdt. Sv't,
JOHN M. CORSE,
Brigadier-General Commanding Forces U. S.

The assault began at once—so soon indeed, that it seemed as if the enemy did not await the return of their flag of truce. The artillery on the south opened a vigorous fire, and a small detachment endeavored to scale the hill from the north. The latter force was speedily covered with the rifles of the Unionists, and found itself unable to advance or retreat.

The principal attack came from the west, Cockrell's rebel brigade advancing up the hill toward the fort,

GEN. CORSE AT ALLATOONA—"NO LIBBY PRISON IN OURS!"

See page 231.

and assailing Rowett's regiments with great vigor. The latter made a spirited resistance, but the exterior line of rifle-pits was entirely too long to be held by so small a force, and the troops fell back, the 7th Illinois Regiment occupying the fort, while the 39th Iowa and 93rd Illinois regiments went into the interior line of rifle-pits immediately in front of it, and upon the right. Colonel Rowett was slightly wounded by a fragment of shell while retiring.

This position was charged by the enemy, in solid column, seven different times. The first assault was repulsed without great difficulty, and upwards of an hour elapsed before the attempt was repeated, the interval being occupied with incessant musketry and artillery firing. The fort was poorly constructed, its weakest point being an opening at about the center of the western face, the most exposed portion of the work. Fortunately, a number of cotton bales were at hand, and these were used to close the gap. The cotton was repeatedly set on fire by shells, making it necessary for a portion of the troops to cease fighting, and smother the flames by rolling the bales over and over.

It was during the slight lull in the battle that General Corse fell, painfully but not dangerously wounded.

In front and to the north of the fort was a house which served as a vantage ground for the rebel sharp-

15

shooters, who had almost succeeded in silencing one of the two pieces of artillery which bore upon their lines. Several gunners had been killed at their post, and the artillerists resorted to many methods of loading the pieces with the least possible exposure. One, while lying upon his back, under the gun, ramming home a cartridge, was wounded in both hands. So thick was the tempest of bullets that the gabions were cut to pieces, releasing the earth, which had furnished a slight protection. At length the one gun which bore upon the house became useless. As was afterward learned, it was actually choked with a sawdust cartridge furnished by some dastardly contractor.

The situation was perilous in the extreme. Calling General Corse to the spot, Captain Flint indicated the position of the sharpshooters, and the useless condition of the piece of artillery, which he suggested should be replaced with one from another face of the fort. Corse rose on tip-toe to view the ground in front, and while in this position a rifle-ball ploughed along the right side of his face, carrying away a part of his ear. Stunned by the shock, the gallant commander fell into the arms of his aide, who seated him upon an ammunition box in an interior corner of the fort. Colonel Rowett, a no less gallant soldier than his chief, at once succeeded to the command.

But Corse made wise dispositions before he fell. The choked gun was replaced by a fresh piece, which

did murderous execution; but this was only after
laborious effort amid soul-sickening scenes. Dead
and wounded men were strewn thick in the way to the
embrasure, and scores were laid aside as tenderly as
was possible before the task could be accomplished.
The General also dispatched his aide to ask reinforcements from Colonel Tourtelotte, who, in the redoubt
on the east side of the railroad cut, was less seriously
engaged.  The aide, having entered the place during
the night, was not aware that a footpath extended
across the cut from summit to summit; and he
made a perilous journey under fire, down one hill
and up the other, happily returning in safety, closely
followed by Colonel Hanna, with his 50th Illinois
Regiment, familiarly known as "The Blind Half-
Hundred."  This command, in moving across the railroad cut, encountered and dispersed a detachment of
the enemy engaged in an attempt to burn the supply
warehouses.

Many of the muskets were now so hot with rapid
firing that they were well-nigh useless; and ammunition for the sixteen-shooters of the 7th Illinois
was becoming scarce.  In this crisis, the defenders of
the fort were counted off in relays, one-half to fire at
a time, at once saving ammunition and giving opportunity for the guns to cool somewhat.  At one time an
officer gave the command to one of the relays, "Cease
firing!"  The lion-hearted Corse, apparently insen-

sible, heard the words, and thought them to mean surrender. Rising to his feet with a bound, the exertion causing the blood to flow afresh from his wound, bathing his face with the crimson tide, he thundered: "No surrender, by God! Hold Allatoona!"

Gallant soldier! Glorious hero! Well might Sherman say, "I know Corse! So long as he lives Allatoona is safe!"

But they were all such soldiers, such heroes! There was no thought of surrender by Rowett and his men.

The enemy was about to make a desperate effort; their preparations were plainly to be seen. The Union troops with the ordinary muskets were directed to fix bayonets to repel an encounter at close quarters; the 7th Illinois to reload their sixteen-shooters and reserve their fire for an opportune moment. The two pieces of artillery had been silent for some time for want of ammunition, but a brave man made the dangerous journey across the railroad cut, swept by the enemy's artillery, and returned with a box of canister.

These dispositions were made none too soon, for the enemy was already advancing to the charge. Night was coming on and Sherman would soon be thundering upon their heels. Allatoona must fall now or never. Fired with the energy of desperation, the rebel columns came on, and as they neared the works

UNION TROOPS DESTROYING RAILROADS.

See page 255.

the two pieces of artillery, doubly charged, fired their deadly contents full in their face, while the troops poured into them a storm of bullets. At this critical moment, General Corse shouted with a voice of unconquerable determination, " No surrender! Officers, draw your revolvers! No Libby prison in ours!"

The enemy's columns halted, shivered for an instant under the pitiless storm, and then fled. About the same moment Colonel Rowett fell with his second wound, a rifle-ball plowing a deep groove through the very crown of his skull, but his pluck was great, and he soon rallied.

The gallant commander, and his equally brave and determined second, were both wounded. But there was little need of commander now ; the enemy was in retreat, and Allatoona was safe.

During this bitter contest, Lieutenant - Colonel Tourtelotte, with the 4th Minnesota and 18th Wisconsin regiments, and a two gun battery, held the redoubt on the east side of the railroad cut. He was able, however, to repulse the attack of the enemy without great difficulty, and afterward rendered material assistance to the defenders of the western redoubt, covering their flank with his artillery, and sending them reinforcements at a critical time. The gallant Colonel, however, suffered a serious wound.

French left behind him two hundred and thirty-one dead and four hundred and eleven wounded and prisoners. Corse's command lost seven hundred and seven men—more than one-third the entire force.

On the night following, a soldier of the 7th Illinois Regiment, Sergeant-Major Flint, by the flickering light of the camp fire, wrote the following stirring lines:

> Winds that sweep the southern mountains
>   And the leafy river's shore,
>   Bear ye not a prouder burden
> Than ye ever learned before?
>     And the hot blood fills
>     The heart until it thrills
> At the story of the terror, and the glory of the battle
>     Of the Allatoona hills.
>
> Echoes from the purple mountains
>   To the dull surrounding shore;
> 'Tis as sad and proud a burden
>   As ye ever learned before!
>     How they fell like grass
>     When the mowers pass,
> And the dying, when the foe was flying, swelled the cheering
>     Of the heroes of the Pass.
>
> Sweep it o'er the hills of Georgia
>   To the mountains of the North;
> Teach the coward and the doubter
>   What the blood of man is worth.
>     Hail the flag you pass!
>     Let its stained and tattered mass
> Tell the story of the terror, and the glory of the battle
>     Of the Allatoona Pass *

General Sherman was so highly pleased with the defense of Allatoona that he issued a general order as follows:

"The General commanding avails himself of the

*From History of 7th Illinois Regiment.—*Ambrose.*

opportunity, in the handsome defense made of Allatoona, to illustrate the most important principle in
war, that fortified posts should be defended to the
last, regardless of the relative numbers of the party
attacking and attacked. The thanks of this army are
due, and are hereby accorded to General Corse, Colonel Tourtelotte, Colonel Rowett, officers and men, for
their determined and gallant defense of Allatoona, and
it is made an example to illustrate the importance of
preparing in time, and meeting the danger, when
present, boldly, manfully and well.

"Commanders and garrisons of the posts along our
railroad are hereby instructed that they must hold
their posts to the last minute, sure that the time
gained is valuable and necessary to their comrades at
the front."

[NOTE.—The author is aware that General Sherman states in his
" Memoirs," that he received General Corse's signal message in full.
But General Corse and his aide are positive that the message was
interrupted as stated at pages 218–219.]

## CHAPTER XXIII.

### A FAMILY OF SOLDIERS.

IN the action at Allatoona fell Dudley Atchison, a private of the 7th Illinois Regiment. This gallant young soldier, in the full vigor of early manhood, and with all the enthusiasm of youth, was not surpassed by any of the heroic band in cool courage and steady determination. He fell in the very heat of the action, pierced by two deadly bullets — one entered his forehead, lodging within the skull; the other passed in above the left ear, and made its exit over the left eye.

But death did not come at once to the gallant lad. For many hours after the battle was over, he lingered in agony, lovingly ministered to by a comrade and kinsman who scarcely left his side. Not a single complaint was uttered by the dying soldier. He answered all questions addressed to him, sometimes rationally, at others, in a careless manner which indicated that his mind was wandering. He spoke of his comrades who were dead or wounded, and when asked as to himself, said that he was " all right." He inquired of the comrade who sat by his side, whether Howell or Howe was attending him, referring to the old family physicians. Then he thought himself to be at home, surrounded by parents, brothers and sisters ; and frequently called for his favorite brother " Aleck," who had fallen more than a year before at Vicksburg. At last, death gave him merciful release from his sufferings, and the same comrade who had ministered to him so devotedly, hollowed out a grave on the summit of blood-stained Allatoona, and laid him tenderly away, wrapped in his army blanket, side by side with a kinsman whose life went out in the same heroic struggle, and there the bones of the patriotic lads rest to this day.

The spirit of the men of that period may be discerned in the words of a brother of the fallen soldier, a comrade in the same company, who, in a touching letter to his parents, said : " The cause is worthy of the great sacrifice." And the dead lad's commander wrote to the heart-broken mother : " He died nobly in the line of duty. He was a brave, obedient and efficient soldier."

" Aleck," the brother to whom the dying boy referred in his moments of delirium, was a lieutenant in the 97th Illinois Regiment. It was during the siege of Vicksburg that this young officer, temporarily in command of his company, led it in a gallant but ineffectual charge upon the enemy. He fell, at his post of duty, with a ball through the brain.

To noble soldierly character he added high moral qualities, which commanded the respect of all about him. Without being in any sense inclined to cant (indeed, he made no pretensions to being religious within the ordinary meaning of the word), he was, both in word and deed, an example of true manliness. Without moral blemish himself, his conduct was a wholesome restraint upon those of his comrades who were inclined to excesses; while, upon occasions when he deemed it expedient, he would drop a word of admonition or reproof, but with so much unaffected sincerity, and kindly personal interest, that it could not be taken amiss. At one time he said: "Boys! Let us be guilty of no conduct that we would blush to have our mothers and sisters know!"

This gallant young officer was held in such high esteem by his company, that its members made up a purse and erected over his grave a handsome monument. Among the devices borne thereon were the unfurled national flag, and an officer's sword; while suitable inscriptions told the story of his death, and summed up his virtues as a soldier and a man. His remains were interred at his boyhood's home, before the war closed, in the presence of a large and deeply affected assemblage of neighbors and friends. The clergyman pronounced a suitable discourse ; and an old, gray-headed man, an ardent unionist, and a life-long friend of the family, brought from his home a handsome national flag, and wrapped it about the burial-casket, and buried it with him.

The aged father of these noble lads early enlisted as a private in the 7th Illinois Regiment, and, about a year afterward, was discharged from the service on account of disability.

Soon after his son "Aleck" had fallen in front of Vicksburg, the sorrowing parent visited the army then besieging that place, in order to recover the body of his son. Seeking the regiment to which the young man had belonged, he lost his way among the numerous roads made for the passage of wagon trains to the various portions of the army. Presently he came to a number of tents without flag or guard, where sat a middle-aged man, wearing what appeared to be the blouse of a common soldier. The old man addressed him, stating his errand, and naming the regiment he sought. The man in the blouse rose from his camp chair, walked with him some distance, pointed to the proper road, bade him a kindly good-day, and then returned to his quarters.

"Who is that ?" asked the old man of a soldier who stood by.

"That's General Grant !" was the answer.

That a great general, his mind burdened with the

plans and anxieties of a mighty military movement, could so simply and unaffectedly enter into sympathy with a plain old man, and assist him to do the last sad duties for the remains of one poor fallen soldier, is of more than passing interest. To this day, General Grant is enshrined in the hearts of that aged man and the sorrow-stricken mother, as one to be loved as well as honored.

This family gave to the country, sire and sons, four in number, every male of arms-bearing age, two of whom found soldiers' graves. Yet it is but a representative of thousands of homes throughout the land, equally rich in patriotic zeal, and equally lavish in the sacrifice of patriotic blood.

## CHAPTER XXIV.

ON THE BACK TRACK.

FTER his repulse at Allatoona, Hood made a detour, and effected a lodgment on the railroad farther north. At Resaca he demanded the surrender of the garrison, and over his own name said, "If the place is carried by assault, no prisoners will be taken." This fiendish threat failed to intimidate the gallant commander, Colonel Weaver, who answered : "I am surprised at the concluding paragraph, to the effect, that, 'if the place is carried by assault, no prisoners will be taken.' In my opinion, I can hold this post. If you want it, come and take it!"

This heroic defiance was in itself a victory. Hood made no attempt upon the post, but continued up the railroad, destroying most of the track, and all the bridges, almost as far as Chattanooga. Besides this damage, he burned about twenty locomotives, and hundreds of cars loaded with subsistence stores and ammunition. So thorough was the work of destruction, that the federal garrison at Atlanta was completely isolated for nearly a month. The writer's journal notes that the first train from the north, after the grand raid, did not arrive until October 29th.

As soon as Hood began his movement, Sherman left the Twentieth Corps to garrison Atlanta, and with the remainder of his army, depleted by casualty and discharge to less than fifty thousand, started north after him. On land as well as at sea, "a stern chase is always a long chase," and the troops, seemingly engaged in a hopeless undertaking, were consumed with anxiety. It is not difficult, now, to discern that even in the early stages of the pursuit, Sherman was paving the way for the famous "March to the Sea." He had telegraphed General Grant that "it would be a physical impossibility to protect the roads now that Hood, Forrest, Wheeler, and the whole batch of devils, were turned loose, without home or habitation," and asked permission to make the march to Savannah, promising to "make Georgia howl!"

But the army was without newspapers or letters, and the General did not take the men into his confidence. Their only information was derived, or inferred, from what they could actually see; and, under the circumstances, the outlook was anything but encouraging. What did it all mean? They were leaving behind them the territory that had been conquered. They were marching North, and their enemy was between them and the Ohio river. Would Hood run over Thomas, at Nashville, or pass around him, and cross the stream, before they could overtake him? Were the plains of Ohio, and the prairies of Illinois, to become battle-fields? Were the homes of the Union soldiers to be devastated, as had been those of Georgia and Virginia? Had Grant been defeated before Richmond? Was a part of Lee's victorious army following close upon Sherman's heels? Would the rebellion prove successful after all, and had the trail of patriot blood from Cairo to Atlanta been made in vain? Such were the gloomy thoughts which filled the minds of the travel-worn and half-starved troops during that apparently hopeless and purposeless march.

October 13th, the Army of the Tennessee passed through Rome. The region was rich in all kinds of supplies, and for a few days the soldiers were again well fed.

It was in this neighborhood that General T. E. G. Ransom died. This gallant young officer was temporarily commanding the Seventeenth Corps, in the absence of General Frank P. Blair. Although stricken with disease, yet he insisted upon accompanying his com-

16

mand. The jolting of the ambulance caused him so much pain, that it became necessary to carry him upon a litter, and he almost died in the arms of his men; those who bore him, when they discovered that death was so near, having barely time to halt, and place the wounded general on a bed in a farm-house, before he breathed his last.

October 21st, the army reached Gaylesville, Alabama, where the pursuit of Hood ceased.

It was near this place that General Sherman received from General Grant permission to march to the sea, together with a hopeful, encouraging letter from President Lincoln; and he immediately perfected his masterly plans, for the campaigns of two great and widely separated commands. While reorganizing his own immediate army at Atlanta, he was also directing a similar effort at Nashville. The mission of the one was to annihilate the war-supporting resources of the "Confederacy;" that of the other, to make possible the mission, by drawing away the only enemy which was to be dreaded. How completely successful were these great and brilliant plans, history records. But the troops, through whose effort success was achieved, were in utter ignorance of these designs, and the momentous results which depended upon them. Yet, with earnest fidelity to the cause, and unshaken confidence in their commander, they cheerfully devoted themselves to the new and unknown task set before them.

ON THE MARCH.

See page 258.

## CHAPTER XXV.

### STRIPPING TO THE BUFF.

VENTS during the last week in October, and the first ten days in November, 1864, were stirring enough. The railroad, which had been completely wrecked by the enemy, was repaired from Chattanooga to Atlanta, where the bulk of Sherman's army was assembling. Every train going north was loaded to its utmost capacity with the wounded and infirm; with surplus artillery, and, in fact, almost everything that the men could not carry upon their backs. Returning trains brought only the most needed articles — hard bread, pork, coffee, sugar, and ammunition. It was evident even to those in the ranks that some important, if not desperate, undertaking was at hand. The acuteness of their perception and correctness of conclusion were surprising. The destination of the army was either east, to attack Lee, or south, to the coast. This was settling the matter almost as definitely as the

General himself could, for he has said, since the war closed, that at the time he had two or three alternatives continually in mind.

The army was now thoroughly reorganized for a new campaign. The Fourth Corps and Twenty-third Corps had been sent northward to assist General Thomas in disposing of Hood. General Sherman's immediate army now consisted of four corps, viz. : Fifteenth, temporarily commanded by General Osterhaus ; Seventeenth, General Frank P. Blair ; Fourteenth, General Jeff C. Davis ; Twentieth, General A. S. Williams. General Dodge having gone North on account of wounds, the Sixteenth Corps was broken up, its two divisions being assigned to the Fifteenth and Seventeenth Corps. The army was divided into two wings, the right wing, commanded by General Howard, and the left wing commanded by General Slocum. The infantry numbered fifty-two thousand. In addition, there was a cavalry force of five thousand men under General Kilpatrick, and about fifty pieces of artillery. The grand total was a trifle under sixty thousand men.

While the work of reorganization was going on, the paymasters were busy with their task. There were many months' arrearages due the troops, the unusual activity of the campaign preventing disbursements at the regular intervals of two months. Payment might as well have been postponed, for the army had little use for money. There were no merchants in the vicinity, and the rapid movements of the army had made the war-risk of the sutler so hazardous that he had retired from business many months before.

The most exciting incident of the day was the presidential election. Most of the States sent to the army sworn commissioners to receive the ballots of those soldiers who would have been entitled to vote if at home. The Illinois troops, however, were debarred this privilege, an anti-war legislature of their State having refused to make the necessary provision. The indignation of the disfranchised troops was intense; and there are yet living thousands of men who will never outlive their contempt and hatred for the political tricksters who put such a wrong upon them. The Illinois regiments, however, appointed judges, and took informal votes, merely by way of expressing their sentiments. In the 32d Regiment, the vote was recorded as two hundred and six for Lincoln, and fifty-eight for McClellan. The McClellan vote in this instance was unusually large, as compared with that in neighboring regiments ; and the Iowa troops, who were almost unanimously Lincoln men, viewed the result with considerable contempt. In this canvass throughout the army, there was no political feeling, in the ordinary sense of the word. Very many of the soldiers who voted for Lincoln were known to be Democrats ; but they recognized the fact that his reëlection meant an earnest prosecution of the war, while there was no assurance of good results coming out of the so-called "peace policy."

The same day, November 8th, General Sherman sent out Special Field Order No. 119, which was as follows :

[Special Field Orders, No. 119.]
HEADQUARTERS, MILITARY DIVISION OF THE MISSISSIPPI,
IN THE FIELD, KINGSTON, GEORGIA, November 8, 1864.

The General commanding deems it proper at this time to inform the officers and men of the Fourteenth, Fifteenth, Seventeenth and Twentieth Corps, that he has organized them into an army, for a special purpose, well known to the War Department and General Grant. It is sufficient for you to know that it involves a departure from our present base, and a long and difficult march to a new one. All the chances of war have been considered and provided for, as far as human sagacity can. All he asks of you is to maintain that discipline, patience and courage which have characterized you in the past ; and he hopes, through you, to strike a blow at our enemy that will have a material effect in producing what we all so much desire, his complete overthrow. Of all things, the most important is, that the men, during marches and in camp, keep their places and do not scatter about as stragglers or foragers, to be picked up by a hostile people in detail. It is also of the utmost importance that our wagons should not be loaded with anything but provisions and ammunition. All surplus servants, non-combatants and refugees, should now go to the rear, and none should be encouraged to encumber us on the march. At some future time we will be able to provide for the poor whites and blacks who seek to escape the bondage under which they are now suffering. With these few simple cautions, he hopes to lead you to achievements equal in importance to those of the past.

By order of Major-General W. T. SHERMAN.
L. M. DAYTON, A. D. C.

Accompanying this was Special Field Order, No. 120, containing directions for the march. These were, in brief, as follows :

1.   The habitual order of march, whenever practicable, to be by four roads, as nearly parallel as possible, and converging at points to be indicated from time to time.

2.   Each corps to have its own ammunition and provision trains. The separate columns of troops to start habitually at 7 o'clock in the morning, and make about fifteen miles per day, unless otherwise ordered.

3.   The army to forage liberally on the country.   Each brigade commander to organize a good and sufficient foraging party, under the command of one or more discreet officers, who will gather, near the route traveled, corn or forage of any kind, meat of any kind, vegetables, corn-meal, or whatever is needed, aiming at all times to keep in the wagons at least ten days' provisions for his command, and three days' forage. Soldiers not to enter the dwellings of the inhabitants, or commit any trespass ; but during a halt, or in a camp, to be permitted to gather turnips, potatoes and other vegetables, and to drive in stock within sight. The regular foraging parties to be intrusted with the gathering of provisions and forage, at any distance from the road traveled.

4.   To corps commanders alone is intrusted the power to destroy mills, houses, cotton-gins, etc , and for them this general principle is laid down.   In districts and neighborhoods where the army is unmolested no destruction of such property should be permitted ; but should guerrillas or bushwhackers molest the march, or should the inhabitants burn bridges, obstruct roads, or otherwise manifest local hostility, then commanders should order and enforce a devastation more or less relentless, according to the measure of such hostility.

5.   Horses, mules and wagons belonging to the inhabitants, to be appropriated freely and without limit by cavalry and artillery ; discriminating, however. between the rich, who are usually hostile, and the poor and industrious, usually neutral or friendly.   Foraging parties may also take mules and horses to replace the jaded animals of their trains, or to serve as pack-mules.   In foraging of all kinds, the parties engaged will refrain from abusive or threatening language ; and may, when the officer in command thinks proper, give certificates, but not receipts, and they will endeavor to leave with each family a reasonable portion for their maintenance.

Many of the troops neither saw nor heard of these orders until after the march had actually commenced ; many more did not hear of them at all, in an official

way.   Army operations did not admit of the perform-
ance of the clerical work necessary to furnish so many
copies of these papers as were needed ; or, of holding
dress-parades, which offered the only opportunity for
promulgating orders meant for the mass of the army.

## CHAPTER XXVI.

### "THE LAST LINK IS BROKEN."

OVEMBER 8th was an eventful day. Lincoln had been elected President, the paymaster had made the grand rounds, and orders had been issued for beginning another campaign.

A veteran regiment occupied the old railroad eating-house known as "Big Shanty," a short distance from the base of Kenesaw Mountain. The building was enclosed by a stout stockade, pierced for musketry. Vivid recollections of scenes at this and similar posts will come back to many old comrades — evenings of sport, followed by midnight alarms which called them out to meet real or imagined foes.

That night, a merry party of soldiers gathered in an upper room of the "Shanty," which served as the adjutant's office. He shared his quarters with the post telegraph operator, whose instruments were on an improvised table. Outside, a severe storm raged, the rain descending in torrents; within, the fun grew fast and furious. The boys—there is no such fitting word to name those dear old comrades of years ago— were indulging in the amusement of a "stag-dance," and when the word came to "swing partners," the "gentleman" grasped the fingers of the one with a piece of cloth tied about his arm, to designate him as a "lady." The figures of the dance were accompanied with the melancholy thrumming of an old banjo in the hands of colored "Jerry," the mess-cook, who had unceremoniously left his master to enter upon a life of freedom. "Jerry," by the way, followed his new-found masters North, after the war ended, went to school for a time, and finally engaged in "preaching," the highest earthly ambition of the male contraband of those days. Three years ago, he was pastor of a colored church in one of the principal cities in Illinois, and wore a broadcloth coat and a silk hat. At that time, he attended a reunion of the survivors of the old army mess, for which he once baked the succulent yam, and brewed the inspiring coffee. The old mess, reunited so far as death and distance would permit, was made up of professional men who were accustomed to a reasonable degree of good-living and "form." In the army, they had all served in the ranks, eventually winning commissions; and one of their number, in the early days, was greatly disturbed to find that the army was "fighting to free niggers !" But so strong was the feeling of companionship, growing out of old army associations, that "the Reverend Jerry," as he was called, was asked to say grace, and took his share of the table, and the conversation, in cordial friendliness with his white comrades.

But to return to Big Shanty,—while the sport was at its height, the telegraph operator called a halt, and handed to the adjutant the following dispatch which he had just received:

*Commanding Officers of all Posts :*
This is the rain I have been awaiting so long. As soon as it is over, we'll be off.
W. T. SHERMAN.

The orders for the great march, quoted in the preceding chapter, had not reached the merry-makers at Big Shanty, whose regiment was temporarily detached from its brigade. Yet the message was readily understood. Hood was so far north that it would be impossible for him to return. There were many large and greatly-swollen rivers between him and Sherman, and his pontoon-train was known to be well-nigh useless. Besides, any movement he might make southward, would bring Thomas' hardy veterans close upon his heels. He could no longer disturb this army, and Sherman need only care for what new enemy he might find in his front, and on his flanks.

During the next three days, the railroad was pushed to its utmost capacity, trains bringing in supplies from the North, and returning loaded with surplus artillery, sick and wounded. Late in the evening of November 12th, the last train bound North rolled past Big Shanty. It would have been a windfall for the enemy. It carried many officers who had resigned, and soldiers whose terms of service had expired. Large sums of money were committed to them by their comrades, for delivery to families or friends at home. One, a surgeon, had not less than twelve thousand dollars in his valise, enclosed in ordinary envelopes endorsed with the amount and the name of the person for whom it was intended. Fortunately, no accident befell the train; but it was more than two months before this was known to the men who trusted so much to uncertain fate.

The passing by of this train awoke strange sensations. Hearty cheers and "God bless you" came from scores of the homeward bound; as hearty cheers and fervent "Good-byes" from those left behind.

But the brave words of both belied their hearts. The former gave an encouragement which was tinged with a feeling of dread; the latter felt an anxiety their shouts did not reveal. The departing train was the sundering of the last link connecting them with country and home. They were about to march out into a great unknown. It was as a voyage upon untried

waters, beyond which might lie no shore. They knew
not what course they were to pursue, what dangers
they were to meet, what enemies were to oppose them.
They expected battle, but what its issue would be,
none could foretell. Those who might fall would
leave their bones in a strange and unfriendly land
forever. Then thought recurred to wife, mother,
sister or sweetheart at home. What would be their
fearful anxieties?

A half-hour after the train was out of sight, the
various troops along the road were set to work
destroying the railroad, and by midnight a glare of
light reaching from Atlanta as far northward as the
eye could reach, revealed the thoroughness of their
work. A regiment would scatter along one side of
the road, each man picking up the end of a tie, then
at the word of command, all would throw the ties end
over end, the fall breaking the rails loose. Then ties
and telegraph poles were piled up and fired, and the
rails thrown across them. The latter were soon red-
hot in the middle, and the men would pick them up
and wrap them around trees, or twist them with cant-
hooks into a corkscrew pattern which it was impossible to straighten. In many instances a dozen iron
rails were twisted around a tree or a telegraph-pole.
The men worked with a will, seeming to take a savage
delight in destroying everything that could by any
possibility be made use of by their enemies. They

attained great proficiency in these methods; and after this fashion they absolutely destroyed three-fourths of the railroad between Chattanooga and Atlanta before beginning the great march; and, afterward, every mile of track they encountered from Atlanta to Savannah.

These were the scenes transpiring as far north as Sherman's army extended. Each detachment, immediately upon accomplishing the work in its own vicinity, marched rapidly toward Atlanta. On the night of the 14th, the troops occupying Big Shanty set the torch to building and stockade, and followed the remainder of the army. There was now not a federal soldier between Atlanta and Chattanooga, and the hills and plains, which had lately echoed the fearful din of artillery and musketry, and had been alive with masses of fiercely contending human beings, were as still and desolate as if a demon of destruction had passed over.

But there were monuments testifying to the fearful struggle—trees riven by cannon shot, and broken-down caissons. Here, there, and everywhere, were graves of those who wore the blue and those who wore the gray, each surmounted by a board upon which were rudely cut by knives of comrades, the name, company and regiment of him who lay beneath. But amid all the graves, not a single epitaph! There was no time for sentiment, and death's work had no novelty here.

On the night of November 15th, the torch was applied to the railroad shops, foundries, and every one of the many buildings that had been used in fitting out the armies of the enemy in this vast "workshop of the confederacy," as Atlanta was called. The flames spread rapidly, and when morning came, it is doubtful whether there were a score of buildings remaining in the city, except in the very outskirts. Sherman had determined to render the place utterly incapable of any more service to the enemy, and with this end in view all the inhabitants had been removed weeks before.

The Twentieth Corps, which had garrisoned Atlanta while the remainder of the army was pursuing Hood northward, were the last to leave the city, and as they marched out, the fine silver band of the 33rd Massachusetts — who that ever heard it, will ever cease to remember its glorious harmonies ?— played "John Brown." The men took up the words wedded to the music, and, high above the roaring flames, above the crash of falling walls, above the fierce crackling of thousands of small arm cartridges in the burning buildings, rose the triumphant refrain, "His truth is marching on!"

For picturesqueness and suggestiveness, the scene was one never to be forgotten.

17

## CHAPTER XXVII.

### ON THE MARCH.

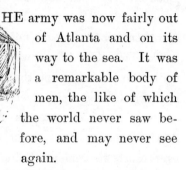

HE army was now fairly out of Atlanta and on its way to the sea. It was a remarkable body of men, the like of which the world never saw before, and may never see again.

Sixty thousand in round numbers—it was an army of veterans, who had served an apprenticeship of more than three years at their profession, and learned nearly all that was worth knowing, at least far more than their generals knew three years before. Their brilliant achievements had already gone into history, furnishing themes for poet and scenes for painter. Their calendar contained scarcely a day that did not commemorate some more or less important battle, skirmish, or march. Each regiment had been re-

duced by the casualties of constant service to less
than one - third its numerical strength at the outset. He was a fortunate colonel who had three hundred men remaining out of the round thousand he
enlisted at home; thirty men made far more than an
average company; there were many which mustered
less than a score. A brigade did not parade a longer
line than did one of its regiments when it went into
service.

This army of veterans was also an army of boys.
The old men and the big men had been very generally
worn out and sent home or to the hospital. It was
the "little devils" (as Sherman once called them in
the hearing of the writer) who remained, and could
always be depended upon to carry their load, march
all day, and be ready for a frolic when they went into
bivouac at night. Very many of them, notwithstanding three years of soldiering, were not old enough to
vote. Many a regimental commander was not thirty
years of age; and the majority of line and staff officers
lacked a great deal of this advanced age. But they
had been in the service from the beginning, and what
they did not know about campaigning was not worth
inquiring into. Each soldier was practically a picked
man. Such had been the ratio of casualties that he
may be said to have been the sole survivor of *four*
men who had set out from Cairo in 1861; all but he
having succumbed to disease or death. He had in-

herited all their experience and added it to his own.
He was fertile of resources, and his self-confidence
was unbounded.  His careless, swinging gait when on
the march was the impersonation of a determination
to "get there," although he knew absolutely nothing
of his destination.  Of that he was careless.  His
confidence in the long-headedness of "the old man"
(General Sherman) was such that he did not disturb himself on that score.  He was heading south
instead of north, and this was ample assurance that
Thomas was taking care of Hood, and that Grant
was "holding Lee down."  He went into action as
unconcernedly as he took the road in the morning
for a day's march; or, if not ordered into the conflict, he would sit on a fence, or lie down in the
road, the image of peaceful contentment, within hearing of a fierce engagement, apparently wholly indif-
ferent as to the result.  On the skirmish line he
frequently advanced without orders, and never fell
back until so commanded, unless it was beyond human
endurance to remain.  He gloried in his strength, and
believed that no effort or hardship was too great.  He
waded swamps, made corduroy roads, and pulled
wagons and cannon out of ruts from which the bottom
had seemingly dropped.  But there was one thing he
did not know, that in all this magnificent effort he was
making immense drafts against his reserve energy,
and that the day was sure to come when he would

THE BUMMER.

See page 267.

find himself far older than his years by reason thereof.

This army, which had been marching light from Chattanooga to Atlanta, was now simply reduced to what it had on, and that was not much. It would have made a magnificent tableau for a "Beggars' Opera" on a stupendous scale. What few tents had been smuggled as far south as Atlanta were now entirely discarded, and only a few "flies" for the various headquarters, and one to each regiment to shelter the field-desks of the adjutant and quartermaster, were retained. A little furniture was supposed to be necessary to the last named officers, but they generally reduced this in about the same proportion as everything else. The greater part of their "office" was carried in breast-pocket and saddle-bags, making more room under the "fly" for comrades who would otherwise have been entirely shelterless. The "fly" was a fair cover in fine weather, when shelter was not needed; but, being open at both ends, it was a sorry makeshift in a rain storm. Each soldier was supposed to carry half of a shelter-tent, which, combined with the counterpart carried by a comrade, made reasonable protection for two, but many of the men regarded them with contempt. The average soldier cared only for a blanket, and this he carried in a roll, swung over his shoulder, the ends being tied together, meeting under the opposite arm. A majority of the men discarded knapsacks altogether; those who yet clung to them carried only a shirt and a pair or two of socks. Each soldier had forty rounds of ammunition in his cartridge-box and one hundred and sixty more elsewhere upon his person. His cooking utensils were a tin oyster can, in which to make his coffee, and some times one-half of a canteen to serve as a skillet, or frying-pan. His haversack contained a liberal amount of coffee, sugar and salt, a very small fragment of salt pork, and three days' rations of hard bread. This supply was habitually to last him ten days. It was expected that he would "skirmish 'round" and levy upon the country for such food as would be a fair equivalent for that large fraction of the army rations of which he was necessarily deprived. It is a matter of record that, without a single known exception, he was equal to the task, and proved to be such an excellent provider, that when he reached the sea he was in better flesh and spirits than when he left Chattanooga. During the greater part of the march, he subsisted mainly upon sweet potatoes and fresh beef and pork, the former baked in the ashes and the latter broiled upon the red embers of a wood fire, or held in the flame on the end of a ramrod, making a very toothsome meal. But even that grew somewhat monotonous after a time.

The soldier's outfit was not complete without a "deck" of cards, and these were carried in the pocket so as to be convenient at any halt on the road. Frequent thumbing had so worn these treasured paste-boards, that in many instances it was an absolute impossibility for one to tell what card he held, if so be he took a hand with a party having a "deck" with which he was unacquainted. It is to be hoped the moralist will not grudge the "boys" the amusement they derived from the game. There were no news-papers, no circulating libraries, no Y. M. C. A., not even a tract in that desolate region.

To sum up, no army ever marched with less im-pedimenta, and none adapted itself so completely or cheerfully to its conditions.

The army marched in four columns, the various corps pursuing parallel roads. These columns were sometimes five, sometimes fifteen miles apart. Their combined front was from forty to sixty miles, for by day the skirmishers and flankers of each corps spread out until they met those of the corps next to them on either side, so that if anything unusual happened in any portion of the army, information was almost immediately given to the other commands. By night the positions of the various columns could generally be distinguished from their fires.

In front of each corps marched a regiment of cavalry or mounted infantry. Frequently these troops, with the aid of the infantry brigade at the head of the column, were able to brush aside the enemy without much trouble, and without halting the main column;

and it was only when crossing a stream, where the passage was contested, that anything like a general line of battle was formed. Each brigade in the column took its turn in the advance, and likewise each regiment in the brigade. A cavalry brigade under the dashing Kilpatrick, with a few light guns, moved on this flank or that, as the emergency required.

The itinerary of the march of the Seventeenth Corps (whose movements this narrative mainly follows) shows the distance traveled between Atlanta and Savannah to have been two hundred and ninety-five miles. The crow's flight would make it much shorter, but he would not make so many flank movements or circuitous routes. The actual march consumed eighteen days. Nine days were spent in crossing streams where the passage was contested, or waiting for supporting columns. The army reached the defenses in front of Savannah, December 10th, but did not gain an entrance to the city until nearly two weeks later.

## CHAPTER XXVIII.

### GENESIS OF THE BUMMER.

OVEMBER 15th, the first day out of Atlanta, the Seventeenth Corps marched fifteen miles, completing that stage of the journey early in the afternoon, and devoting the remainder of the day to destroying the railroad. The Fifteenth Corps pursued a parallel road to the right ; and, still farther in that direction, on separate roads, were the Fourteenth and Twentieth Corps. The next day the columns marched sixteen miles, and resumed the work of railroad wrecking. On the 17th, twenty miles more were left to the rear, and the troops bivouacked on the banks of the beautiful Cahawba.

This was a section of country which the war had not disturbed until this moment. It was literally a land overflowing with milk and honey, and well was it for the army that such was the case. The three days' rations of hard tack which the men had placed in their haversacks were already exhausted, and there was no assurance that more would be issued from the commissary train for seven days to come; indeed, there was every reason to believe that there would not be such an issue.

The emergency produced the forager, commonly known as "the Bummer." He was not a development; he was a creation; and no history of this most romantic and frolicsome of campaigns can be complete without recognizing the personality and characteristics of this unique type of the army.

The Bummer had abundant warrant for his being. Sherman had given him a personality, and specified his duties ; but certainly no one could have been more surprised than the General himself, to see the aptitude of this creature for his task, and the originality of his methods.

Under general orders for subsisting the army upon the country, as far as possible, regular foraging parties, properly officered, scoured every road on the flanks of each column, gathering horses and mules from the plantations to replace those which had given out on the march, together with grain and hay for the animals, and meat, meal, etc., for the troops. These supplies were turned over to the commissary and quartermaster's departments, for issue in the reg-

ular way.  The result might have been foreseen.
There was general dissatisfaction, for there were not
enough hams, or chickens, or syrup, for all.  Those
who were obliged to put up with side-meat were filled
with indignation ; and, under color of the license
given by Sherman's orders, every regiment in the
army sent out an independent foraging party, whose
duty it was to see that its particular command was
furnished with all the delicacies the country afforded.
These men were the most venturesome in the army,
and in their keen competition to outdo each other,
and capture something that the others would envy,
they took great risks and experienced many startling
adventures.

When the Bummer left the column on his first day's
excursion, he either went on foot, having just quitted
the ranks, or bareback on some broken-down horse or
mule, which had been turned out from the wagon train
utterly exhausted.  At the first farm house he came to,
he looked about for a fresh mount.  If it was to be had,
he helped himself ; if not, and some rival Bummer
had not been there before him, nine times out of ten
some darkey belonging to the place would pilot him to
where the stock was hidden in the woods or swamp.
Then he would search the place for provisions, and
soon have his animal, and perhaps two or three others,
loaded down with poultry, meats, meal, sweet potatoes,
honey, sorghum, and frequently a jug of apple-jack;

or he would find a wagon and load it, with the aid of a few negroes, and hitch together mules and horses indiscriminately with such improvised harness as he could make out of old ropes, chains and leather straps. But he worked hard for what he obtained. In many cases, smoke-houses and barns were empty, and when he had nearly abandoned all hope of finding anything, some old darkey, belonging to the premises or the neighborhood, would direct him to search under the house. Often a hint from the same source would lead him to open what appeared to be a newly-made grave, but which proved to be the repository of the provisions he had been vainly seeking.

In few instances were the inhabitants found "at home." The majority, terrified by the horrible stories published by their newspapers, of the rapine and rapacity of the dreaded " vandal Yankees," had fled, taking with them what they could.' Where the premises were abandoned, the Bummer made a clean sweep, appropriating everything he wanted, and a great many things he did not want. If the negroes on the place told stories of great cruelty they had suffered, or of bitter hostility to the Union, or if there were blood-hounds about, which had been used to run down slaves, the injury was generally avenged by the torch. Where the Bummer found women and children, he was usually as courteous as circumstances admitted. He would " pass the time of day " with the old lady, inquire when she had heard from "the old man," and whether he was with Johnston or Lee, winding up with kissing the baby. Behind this excess of good nature, it must be confessed, lay, in part, a selfish motive. The Bummer was a wily diplomat, and having established " an era of good feeling " between himself and his unsuspecting victim, he cross-examined her in an innocent and insinuating way, managing to acquire a great deal of valuable information. He ascertained what enemy had been in the vicinity, how recently, their course on departure, and their probable designs. He learned all that was to be known of the neighbors farther down the road, whom he expected to " raid " the next day — the quantity and description of supplies, and where they were to be found. Information under this head was usually yielded more willingly than upon any other subject; for it is a curious trait of human nature that a man (or woman) who has been robbed, or swindled in a trade, takes a keen enjoyment, perhaps disguised, in seeing his fellows made fully as miserable as himself. In return for the information acquired, the Bummer compensated his informer with Munchausen narratives of what he and his comrades had already done ; never failing to draw strongly upon a vivid imagination as to what they expected to do.

In taking supplies the Bummer generally drew a fair line between rich and poor, and what could be spared and what could not. His depredations were usually confined to the country on either side of the road traveled by his own column, and he would cover five or ten miles until he met the bummers of another corps; thus, these men actually swept over a breadth of country from sixty to eighty miles. They would often dodge past their own cavalry advance; and in many instances they attacked and dispersed the enemy.

Having loaded his horses or wagons, as the case might be, the Bummer would head for the road upon which his own column was marching. By discreet queries he would soon learn in what direction his regiment was at the time. If rearward, he waited inside a field until it came along; if, in front, he endeavored to place his outfit in the wagon train as early as possible, in order to follow into camp. In this he was sometimes disappointed, and his acquisitions, teams, supplies and all, would be confiscated by some grouty quartermaster or commissary who did not believe in such irregular proceedings. But generally the Bummer knew whom to suspect, and when he hesitated to trust his wagon or horses in the train, he would conceal them near the road, and dispatch some one to the regiment for re-inforcements. The needed help soon arrived, and a score of zealous chaps would distribute the coveted eatables among themselves in a prompt and business like manner.

One would swing a couple of hams from the end of his gun and trudge into camp, while others labored with the turkeys and chickens, or a jug of molasses, or a gum of honey. Sometimes an officer would attempt confiscation, and then the Bummer would announce that he was purveying for the mess of General This-or-That, naming some one notorious for ill-temper and a determination to stand up for what belonged to him. The fiction generally saved the provisions.

The author recalls one who was the most perfect type of the Bummer he ever met. "Snipe," which by the way, was not his name, was a square-built fellow, with light complexion, and a tuft of red beard on his chin. He did duty as an orderly for the adjutant of an Illinois regiment. When rations became scarce, Snipe, of his own motion, and from a real love of adventure, added to the duties of his position, those of purveyor of the mess to which his chief belonged. As soon as the troops left camp in the morning, he would strike out for a day's excursion. It was his particular delight to bring in a fresh horse for his chief almost daily; and truth requires the admission that he knew a good one when he saw it. If the animal was particularly fine, it was utilized at once, the one displaced being relegated to the artillery or wagon train. Snipe was often absent a couple of days or more, and when it came to be believed that he had fallen a victim to his venture-

18

someness, he would "bob up serenely" with an unusually large and excellent supply of provisions.

On one of these excursions, Snipe's absence was protracted into the third day. A short time before this, some of the bummers had been killed by the enemy's cavalry, and their bodies left on the road, with cards pinned to their jackets, reading "Death to Foragers!" Taken in connection with this incident, Snipe's demise was commented upon as a matter of fact, and a new orderly was duly installed in his stead. About midnight the voice of Snipe was heard arousing the camp. Seen in the flickering light of the pine-knot camp fires, he and his outfit presented a ludicrously striking appearance. He had six animals, horses and mules, strung together with a motley assortment of improvised harness, made up of all sorts of odds and ends of leather, rope and iron chain. He bestrode one of the wheelers, and swayed in the saddle with an excitement which was in some degree the exhilaration of victory, but in greater part the effects of applejack. His wagon was an immense box of the Tennessee pattern, high at each end and low in the middle, similar to an old Dutch galliot, loaded to the guards with the choicest of wines and liquors; and, by fortunate chance, there was in the cargo a small box of glass goblets. Snipe at once had his wagon unloaded, with the boxes extemporized a bar, and grandiloquently called upon all hands to walk up and take a drink. It is curious to note that every man in the regiment at once awoke and accepted the invitation. If they had been wanted for guard duty, or fatigue, it would have taken the sergeant-major, an orderly-sergeant, and a stout pair of boots, to have awakened the very same men. Samples of the wine were sent to corps headquarters, and the general pronounced them excellent, at the same time intimating that a further supply would be acceptable. Snipe, however, failed to discover any reason for complying with the request, and by the assistance of some men from a couple of neighboring regiments, his stock was exhausted before daylight.

A prank perpetrated by Dick Rucker, of the same regiment, had a more serious side to it. Rucker was not a "bummer," but a quartermaster, and as such was one of the regularly authorized foragers contemplated in General Sherman's orders at the beginning of the campaign.

One day, when near Savannah, Rucker, who was looking for horses for his wagons, took an animal belonging to a clergyman, whom we will call Taylor. The story may be written in three scenes :

"Can't help it, Mr. Taylor," said Rucker.

"But," remonstrated the clergyman, "it's the only horse I've got."

"It don't make any difference," said Rucker, and he took the horse.

"But, Lieutenant, General Sherman and I are old friends ! If you won't leave me my horse, at least give me your name, and I can get an order from the General to have it restored to me !"

"Oh ! yes, if that'll do you any good," said Rucker, as he rode off with the animal. "My name is Lieutenant Smith, adjutant of the —d Illinois."

The second scene was at Thunderbolt Inlet, and Lieutenant Smith (although that was not his name) was directing the embarkation of his regiment on a gunboat for passage to South Carolina, when a mounted officer rode up and accosted him.

"Lieutenant Smith, General Sherman has directed General Howard to have you return the horse you took from Rev. Mr. Taylor, near Savannah. Please turn it over to my orderly."

Lieutenant Smith, who was entirely ignorant as to the horse or the trick Rucker had played upon him, was naturally indignant, and hotly answered :

"I don't know anything about Mr. Taylor's horse, and you can give General Howard my compliments and tell him to go to the devil !"

And Smith went aboard the gunboat, while the staff officer rode away.

The third scene was in the vicinity of Pocotaligo, a couple of weeks later. As soon as the regiment came within easy reach of General Howard, Smith was ordered to report at the General's headquarters.

"Lieutenant, you sent me a very insulting message. What have you to say?"

"General, I beg pardon for sending such a message, but I didn't steal any horse, and it made me angry to be accused of such a thing."

"Well, Lieutenant, the evidence seems to be that you did take the horse. You will report to your commander as under arrest."

Lieutenant Smith went back to his mess sadly crestfallen, and to add to his discomfort it became apparent to him that his messmates, among whom was Rucker, were having a great deal of fun at his expense, concerning something he knew nothing about. After some days, one of the number told of the prank that Rucker had played upon him, and the lieutenant at once wrote an explanatory note to General Howard, who released him from arrest.

But it was now too late for Mr. Taylor to recover his horse. The army was by this time a couple of hundred miles away from where the animal had been taken. Besides, the animal had been used up and abandoned by the wayside. Furthermore, he was a worthless, disreputable beast at best, not of sufficient value to justify the trouble he had caused.

# CHAPTER XXIX.

## THE EVENTS OF A DAY.

OON after day dawns, the bugler sounds the reveille, and the sleeping army bestirs itself for another day's march. The men turn out unwillingly, half-dressed, to roll-call, and then gather in little knots to prepare the morning meal. One reawakens the all but dead embers of last night's camp-fire, and piles on fresh wood ; others take a bunch of canteens and go in search of water. Each man makes his own pot of coffee. The berry is laid inside a piece of cloth, and broken on a stone under the blows from the butt of a musket ; and the delicious beverage is soon brewing in the old tin oyster-can held over the fire at the end of a ramrod. If the foragers have been successful the day before, sweet potatoes are baking in the ashes, and a piece of beef well-salted is broiling

MAKING CORDUROY ROAD.

See page 286

upon the glowing embers. Meat thus cooked would satisfy the appetite of the veriest gourmand. Scorching by immediate contact with the fire, imparted a delicious flavor ; besides, all the natural juices were retained within. If the country was barren, the hunger of the men was satisfied with " hard-tack," and a fragment of army bacon " sizzled " in the fire.

An hour later the bugle sounds the " assembly," and the troops fall in on their color-line; each regiment, brigade and division has its appointed place in the column, and all move in an orderly way. The head of column marches out promptly at the appointed hour. This is a coveted place in the line of march. The troops occupying this position have no interruptions, except the occasional delays necessary for brushing away the enemy in front; and they usually reach their stopping-place for the night early in the evening. Those who constitute the rear-guard are less happily situated. They must await the movement of the wagon-train and fall in behind. It is generally noon, oftentimes later, before they are able to move; this delay involves a corresponding lateness in reaching their camping-ground, and frequently they do not settle down until nearly midnight, and sometimes even later.

Well in the advance is a small detachment of cavalry, or mounted infantry, moving at a good pace. But they are argus-eyed, and frequently halt to ascertain the occasion of a suspicious circumstance, or to reconnoitre the road. Two or three ride in advance, their reins held in the left hand, their repeating carbines or Henry rifles resting across the pommel of the saddle, or held at the side, muzzle downward, ready for instant pulling to the shoulder.

A detachment of the enemy, also mounted, is discovered, and the main body of the Union troopers are notified. Down the road the regiment charges, at a sharp trot, then at a gallop, until well within range of the enemy, when they break into a wild rush, urging their horses to the utmost speed, firing as they go. The enemy turns and retreats until he reaches his supports, and then the federal advance is checked. The Union skirmishers dismount, seek such shelter as the ground will afford, and keep up a sharp fire until the infantry supports hurry forward and seek the enemy's flanks. Meanwhile a few pieces of artillery open fire down the road, over their heads. In half an hour the enemy vanishes. The Union troops resume their place in the column; an ambulance drives rapidly forward and receives a load of bleeding sufferers; a grave or two is hastily dug under the shadow of the trees, and the march is resumed until the next turn in the road, a small stream, a swamp, or a clump of timber, offers opportunity for a repetition of the scene.

These events do not disturb the main column. At

the halt the men scatter to the sides of the road;
some drop into a doze, others reach into their haversacks and munch a piece of hard tack, while here
and there little knots engage in the mysteries of
euchre or seven-up. Presently a general and his staff,
or a mounted officer, passes by, and a running fire of
interrogatories is discharged: "How far is it to
camp?" "What's up ahead?" "What in the ——
are we stopping here for?"—followed by sarcastic
remarks upon his appearance, or possible errand, concluding with the inevitable injunction to "Grab a
root!" Happy the man who, under such circumstances can, either by a soft answer turn away wrath,
or keep his tongue to himself; for an impatient retort,
or an indication of annoyance, will provoke some keen
remark that will pass from regiment to regiment, and
follow him the length of the entire column, no matter
how fast he speeds his horse.

The enemy in front has been brushed away by this
time, and the column is again in motion. The men
plod along in a go-as-you-please fashion. Conversation, quip and badinage, interspersed with fragments
of song and school-day recitations, enliven the hour.

There is no such place to learn character as here.
Every man is weighed by his comrades and his true
value ascertained. His weaknesses may be concealed
in society—here they stand fully revealed. Any peculiarity, good or bad, physical or mental, is detected,

and fastens upon him some significant appellation, from which he can not escape. A particularly tall man goes by the name of "Fence-rail," or "Ramrod;" a short one by that of "Stunch," or "Shorty;" while one of square build is known as "Chunky" or "Fatty."

But traits of character are more readily recognized than those of person. Here is "Shakspere," so called from his habit of interlarding his reflections upon current events with quotations from books read in boyhood. There is "the Professor," who at home was a country school-teacher and cross-road lyceum debater. He commits what is the unpardonable sin in the eyes of his comrades, that of using a big word where a small one will answer equally well. He affects superior wisdom, and the initial movement of a campaign is as much information as he needs to enable him to tell all about what the outcome will be. If he does not know just how things are, he knows just how they should be. In camp, on Sunday, if there be no chaplain, he will expound a passage of Scripture before a jeering and skeptical audience, but is in no wise disconcerted at the unfavorable reception given to his well-meant effort. Here, too, is "Grunty," whose life is a perpetual torment to himself, for he becomes a butt for the jeers and pranks of all his comrades. To him nothing is as it should be, but everything is as it ought not to be. "Hog" cares only for himself. Never a cracker or piece of tobacco will he divide with a comrade, and a dying man could scarcely hope for a drink of water from his canteen. "Slouchy" never carries a blanket or overcoat on the march, but depends upon stealing one or both when he reaches camp. He is intolerably filthy, and has not a friend who would sleep under the same blanket with him.

But these are the exceptions. The great majority have been formed in other moulds. Among them is "Old Bully," generally a boy, and who otherwise belies his name, by not being a quarrelsome or overbearing brawler, but the personification of companionability, ever good-natured, abounding in kindly deeds for his fellows. Here, too, is " Old Reliable," a slow-but-sure sort of a fellow, usually older and more staid than most of his comrades. He has but little venturesomeness in his make-up, but is ever one to be depended upon. At the end of the day he is always in camp, and is one of the first to be ready for the march in the morning. He is never without a needle or button, or piece of tobacco, that can not be had elsewhere in the regiment, and is ever willing to do a kind turn for a comrade, and make no fuss about it. Here, also, is " Fire-Cracker," a light-hearted chap, with a sharp tongue and a ready wit, full of quaint conceits, firing his jokes and repartees at his companions from one end of the day to the other. One such man in a company does better service in keeping his fellows in good health (so much does health depend upon animal spirits) than a dozen surgeons.    He takes pride in "keeping up with the procession," and no matter how many may be the stragglers on a hard day's march, he is always in his place.

Now the column descends from the high land into the swampy bottom, which tells of the nearness of a formidable stream.   A small but well equipped pioneer corps, generally composed of negroes, has worked manfully to put the road in repair, but here the greater part of the army must lend a helping hand.   Entire brigades stack arms and tear down miles of rail-fences, and carry them to make a corduroy road where the bottom has dropped out of the country, or fell trees by the roadside, if rails are wanting.   The heavy army wagons and trains of artillery rumble across, the poor animals suffering cruelly as their feet plunge between the rails.   Soon the extemporized road disappears in the soft ooze, and a second, and even a third, roadway is laid, before all the trains are able to pass through the swamp.   Meanwhile, other large detachments are struggling with wagons or guns whose teams are exhausted, or which are sunk in the mud almost beyond recovery—lifting them out by main strength.

Farther on is the river.   The skirmishers are exchanging shots with the enemy on the other shore. Now a couple of pieces of artillery are hurried forward and pitch shells across. The pontoon train is brought up, and under the protection of this fire the pontooniers launch their canvas boats, one after another, and connect them, until they reach the other side. The skirmishers rush across, an infantry battalion close at their heels, and drive the enemy from the river bank. Planking is then laid upon the boats, upon which troops and trains pass over.

On the other shore the ascent is steep, and the roadway is through thick, sticky clay. Hundreds of men apply themselves to the wheels of the heavy wagons and guns, while the army teamster cracks his whip and urges forward his weary animals with the choicest oaths known to the language. Here is a fertile field for a word-picture, but the pen quails in view of the immensity of the task. Nothing that ever fell upon human ear is to be likened to the complexity and comprehensiveness of the vocabulary of the army teamster. He knows the pedigree and performances of the mule, and every detail of its anatomy ; and he anathematizes it from one end to the other, giving a full bill of particulars. He runs the gamut of oaths in every key, and with every possible inflection of voice, and then profanely apostrophizes himself because of his inability to express himself as vigorously as he thinks circumstances justify.

So the day wears away. There is no halt made for the noon-day meal. The men eat as they march, or when there is a stop because of the road being blocked; the provident soldier limiting himself to the fractional part of his ration, in order to make his provision last until a new issue is made ; and the reckless eating until all is gone, trusting to good fortune to provide for him on the morrow. As evening comes on, the steps of the men grow laggard, and they drag themselves painfully along the dreary road. The jibes and jokes which have been bandied from man to man have died out, and there is only sullen silence or profane complaint. Then the foragers rejoin the column, and their treasures of eatables unloose the tongues of the men, and cause them to chirrup gleefully in anticipation of the feast to come with camp and night. Anon the martial music strikes up, a tremendous shout is raised, and the column regains its buoyancy of spirit and elasticity of gait.

At length the camping - ground for the night is reached. If the foragers have been successful, the men now enjoy the real meal of the day. Turkeys, chickens, beef and pork, vegetables of all descriptions, sorghum and honey, make a toothsome meal, and the severity of their labor gives to the men the heartiest of appetites.

## CHAPTER XXX.

### A REAL CAMP-FIRE.

HE day's march over, the men gather in little knots about their camp - fires, without thought of the weather making it necessary to huddle over the glowing embers. Habit has made this the rendezvous; besides, the bright blaze is conducive to companionability.

The men are variously engaged. Some repair garments falling into pieces through long and hard service. Many beat the sand and dust of the march out of their shoes, and patch up, as best they can, the stockings which are so worn and ragged as to be little protection to their blistered, travel-worn feet. Others cook a fragment of meat or a potato for the mid-day meal on the morrow, while not a few industriously thumb a "deck" of cards. Euchre and seven-

19

up are the favorite games; but occasionally poker is played, grains of corn standing for "chips."

The men produce their pipes and tobacco — was there one who did not smoke, and call it "solid comfort ?" — and discuss the events of the day. In this symposium, the Bummer who has been out foraging that day, occupies a conspicuous position. He is the gazette of the army. His rambles have led him among comrades belonging to other commands traveling far distant roads, and he knows all about what Slocum or Kilpatrick has been doing. This narrative, and his encounters with citizens on the plantations he has visited, he relates in a graphic manner, the only interruption being an occasional quip interjected by a listener, and at times a profane reflection upon the veracity of the narrator. But amid all the running fire of sharp retort, there is rarely anything but good humor. The thin-skinned man, who could not take a joke, wore himself out with homesickness, and was discharged, and the quarrelsome camp-bully deserted, long ago.

Then conversation turns upon the morrow, — which way are we going, and what will we do when we get there ? It is a curious commentary upon the practical side of our system of education, that few soldiers in the ranks, (and nearly all had at least attended public school,) had any sufficiently clear recollection of geography to be able to figure

out their actual position. They knew they were
heading south, or southeast, as the case might be ;
they had gathered from citizens that their direction
was towards Savannah or Mobile, but that was all.
Even the large rivers they crossed were not conspicuous enough landmarks to give many their
bearings.

This subject disposed of, the boys would fill up the
evening with such anecdote and song as grew naturally
out of the conversation.

There was less singing in the army than the latter-
day "Camp-Fire" would lead the uninformed to
believe. In the early days it was different. Then,
a prayer meeting was held almost nightly in some
quarter of the regiment, and the songs sung were
of the "I'm going home !" and "When shall we
meet again ?" order, but these soon outlived their
usefulness. They were too suggestive of death and
the judgment, and the realities of active service in
the face of the enemy was sufficient. For similar
reasons, the boys did not take kindly to songs of a
mournfully domestic order, such as "We shall meet,
but we shall miss him," and "We are sitting by
the cottage door, brother." Neither did such as
"We are coming, Father Abraham," or "Down with
the traitor, and up with the star," attain any great
popularity in active war-days. The one was a rallying
song for recruits, and these were veterans; the other

was a sentiment which could be safely sung a thous-
and miles at the rear; but those who were at the
front had learned the magnitude of their contract, and
they did not care to do any unnecessary boasting.     A
new love ditty with a taking melody was favorably regarded, but what the boys really ached for, and sang
with a joyous abandon, was some comic song such as
" Darkies, hab you seen de massa ? " or " Brigadier
Bralaghan; " or such roystering verses as " The
Bould Sojer Boy," or " Benny Havens, oh ! " and it was
rarely that a really ribald song met with much favor.
Johnny ——, a sadly illiterate but true-hearted boy,
furnished great amusement with his one solitary song,
not exactly of a Sunday-school pattern, something
about his grandfather's ram, which he sang daily and
nightly for nearly four years, until, poor fellow, he
was killed at Bentonville.     In his innocence he never
suspected that his comrades were " guying " him when
they asked him to sing.     Then there was " Jerry,"
the cook for an officers' mess — the " Fine-Haired
Mess " it came to be known, but why, is scarcely
apparent — who also had but one song, but that one
a great favorite, which he sang in a most melancholy
heart-broken way, with up-rolled eyes, to the dismal
thrumming of an old banjo:

> " O ! far' you well, my Mary Ann,
>      Far' you well my dear !
> I've no one left to love me now,
>      An' little do I keer !

" O ! if I had a scoldin' wife,
    As sho' as you is bo'n,
  I'd take her down to New Orleans,
    An' trade her off for co'n ! "

But anecdote growing out of the events of the day
was the principal pastime, and every regiment could
yield sufficient to furnish themes for poet and scenes
for painter.

One evening a soldier displayed the picture of a
fair young girl. He had taken it from an enemy,
dead on the field of battle. "Blame me !" said he,
"but it just made me sick. And he was a nice-look-
ing young feller, too. Why, he had the picture held up
right before his eyes, and he had just as natural and
sweet a smile on his face as if he was alive ! "

"Well," said a comrade, "at least I'd a let the
poor chap been buried with his picture! "

"Stealin' that picture," said another, "was about
as mean a trick as Jack Ruggles did the other day.
Why, he came across a dead Johnny, lyin' flat on his
face, and he turned him over and took a plug of black
navy out of his pocket and took a chaw, and smacked
his lips and said it was mighty good. I've been
hungry for tobacco, but —— me if I want any out of
a dead man's pocket."

"Say, Stunchy," said another, "don't you remember the Johnny we buried in front of our lines at
Shiloh, with a cartridge between his teeth? A bullet
hit him in the head and killed him. He never fell

over nor moved a muscle, and there he was, dead on his knees behind a stump, his gun in one hand, his hand up close to his mouth, with the big part of the cartridge in his fingers, and the paper he had bit off the end still 'tween his teeth. We couldn't straighten him, and we buried him just so."

"You bet I remember that, and I mind a derned hard jolt I got on Monday night, when the battle was over. The Johnnies run us out of our camp the first day, and when we got the bulge on 'em and whooped 'em out, I went to my tent to see what was gone, and there was a blamed Johnny lying there asleep, at least that's what I thought he was doing. I shook him and hollered at him, but he didn't answer, and then I found he was dead. He was shot bad, and crawled in there after he was wounded, I reckon. But he might have gone in for plunder and been killed while he was in there. There was an awful stiff fight in that camp, and the tents were riddled full of holes."

"Talking about men being killed," remarked another," reminds me of Colonel Jones, of the 53d Indiana. You all remember how he was wounded that awful hot day McPherson was killed. While they were carrying him off the field a shell exploded close by and killed him. He was a fine officer and a nice man, and I heard some of the officers up at division headquarters telling a pretty good story that he was responsible for. It seems that when Lincoln was a

A REAL CAMP FIRE.

See page 289.

young chap he was working for an old skinflint that kept a cross-roads store. Lincoln wanted a pair of boots, and as the storekeeper didn't owe him enough to pay for them, Lincoln asked him to let him have the boots and take the pay out of his wages when he owed him enough.

"'No,' said the storekeeper, 'you just wait till you earn the money, and then you'll get the boots!'

"Well, when Lincoln was elected, the old man wanted to be postmaster, so he wrote, telling the President what he was after, and for fear Lincoln wouldn't remember him, said that Lincoln had been his clerk once.

"After a while he got a letter from Lincoln, saying he was very sorry the office had been promised to another man. And he also wrote:

"'You need never fear that I will forget you, old friend. I remember you very well, *especially the boots!*'

"Lincoln wasn't a bit malicious about it, but you see he couldn't lose so good an opportunity for a joke."

"It's all very well, you fellows talking about dead men, but I tell you, boys, I'd just as lief be killed as scared to death, as I was almost at Vicksburg." The speaker continued:

"You see, I went home from Memphis on a furlough, and when I got back there my division had

gone to Vicksburg.   I was corralled at Fort Pickering
and put to work on the fortifications until there was a
big enough squad of us to put on a boat and send
down river.

"Well, we got started, and went up Yazoo river to
Haines' Bluff.   We landed there about five o'clock in
the evening.   There were two others besides myself
who belonged to Lauman's division, and we asked
where it was.   They told us it was about six miles on
the left, and we made up our minds to reach it that
night.

"We walked along pretty briskly, and it got to be
dark, and finally we ran up against some tents, and
asked who lived there, and the guard said it was
General Hovey's headquarters.   We asked where
Lauman's division was, and he said we were heading
for it, and to go straight ahead.

"Well, after awhile we saw some camp fires, and
we walked towards them, but they were a good ways
off.   Then we got into a hollow where we couldn't see
them, but supposed we were going in the right direction.   Pretty soon we came to a hill and commenced
climbing it.   We were all singing a new song we had
learned while at home on furlough, and were just in
the middle of the chorus, "Dear Annie, dear Annie of
the Vale," when a blaze of fire jumped right out of
the hill and the bullets whistled around by baskets-
full.   We all turned to run, and my foot caught some-

thing and I fell. The hill was pretty steep, and my knapsack, full of goodies from home for the boys, made me top-heavy, and I rolled down hill, end over end, and landed, ker-chug, in a ravine lined with underbrush. The other boys were nowhere to be seen, and I tell you I was scared. The bullets came raining through the brush from both sides.

"Well, I lay all night in a cold sweat. The idea of being killed down there, all by myself, and mother never know what had become of me, was awful.

"Next morning I made up my mind to reconnoitre, but the guns began to crack again from both sides, and then artillery, and I found that I was between the Union and rebel lines, and I tell you I hugged the ground close.

"After a while the artillery let up, and then there was only a few rifle shots. I had studied the lay of the ground and got the points of the compass, and made up my mind which way I ought to go to get into the Union lines. Then I rose up on my knees and looked through the brush, and on both sides of me I saw earthworks, and noticed that farther to the south they bent away from each other. So I concluded to follow the ravine farther that way, and I did so, crawling on my hands and knees for fear I would be shot at. Then I took another observation, and found that the works on my left, which I took to be the Union side, had run out.

"Then I took a white pocket-handkerchief out of my pocket—you see I was just from home—and tied it on a stick, and made up my mind to surrender to the first man I came across, Yankee or Johnny. So I marched along to the left, at right angles from the ravine, when somebody halted me—he was about two hundred yards off—and I waved my white flag. It was a squad of cavalry, and, great Scott! but I was glad to see that they wore blue coats!

"Well, I told them my story, and who I was, and showed their officer my furlough, and he told me how to get to the division. On the road there, I came across a camp where the men were at dinner—it was noon, now—and as I was hungry, I asked for something to eat. They told me to sit down with them, and while we were eating they told about a desperate charge the Johnnies had made on them the night before. From the way they described it, I knew it was us three fellows singing, 'Dear Annie of the Vale!'

"Then I found my division. It seems it had not moved up so as to complete the line of investment, but was well back in the rear and to the left of the line, and we wanderers had gone clear around the left flank of our own lines, and got in between them and the rebels. Then we got turned around, not knowing where we were, and marched right up in front of our own rifle-pits!

"One of my comrades that night, got into camp all safe. The other was never heard of, and he was probably shot and died somewhere in the thicket where I spent such a miserable night. But for nearly three months that ground lay half-way between the two lines, and there was no chance to go and look for a body; besides, the underbrush was so thick and covered so much space, that it might never have been found anyway."

"Yes," said another, "there were some curious circumstances in that Vicksburg campaign. I mind that General Hurlbut had a scout whose name was Bell. He was from Galesburg, and an awful smart chap. You remember we had Pemberton cooped up in Vicksburg, and Jo Johnston was out behind Black River, in our rear, and they were trying to agree upon a concerted movement to smash Grant, who was in between them. This Bell deserted and went to Johnston, and somehow or other got into his confidence, and undertook to carry a dispatch through Grant's lines to Pemberton. He also took along a lot of gun caps, which were badly needed by the Johnnies in Vicksburg. Hurlbut knew all about the scheme, and when Bell tried to get through the lines he was captured by Hurlbut's pickets and taken to the General.

"The officers had a hard job making out the cipher dispatch, but they finally read it as follows :

" 'My last note was brought back by the messenger. Two hundred thousand caps have been sent. It will be continued as they arrive. Bragg is sending a division. When it comes I will move to you. Which do you think the best route? How and where is the enemy encamped? What is your force?'

" Well, Bell's gun-caps were dampened so as to be useless, and he was allowed to go into Vicksburg with them and his dispatch. The next day he came back with an answer from Pemberton, and that gave away the whole job. Grant had found out where Johnston was to make his rear attack, and he fixed for him. The upshot was, that Vicksburg surrendered before Johnston knew it, and then Grant turned and smashed him."

"Say, boys," broke in a comrade in the uniform of a lieutenant. " You don't know how near I came to having a commission long before I did, do you ?

" While we were laying at Natchez, General Lorenzo Thomas, Adjutant-General of the Army, came down to look after his pet hobby of arming the negroes. I was chief clerk for General Crocker's adjutant-general then, and one morning General Thomas came into the office when I was alone. Says he, 'General Crocker gives a good account of you. How would you like to have a commission as adjutant of a negro regiment?'

" It came so bluntly, and his voice was so kind,

Jackson May 25th 1863—

Lieut: Genl Pemberton.

My XAFV-USLX am VVIFLSJP by the BRCYAJ
2ITVVV VEGT-SUAJ-NERP-ZIFVL: It
will be GTOECSZQD as they NTYMNX
Bring MU-TPHINZG a QKCMKBSE.
Will it-DZGJX I will VOIG-AS-QHK.
NITWM do you YTIAM the IIKNI-
VFVEY. there + where is the JSQML-
GUGSFTVE? HBFY is your ROEEL?

J. E. JOhnston

it took me off my feet. After a few moments I said :

" 'General, I am proud to have the confidence of General Crocker and yourself, but I can't take it.'

" The General looked as if he did not know what to make of it, and I went on :

" ' General, I am very grateful to you; and I want to say that I am fully in sympathy with the purpose of arming these people. I am an original abolitionist, having been brought up on Greeley's *Tribune ;* but I started out in this war with my schoolmates and work-shop companions. If I can win a commission serving with them, I will be glad of it. But if I can not, I will serve with them as a private to the end.'

" The General didn't speak for a few minutes, and then he said :

" ' Young man, I respect your feelings, and I hope and believe you will gain your desire before the war is over. Now, I will be here for a couple of weeks, and if you know of any corporals or sergeants who would make good company officers, and take commissions with negro troops, let me know.'

" Well, boys, I remembered that, and most of the men in this regiment who received such commissions, were appointed largely upon my recommendation.

" I had another good chance," he continued, " just after the siege of Vicksburg. You remember that

20

division commanders were instructed to report the names of young soldiers who had behaved themselves, for appointment to West Point cadetships. Well, my name was sent in, but I would n't accept. I started in to see this war through, and here I am."

"Now, byes, it's domd sthrange how aisy the shoulder-sthraps came to some of yees, and how harrud it was for some of the rist of us." The speaker was a tall, raw-boned Irishman, wearing the chevrons of a sergeant. He continued :

"I was on garrud juty at Gin'ral Chrocker's hid-quarthers, back of Vicksburg, and wan day some uv the byes made up their minds for a little spoort. So we sint to Boviny for a gallon of whishkey, and put it away in a tint, ready for night. Well, it happened that some of the eshcort company shmelt it, an' they sthole it, and had the divil's own time. Some uv thim was quarrelsome chaps, an' they had a bit of a shindy.

"In the mornin', the Gin'ral — he was a fine sowl-ger, an' a mighty good man, but cross as the very divil sometimes — he had thim brought up afoor him, an' sint thim to the garrud-house.

"Now, you say, we did n't intind to be lift widout our fun, so we got another jug of whishkey, an' that night we had some rare spoort. The Gin'ral's wife had come down river that day, an' was quarthered wid him at the big brick house, an' it's aisy to belave that she was dishturbed by the noise. Anyhow, it was n't

long afther I crawled into me tint, afoor I hurrud
somebody a-thumpin' on the canvas from the outside,
an' thin the Gin'ral — I knew his voice in a minit —
says he, 'Corporal of the Garrud!' — you see the
corporal shlept in the same tint wid mesilf —'Corporal
of the Garrud! In the mornin' bring thim drunken
divils to me office! I'll tache thim a lesson! If
there's any gittin' dhrunk and raisin' ——— to be done
about these headquarthers, I'll do it mesilf, be gobs!'
says he.

"Well, byes, I was mighty bad scared. The Kur-
renal had ricomminded me for promotion, an' he was a
Prisbytarian, an' awful sthrict, an' I knew if he got
howld of this schrape it was all day wid me prospicts.
You may belave I did n't slape a wink, but did a powerful thinkin', an' made up me mind what I wud do.

"In the mornin' I got up airly an' took a drink to
sthiffen me narves, an' wint sthraight to the adjutant's
office, an' as good luck would have it, there was the
Gin'ral all by hisself.

"I made my best shalute, an' says I, 'Good mornin',
Gin'ral! I hope your honor is well this fine mornin'.'
An' then I says, not givin' him time to spake back:
'Gin'ral,' says I, 'I desire, sir, to repoort mesilf as
wan of thim drunken divils that raised ——— last night.
I just made a domb lamb's-tail of mesilf, sir, an' I
hope your honor will excuse me this wanst!'

"It took the Gin'ral just right, an' he begun to

laugh, an' says he, 'Was there any fightin' last night ? '

" 'Divil a bit, your honor,' says I.

" ' An' are yees an Irishman ? ' says he.

" ' By no manes, sir,' says I. 'Me father was from County Corruk, but I was borrun in this counthry,' says I.

" An' thin the Gin'ral laughed all over, an' says he :

" ' It's domb lucky for yees,' says he, 'that you was borrun in this counthry. I've always noticed whin a full-blooded Irishman gets dhrunk, he wants to fight. I don't want to interfare wid anybody's innocent amusemints, but I won't allow anybody around these headquarthers to get dhrunk *and fight !* Go to your quarthers, sir !'

" That was the last av it, but the sthory got out, an' divil of a commission have I sane ! "

Meanwhile the men drop away gradually to their shelter-tents and blankets, each one seeking such spot as may suit his convenience, preferably snug up against the root of a great tree. So little semblance is there of the permanent camp, with its color-line, its officers' tents, and the avenues separating the quarters of the various companies, that the sergeant-major has no little trouble to find the orderly-sergeants, and they the men, when a midnight call is made for fatigue or picket duty.

The camp-fires now die down ; and, environed by hundreds of vigilant sentinels, the army sleeps upon another of its countless bivouacs.

Far along in the night, an orderly from brigade headquarters rides into camp, and calls for the adjutant, to whom he hands a circular order directing the command to march in a certain direction at a designated hour on the morrow. The adjutant acknowledges receipt, by writing his name on the back of the order, which the orderly takes to the next regiment, until all have been notified. The men neither know nor care anything about the incident, and the bugle-sound in the morning is their only warning that another day's march is to begin.

## CHAPTER XXXI.

### WORKING A PASSAGE.

OVEMBER 18th, the troops marched eighteen miles, crossing the Ocmulgee river on pontoons. Here some extensive cotton factories were destroyed. On both sides of the stream, for many miles, the roads lay through low, flat ground, sodden with recent rains, and the heavy wagon trains soon converted them into almost bottomless abysses of mud, entailing upon the men severe labor in corduroying, and extricating artillery and wagon trains — work to which necessity had already accustomed them, and which was to be almost a daily experience henceforward to the close of the war.

The next day the troops passed through the beautiful town of Monticello. No male inhabitants were to be seen, except young boys and infirm old men. The rebel conscription act had literally "robbed the cradle and the grave," as the expressive phrase of the day had it, driving into the ranks all who could possibly do any manner of military service, whether in the field, in garrison, or guarding prisoners. A few women occasionally peered curiously from their windows, but usually they kept themselves well hidden from sight. The negroes turned out in full force to hail their deliverers. It was remarkable that the federal army found among the most ignorant of this enslaved people, who had been continually told that the dreaded "Yankees" were demons and not men, an unshaken faith that the coming of this army was to bring to them freedom from bondage, and many extravagant scenes were witnessed. It was not an unusual occurrence to see negroes fall upon their knees by the roadside, as the troops passed by, and hear them bless God and the boys in blue in one and the same breath. They manifested an ardent anxiety to see General Sherman, and in some instances addressed him or spoke of him with a reverence and extravagance of expression which they could not have exceeded had he been the Savior of mankind. Thousands of these poor people left their humble homes, carrying their children and a few household effects, and, falling in behind the soldiers, trudged along, with no idea of where they were going, except that they were on the highway from slavery to freedom. It was useless to tell them to stay at home; that they would be freed by the war wherever they might be, and that the troops could not feed them. With a blind faith, they persisted in the journey, braving all hardships, until they reached the coast and were provided for.

There was another remarkable trait in the slave character—their entire devotion to the soldiers of the Union. The writer has never heard of a single instance where one of these blacks, man or woman, ever betrayed a blue-coated straggler, or escaping prisoner, into the hands of the enemy; but, on the other hand, they gave them every possible assistance, secreting them by day, feeding them and assisting them on their journey by night. Still more wonderful was the knowledge these ignorant people had of military movements. Much sport was made in early war times of the "intelligent contraband," whose narratives were given to the press by war correspondents; but his news was usually reliable in its general terms, although ignorance led him into exaggerations whenever a numerical force was in question. In countless instances, the negroes along Sherman's line of march through Georgia and the Carolinas had information of the advance of his troops, and of their achievements,

long before seeing them, and knew of victory or disaster in Tennessee, Virginia, or on the coast, before
many of the white people about them did. It was
believed by the Union soldiers that the negroes trans-
mitted the news by swift runners, traveling day and
night, and the belief is plausible in view of all the
facts.

The next four days after leaving Monticello, the
army marched fifty-five miles, reaching the Oconee
river.

Hitherto, the cavalry and mounted infantry in
advance, with occasional assistance from the leading
brigade of each column, had been able to brush aside
the enemy in front; but here the passage of the
stream was disputed by a strong force of infantry and
artillery on the opposite bank. Deserters and prisoners stated that among the enemy's troops were six
hundred convicts from Southern penitentiaries who
had been put under arms. Many of the latter were
taken prisoner, but General Sherman at once ordered
them to be liberated, shrewdly concluding that they
would trouble their own people more than they could
him.

November 23d and 24th, the opposing forces skirmished incessantly, and there was considerable artillery firing. The next day a sharp little engagement
occurred, in which Belknap's brigade took the principal part. Under cover of its fire, three miles of

high railroad trestlework through the swamp were
destroyed. Later in the day a crossing was effected
at Fall's Ferry, higher up the stream, with little
opposition.

Near the Oconee river the troops came in possession
of some late Southern newspapers containing the first
information they had received from the outer world in
nearly two months. The ill-looking pages, imprinted
upon dingy paper, almost as dull in color as that in
which the butcher wraps his meat, was of a verity,
" *lux lucet in tenebris*," a light shining in darkness.
Loud-voiced readers were called into requisition, and
the contents were listened to by thousands, who
drowned the voice of the reader, ever and anon, with
exultant cheers, or howls of derision, as the para-
graphs pleased or displeased them.

First, and all-important, was the news that Lincoln
had been re-elected to the Presidency, and the Government had called out more troops. Referring to this,
the editor denounced the Northern democracy bitterly
for " permitting the election of the hated despot," and
said that there was now no longer hope from without,
but the Southern people must achieve their own freedom. It was a curious fact that among the means to
this end was urged the freeing and arming of half a
million slaves—this, too, by a people who had set out
to establish a government with slavery as the corner-
stone. This, however, would require time, and the

A HUNGRY PARTY.

See page 328.

immediate emergency demanded that the white people
of the South, men, women and children, should rise
against the invaders. In order to inflame their passions, the paper contained many horrible falsehoods
with reference to "the great raid," as they termed
Sherman's march, giving scandalous narratives of rob-
bery, rapine and murder. They spoke of Sherman as
"the great raider, horse-thief and murderer," and pronounced awful curses upon him and his vandal fol-
lowers. In other columns were found inflammatory
appeals from military and civil authorities, calling
upon the inhabitants to harass the troops in every
conceivable way ; to fire upon them from behind every
barn and stump; to burn bridges, and fell heavy trees
across the roads in their line of march ; and to remove
or destroy all provisions and forage in their track.
Frantic efforts were made to comply with some of these
requests, and the movement of the army, from the
Oconee river to Savannah, required redoubled effort.
The citizens were too discreet to carry out the guer-
rilla warfare urged upon them, which, while delaying
the army in no great degree, would have made it necessary to hang a few of their own carcasses from the
trees lining the roads. But the roads were blocked
with felled trees almost the entire distance, and it became necessary to send large working detachments
from the marching column to assist the pioneer corps,
which, under usual circumstances, were able to keep

the way sufficiently clear to admit of the passage of artillery and supply trains. Again, throughout this same region, so thorough was the destruction or removal of provisions, that for many days the troops were obliged to subsist almost entirely upon peanuts and parched rice taken from the fields, the contents of the supply trains being well-nigh exhausted.

## CHAPTER XXXII.

THE OGEECHEE.

OVEMBER 28th, 29th and
30th, the army marched
forty - six miles, entering
upon the region of the
savannas.    Here the great
pine trees rose straight in air nearly
a hundred feet, surmounted at the top by a
crown of brilliant green.    But few branches projected
from the trunks, and these far from the ground.    The
trees were not thickly set, and the ground was remark-
ably free from undergrowth, permitting the troops to
march on either side of the road, which was left clear
for the wagon train, thus shortening the column fully
one half.

December 1st, the army crossed the Ogeechee river
and engaged in its old task of destroying the railroad.
This piece of track afforded unusual opportunity for

the most thorough exercise of the destructive propen-
sities of the troops.   The rail was of the light pattern,
such as is generally used now for horse-car tracks,
laid upon wooden stringers about eight inches square,
which rested on the usual ties.   Both stringers and
ties were of pitch-pine, and burned readily, while
the iron was so light that it soon heated to cherry
red, when it was readily wrapped around fence posts
and trees, the men exercising their fancy in the
construction of iron "neckties" of curious pat-
terns.   Particular attention was given here, as at other
points where railroads were destroyed, to the glass
insulators on the telegraph poles.   These were either
broken with axes, or thrown into the waters of the
adjoining swamps, and were not readily replaced by
the enemy.   In fact, the whole mechanical system of
the South was an importation ; and as soon as armies
drew a line between North and South, that moment
the South began to go down.   With Northern mar-
kets closed to it, railroads, cotton-works, and nearly
everything in the way of machinery, fell into decay;
scarcely a cog-wheel could be replaced by Southern
mechanics.   Their railroads were wonderfully run
down; and in very many instances a train might be
heard at considerable distance, from the creaking of
the wheels in the axle-boxes, because of the absence
of oil.

December 2nd the army came to Millen, which had

been a large prison-pen for the safe-keeping of Union prisoners. The cavalry advance made a rapid movement upon the place, hoping to release their unfortunate comrades, but were dismayed to find that they had been removed to a less accessible point.

December 9th, the troops reached a point seven miles from Savannah, having marched forty-five miles since the 3d. At this place the soldiers were greatly rejoiced to hear the guns of the Union fleet; and to learn from citizens that the ships had been sending up signal rockets nightly for some time past, in anticipation of the arrival of the army. It mattered little that the principal obstructions, an hostile army and strong fortifications, yet separated soldiers and sailors. The former felt that their success was assured, and, at the worst, only a few days would pass until the two would clasp hands.

The next day, December 10th, the march was resumed, Belknap's brigade leading the Seventeenth Corps. Here the troops ran hard up against the enemy at a point near the stone reading "4 miles to Savannah." At this place torpedoes had been planted in the road, and the cavalry advance exploded some of them in passing along. General Sherman was greatly enraged at what he denounced as conduct not justified by the laws of war, and he caused prisoners to pass up and down in order to test the road. It was, however, the opinion of the writer of these pages, that the

21

torpedoes were placed, not so much for the loss of life they might occasion, as to give notice of the occupancy of the road, their explosions serving as signals for the enemy to open fire with their heavy guns. This conclusion seemed reasonable from the fact that the guns were trained directly down the road, which was screened from sight of the artillerists by the heavy growth of trees, and that fire was opened immediately after the explosion of the torpedoes. These engines were used, however, at some points where the explanation would not hold good.

The line of march lay down a broad sand road, lined on either side with live-oak trees whose branches met over-head, forming a beautifully arched avenue, straight as an arrow. Suddenly the troops came to a clearing perhaps a quarter mile wide. The 32d Illinois Regiment was in front, and as the adjutant and the old grizzled major who was in command, riding side by side at its head, left the wooded avenue and entered the clearing, a shell rose from over the timber in front. It had evidently been projected from a great distance, for it was falling fast in its trajectory, and in a direct line for the regiment. Usually these missiles were heard, but not seen, and familiarity with the sound had bred a certain degree of contempt. But this shell is plainly visible, from the instant it rises over the timber in front, and it holds the gaze as did the glittering eye of the gray-beard

Ancient Mariner that of the wedding guest. It seems
to be charged with a personal message. Its motion
appears to be slow and deliberate; it is so sure of its
mark that there is no need for haste. At first it is
a small black blotch on the sky. It grows. It is as
large as a tin-cup—as a plate—a barrel. Now its
immensity fills the entire field of vision, shutting out
trees and sky. Will it explode before it comes
near enough to do damage? Why don't we "flank
off" to one side of the road, and give this demon of
destruction a clear right of way? There are no
orders. Shall we "dodge," and allow it pass over-
head, rather than sit up straight as a target for it?
Certainly, if the major will only "dodge" first. But
he does not, and pride will not permit his companion
—when, sh-sh-sh—the shell passes over, very low
down. Thought has traveled far more rapidly than
iron propelled by gunpowder. The danger is past.

A few moments later the troops left the road,
formed line-of-battle through the timber on the left,
and deployed skirmishers. This was scarcely done,
when some one brought word that the shell whose
course has been noted, had played havoc with the
color company of the regiment. Riding hastily back
to the road, the adjutant found Ed Lawson, the
captain, with five men of the company following his
own, stretched out upon the ground, all wounded,
but none killed. The shell had exploded at the head

of Lawson's company, the center of the regiment, and a fragment struck him in the lower part of the stomach, bruising him severely. He subsequently recovered, yet it is not too much to say that this injury hastened his death, which occurred a few years afterwards. He was one of a squad of noble fellows who formed the nucleus of the company mentioned in the opening chapters of this volume; a most conscientious soldier, as well as a man of excellent deportment, and unimpeachable personal character. He rose from the ranks to the grade of orderly sergeant, and finally became captain of the company in which he had enlisted as a private.

Near the point where the troops entered the timber and went into line-of-battle, was General Sherman. He had dismounted, and was walking nervously up and down the side of the road, his head bent over on his breast, his hands crossed behind him. He seemed intent upon his own thoughts, and oblivious to the volleys of shell and shot which tore down the road. Those who saw him in this situation thought that he was exposing himself unnecessarily, and heartily wished, for the sake of all concerned, that "the old man" would seek a safer place, at least until the Savannah problem was solved, and the cracker-line re-established.

For ten hours the troops lay under as hot an artillery fire as they ever experienced: a cannonade from field pieces in actual action, would have been far preferable. As it was, they were posted in dense pine timber, and the heavy missiles from the 32-pounder and 64-pounder guns of the enemy's permanent fortifications, tore through the immense trees, hurling branches and splinters in all directions. It was very demoralizing, but fortunately the casualties were light.

With night came a novel experience. The command was ordered to extend to the right and reach the Ogeechee river, preparatory to a complete investment of Savannah. The only route was a narrow causeway built up through the rice swamp, parallel to, and within plain sight throughout its whole length, of the enemy's heavy works, about eight hundred yards distant. The troops were massed in the heavy timber at the approaches to the causeway. As soon as darkness should well settle, they were to pass over and in a hurry.

Fortunately the moon, which stood high and was near the full, was obscured by heavy clouds. The moment came, the word was given, and the head of column left its shelter, the troops marching in close order. They had made but a short distance, when suddenly, on the left, from down in the water, rose a shrill whistle, which was repeated again and again, until the sound was lost in the distance. It was a line of the enemy's picket-boats signaling the movement back to the forts.

The response was prompt. The enemy's gunners had excellent range, and a storm of shot and shell flew across the water and over the causeway. The fierceness and suddenness of the attack accelerated the pace of the troops to such a degree that, in the darkness and confusion, many were pushed over into the water ; but in every such case, so far as heard from, the men who came to grief received their baptism on the side of the causeway farthest from the enemy's batteries — an unanswerable argument showing the natural instinct of men to recede from gunpowder rather than advance toward it. Fortunately, no lives were lost, but there were more guns and drums abandoned that night in the rice-swamp than during all the previous six months from Atlanta thus far.

Such experiences as these were the severest strain upon the nerves, and put discipline to a hard test. These troops would stand comparatively unconcerned amid a torrent of shot and shell, when so posted as to be able to fight back. But to take a severe fire, on unknown ground, in the darkness of night, without opportunity of defending themselves, was a very different matter.

# CHAPTER XXXIII.

## SAVANNAH.

ECEMBER 10th, the investment of Savannah was almost complete. The extreme right (Blair's Seventeenth Corps) rested on the Ogeechee river, seventeen miles from the city.

Near that point were standing huge live-oak trees, which antedated the memory and legends of "the oldest inhabitant." Their great branches, as large as the trunks of trees in our own latitude, spread so widely that a good-sized regiment might form a line of battle beneath them. From their boughs drooped graceful festoons of moss. Just beyond, flashed the billows of old ocean, its surf falling upon the ear distantly and hoarsely.

Under the moonlight, the scene was yet more im-

pressive. It might have been the picture so beautifully described by Longfellow :

" The murmuring pines
Bearded with moss, and in garments green, indistinct in the twilight,
Stand like Druids of eld, with voices sad and prophetic.
Stand like harpers hoar, with beards that rest on their bosoms.
Loud from its rocky caverns the deep-voiced neighboring ocean
Speaks, and in accents disconsolate answers the wail of the forest."

For many days the troops had been reduced almost
to starvation. The rations in the supply-trains were
exhausted ; and, in compliance with orders from the
authorities, the citizens had either removed or destroyed all provisions and forage along the line of
march for a week past. In this strait, the army, officers and men alike, subsisted upon immature "goober-
peas" (peanuts) dug out of the sand-hills, whose ster-
ility yielded nothing better, and rice gathered from
the swamps, beaten out and parched. Even this poor
makeshift for food soon failed, as the army massed
close about Savannah ; and the hunger of the men was
heightened by recollections of the good living they had
indulged in but a few days before, when in the region
of sweet potatoes, pigs and beeves. The mules and
horses were worse off — they either had no corn at all,
or the little doled out was stolen from their troughs
and nose-bags by hungry soldiers.

At this period of general suffering, the adjutant's
faithful "Bummer" succeeded in acquiring a few
sweet potatoes, a small piece of fat pork, a solitary

onion, and something in a canteen. Just as this tempt-
ing repast had been spread out upon an empty hard-
tack box, and the writer and a mess-mate were seating
themselves for "a square meal," Frank Orcott, of the
7th Illinois, one of the best fellows living, appeared in
sight. He was mounted on an under-sized mule, with
a dear-mother-I've-come-home-to-die expression in its
eye; and absence of flesh made its anatomy resemble a
wind-wrecked "prairie-schooner." Frank himself
seemed as if he had lost every friend in the world, and
when hailed, he looked around with a glad surprise.
He joyously accepted an invitation to dinner, and
although the two have eaten many a sumptuous meal
at each other's tables since, they have never met upon
such occasions without adopting, unanimously and
enthusiastically, resolutions setting forth that their
best dinner was eaten on the banks of the Ogeechee
river, that December day, more than twenty years ago.
It is such an episode as this that makes the heart of
the old soldier throb, and the water dim his vision,
when he hears those beautiful lines of the soldier-poet,
Miles O'Reilly :

> " There are bonds of all sorts in this world of ours,
>    Fetters of friendship, and ties of flowers,
>       And true-lovers' knots, I ween.
>    The boy and the girl are bound by a kiss,
>    But there's never a bond in the world like this,
>       We have drunk from the same canteen.
>
> " It was sometimes water and sometimes milk
>    And sometimes applejack, fine as silk ;
>       But whatever the tipple has been,

We shared it together, in bane and in bliss,
And I warm to you, friend, when I think of this,
We have drunk from the same canteen."

December 13th, General Hazen's brigade of the
Fifteenth Corps, made its magnificent assault upon
Fort McAllister, which blocked the Ogeechee. Un-
mindful of the great belching guns of this formidable
fortress, the rattling volleys of musketry, the entangling abattis and *chevaux-de-frise*, the interlacing wires
which snared their footsteps, the exploding torpedoes—
this gallant band rushed on, and in a few moments the
national flag flying over the ramparts told the story
that the great river was again open. Then the supply
boats, which had been gathering below to succor the
famishing army, pushed their way up, and were
received with tremendous enthusiasm ; while soldiers
and sailors, who had never seen each other before,
grasped hands as if they were own brothers. Now
supplies were distributed in lavish profusion, and col-
lapsed stomachs assumed aldermanic proportions.
Here, too, heavy mails were received, and "the boys"
made happy by the receipt of letters from home, in
answer to those written from Atlanta two months
before.

But there were letters which found no owners. One
came addressed to a comrade who was particularly dear
to the writer of these pages. He was a soft-cheeked,
girlish-looking lad from the interior of Ohio. He had
a romance — who of the boys had not ? — and this had

been confided to his friend. But the poor fellow fell in a skirmish a few days before reaching Savannah, and it was the sad duty of his companion to return the letter to an anxious maiden at home, and with it give the sad tidings of the loved one's death. God pity the mothers, wives and sweethearts whose heavy eyelids were held up by dreadful anxiety through those weary months when no tidings came, and hallow in their hearts the memory of those who died.

The Union lines were now in constant action, pushing steadily forward against Savannah. Several heavy guns from the fleet were put in position, and when all was in readiness for bombardment, General Sherman made a demand for the surrender of the city, enclosing a copy of the bloodthirsty demand of General Hood at Resaca (similar to that of General French at Allatoona), and said : " Should I be forced to assault, I shall feel justified in resorting to the harshest measures, and shall make little effort to restrain my army, burning to avenge the national wrong which they attach to Savannah and other large cities which have been so prominent in dragging our country into civil war." The demand was refused, and siege operations were prosecuted vigorously.

On the night of December 20th, the Seventeenth Corps was well up in front of the enemy's works, General Belknap's brigade succeeding in advancing within three hundred yards of the fortifications immediately outside the city, making its approach under a severe fire of musketry and heavy artillery. Next morning the skirmish line was farther advanced, when the works were found to be deserted, the enemy having retreated across the Savannah river, into South Carolina.

The writer immediately rode into the city and down to the river front. Two miles below lay a couple of dark hulks which a citizen near by said were a ram and iron-clad gunboats belonging to the "Confederate navy"—the soldiers supposed them to be national vessels. The Union flag was soon flying from a dozen prominent buildings, and the rebel vessels defiantly fired a few ineffective shots toward the city. A battery of heavy Parrott guns was brought to the river front, and returned the fire for a short time, but with as little effect. A few minutes later, a blaze of flame leaped from the portholes of the vessels, and there was an irruption as of a volcano, followed by a dull, muffled roar. The enemy had blown up his "navy."

General Sherman, a day or two afterward, wrote to President Lincoln : "I beg to present you, as a Christmas gift, the city of Savannah, with one hundred and fifty guns and plenty of ammunition, and also about twenty-five thousand bales of cotton." He further said, in his official report : "I estimate the damage to Georgia at a hundred millions of dollars, at least twenty millions of which has inured to our advantage, and the remainder is simply waste and destruction. This may seem a hard species of warfare, but it brings the sad realities of war home to those who have been directly or indirectly instrumental in involving us in its attendant calamities. . . . As to the rank and file of my army, they seem so full of confidence in themselves that I doubt if they want a compliment from me ; but I must do them the justice to say that, whether called on to fight, to march, to wade streams, to make roads, clear out obstructions, build bridges, make 'corduroy,' or tear up railroads, they have done it with alacrity and a degree of cheerfulness unsurpassed. A little loose in foraging, they 'did some things they ought not to have done,' yet, on the whole, they have supplied the wants of the army with as little violence as could be expected."

President Lincoln, in reply, said : "Many thanks for your Christmas gift. When you were about leaving Atlanta for the coast, I was anxious, if not fearful. Now, the undertaking being a success, the honor is all yours." General Grant wrote : "I congratulate you and the brave officers and men under your command on the successful termination of your most brilliant campaign. I never had a doubt of the result. When apprehensions for your safety were expressed by the President, I assured him that, with the army you had, and with you in command of it, there was no danger but you would reach salt water in some place." And

General Halleck said : "Your march will stand out prominently as the great one of this great war."

Some days after entering Savannah, the troops were overjoyed to learn of the glorious victory won at Nashville, under General Thomas, by their former comrades. The Army of the Tennessee had particular reason to be proud of their own Sixteenth Corps, which bore so gallant a part in the action, under the leadership of General A. J. Smith, that General Thomas telegraphed to the President : "General Smith, with McMillen's brigade of McArthur's division, charged and captured the salient point of the enemy's line, with over a thousand prisoners." This was the turning-point in the Battle of Nashville. Half an hour later, the shattered remnants of Hood's army were in full retreat.

LAYING PONTOONS.

See page 286.

## XXXIV.

### "ALAS. POOR YORICK!"

T Savannah, the troops lived at high-pressure, and their short stay was a continual round of merry-making. If the few male inhabitants remaining, were somewhat formal and distant, ample amend was made by the ladies, who were generally cordial; and each little knot of soldiers made acquaintance with fair ones, glad to entertain and be entertained with cards, dance, and song. The poor Confederate soldier, fleeing before the Nemesis pursuing, might well say, in the words attributed to him near Memphis, two years previous, by a Union soldier who parodied "Maryland, my Maryland : "

22

" The Yankee's foot is on thy shore,
  Tennessee, my Tennessee !
They riot run thy country o'er,
  Tennessee, my Tennessee !
How can our hearts be light and gay,
  When Yankee hands hold here their sway,
  And Southern girls their 'hests obey,
  Tennessee, my Tennessee !

" They steal and eat thy pork and beef,
  Tennessee, my Tennessee !
For cotton, too, thou'rt come to grief,
  Tennessee, my Tennessee !
Thy daughters fair, they're courting strong,
  With dance and marriage, card and song,
  Woe is the day ! for all goes wrong,
  In Tennessee, my Tennessee !

Thou mak'st them all so light and gay,
  Tennessee, my Tennessee !
With liquor good to wet their clay,
  Tennessee, my Tennessee !
With the true spirit of the vine,
  The brightest of thy native wine,
  Blackberry juice and muscadine,
  Tennessee, my Tennessee ! "

Among these people of Savannah was one who became particularly dear to the writer of these pages,
and a number of his companions, many of whom will
learn of his tragic death with deep sorrow.

In casting about for a sheltering roof, in the absence of a tent, a young officer happened to note a
small cosy cottage standing somewhat back from the
street, in the outskirts of the city. The door stood
open and he entered. The parlor was just what he
wanted, and his field desk was speedily set up in one

corner and his pair of blankets and valise deposited on the floor. A well-filled book-case stood at one side, and in this he was delighted to find his favorite author, rare Bobbie Burns, nature's own poet. With the book in his hand, and a good cigar between his lips (it was taken from an adjoining side-table), he was the picture of contentment, when a middle-aged lady entered the room. "Ah, sir!" said she, "you Northern gentlemen do not wait for invitations when you are away from home!" This in a tone which was a refined sneer.

"Beg pardon, madam," was the response, as the cigar was laid aside, "I did not find anyone at home, and the door stood open. We are without tents, and must seek shelter, and I promise to disturb you as little as possible. Any room in the house will be acceptable, and I will adapt myself to your convenience as much as possible. Perhaps your having an officer of the Union army as a lodger may insure you against other intrusions. I have taken the liberty to examine your book-case, and with your permission would be glad to make use of it during my stay."

Glancing at the volume in the hand of her unbidden guest, the lady said, "Ah! Burns! Is he a favorite of yours?"

"Yes, indeed, madam; for I have heard his songs sung in his own land."

"Indeed! Are you Scotch?"

"I can not say as to that, madam. I was born at Berwick-upon-Tweed, but there seems to be a doubt as to whether the old town is English or Scotch. At one time it was called a free city, and one of the British sovereigns wrote himself King of England, Scotland and Berwick."

Thereupon followed a conversation in which it was made known that the lady was a Scotchwoman, and had known her guest's father (then deceased) beyond seas. A most cordial feeling at once arose between the two conversationalists, and a lasting friendship was established.

Somewhat later in the day, the lady's husband reached home, and to him was introduced the young officer, with an explanation of the friendly ties existing between him and the wife. He was most cordial from the moment. Even without such an introduction, he was disposed to a spirit of gentlemanly toleration, based upon the idea, as he expressed it, that "to the victors belong the spoils ;" but the kindly interest of his wife led him to the utmost cordiality of word and act, and the two became fast friends. He had understood that the army came through very light ; would his guest accept such needed furnishings, as his wardrobe would supply ? and accept such a loan of money as would be acceptable until he could supply himself through the customary channels ?

Mr. Warren was then about forty years of age, a

bank officer, and a large landholder ; but the disasters of war, and the exorbitant exactions of the Confederate authorities, had left him but little of his previously ample fortune. He was a misanthrope, a cynic ; but whether his melancholy had other cause than financial disaster, the writer never learned. Yet he was capable of warm attachments, as this acquaintance amply testified ; and his regard, when once won, was far deeper than that common to men who are on familiar terms with everybody. Of studious habits and considerable culture, he had surrounded himself with all that could seemingly make life enjoyable. His pictures were exquisite, and his books the choicest. He was a writer of no mean ability, and many gems of true poesy fell from his pen and found their way into the columns of leading Southern journals.

The time came for the young officer to leave Savannah with his command, and the regret of parting was mutual. An irregular correspondence was maintained between Warren and his former guest until about ten years ago, when the latter was surprised to receive from Warren a letter written from St. Louis, but a few miles from his own home, requesting a meeting in that city. The summons was answered in person by the next train, and Warren was found with his wife at a private boarding house. He said that he had broken up his home at Savannah, but gave no reason, and came to St. Louis hoping to find employment. The friend to whom he appealed for assistance being then on his way East on an urgent errand, left with him money to supply his immediate necessities, promising to aid him as he wished upon returning. A few days later, he learned from the newspapers that Warren had found his death by the deadly morphine, and that the widow had returned to her Southern home with his lifeless remains. The published account said that his taking off was " accidental." Let us believe that it was, nor grudge him his rest.

As the writer pens this narrative, the portrait of Warren lies before him, recalling to mind the lines penned by the poor fellow at the field-desk of the former in Savannah, on New Year's Day, of 1865 — alas, how sadly suggestive, when read in connection with the circumstances of his unhappy death !

> One day, one day,
>   Oh, troubled breast,
>   Thou 'lt be at rest !
>
> If love's disdain
>   Of thee makes mirth
>   Six feet of earth
> Will end his reign.
> Rended his chain,
>   Oh, troubled breast,
>   Thou 'lt be at rest.
>
> The life uncrowned,
>   The true love crossed,
>   The peace here lost,
> Will there be found !
> Beneath the ground,
>   Oh, troubled breast,
>   Thou 'lt be at rest !

## CHAPTER XXXV.

THE SOLDIER ON HIS SEA-LEGS.

HE capture of Savannah was the close of the actual "March to the Sea." But, as was remarked in an earlier chapter, so closely did the Campaign of the Carolinas follow upon that of Georgia, and so intimately blended were the consequences of these historic movements, that the "Great March" may be said to have actually begun at Chattanooga, ending only upon the arrival of the army at Raleigh, North Carolina, where Johnston surrendered to Sherman.

It had been decided that Sherman's army should be transferred to South Carolina, to operate against Lee's communications. The itinerary of this campaign shows that it occupied upwards of three months, and involved a march of four hundred and eighty miles to Goldsboro, North Carolina. To this was supplemented the march to Washington City, via Raleigh, three hundred and sixty miles farther, making eight hundred and forty miles in all. The figures look commonplace, but it was a great undertaking. The roads were continuously bad, the army had never traveled worse, and the weather, with but slight exception, was horrible beyond description, rain falling almost incessantly.

A portion of the army made its movement from Savannah by land, crossing the Savannah river, and traversing the low ground lying near the coast-line ; while another part was transported by water to Hilton Head. It is difficult to say which of the two had the worst end of the bargain—the one, floundering for days and days in bottomless mud, or the other, churned and thumped about in rickety vessels on salt water. As it was, both agreed that they had never before experienced such misery.

On the morning of January 6th, Smith's division of Blair's corps marched from Savannah to Thunderbolt Inlet, on Wassau Sound, eight miles, under a beating rain. There the troops embarked, the regiment which the narrative principally follows, taking passage on the "Winona," a wooden gun-boat the troops first made acquaintance with on the Mississippi river, at Vicksburg and Natchez, in 1862–3, when it belonged to Farragut's squadron. It was a light draft propeller, carrying several heavy guns, all on the spar-deck. Of course there were no accommodations below except for the ordinary ship's crew, and the soldiers were disposed on deck, "out of doors," as they expressed it, as best could be. Soon after noon the vessel got under way, and it was not long before the trouble began. There was an unusually heavy sea, and what with that, and the heavy deckload of guns, anchors, and the like, the crazy old "Winona" pitched about at a terrible rate. Most of the men were dreadfully seasick; and, without strength to hold on to anything, they tumbled from one side of the vessel to the other, with its every motion, being so thumped and pounded that many of them were sore with bruises for days afterward. The scene was distressing enough, but had its comicalities. In the working of the ship, the officer of the deck frequently called out the "steady" which served as a direction to the man at the wheel, who echoed the "steady" as he plied the spokes of his helm. The untutored sons of the prairie, ignorant of the meaning of the words, took them to be sarcastic injunctions addressed to themselves, to stand up straight while the decks were wobbling forty-five degrees port and starboard in as many seconds; and they replied with elaborate profanity between the gulps which signalized the commotion beneath their waistbands.

Some time after dark, Hilton Head was reached, and anchor cast, but the vessel continued to roll wildly all night, making sleep impossible to the sore and weary landsmen. In the morning the "Winona" steamed into Beaufort, and the men disembarked, thanking God that they had escaped from an experience compared with which plain soldiering was heavenly happiness.

Beaufort was a beautiful little town, extremely southernish in every respect. The houses, all of wood, were low, covering considerable ground, and encompassed on all sides with spacious verandahs. The fortifications were garrisoned by Foster's corps, all negroes, well clothed, well armed, and in a high state of discipline. Large numbers of freedmen were in the vicinity, cultivating abandoned plantations.

In the harbor lay ships, displaying the flags of almost all nations, and among them, flying the American stars and stripes, were several captured blockade runners—Clyde-built, long, narrow, dull-colored vessels, lying very low in the water — evidences of "British neutrality."

January 10th, the troops marched out of Beaufort, and after making five miles, ran against the enemy. He was driven without much difficulty, however, and, after penetrating the country fifteen miles, the command halted at Pocotaligo, near the Charleston and Savannah railroad, to await the arrival of that portion of the army which was marching overland, or, to be more exact, wading through water, from Savannah. Pocotaligo was an inlet, navigable by light-draft vessels at high tide, and the works abandoned by the enemy were very complete.

There, a few days later, large numbers of recruits and drafted men were received for various regiments. Many were substitutes, furnished by drafted men, receiving bounties ranging from eight hundred to two thousand dollars each. The arrival of the latter class occasioned much feeling among the old soldiers, who had been paid only the four hundred dollars government bounty allowed for re-enlistment as veterans, and had been cut off from all local bounties.

These recruits were also the cause of other complications. The regiments to which they were assigned had been depleted, by the casualties of service, below their minimum strength, and these accessions were not sufficiently numerous to bring them up to the standard to admit of the muster-in of subalterns who held commissions. As there were not enough of these recruits to fill up all the companies, it was plain that some must secure the necessary number, while others could not. So far as memory goes, the officers whose duty it was to make the apportionment, very properly filled up the companies having the most worthy and capable subalterns to be advanced.

Every regiment had its "bob-tail" companies, and from these came cries of partiality and favoritism.

Until January 29th, the troops lay in fathomless mud, drenched daily with the worst rains they had ever experienced. The enemy was immediately in front, and the skirmish-line was engaged day and night. On the 30th, the troops broke camp and set out in earnest for the interior of South Carolina. The enemy contested every foot of ground, but fortunately the sun again shone out, the roads dried up somewhat, and the spirits of the men rose, so that, on the whole, favorable progress was made.

# CHAPTER XXXVI.

## OLD FRIENDS HEARD FROM.

OTWITHSTANDING the discomforts of the voyage from Savannah to Beaufort, the regiment whose movements have been noted, had cause to remember with gratitude the officers and men of the " Winona," who made every effort to mitigate, as much as possible, its unpleasantness. Hence, in recognition of kind treatment, the adjutant, on behalf of his comrades and himself, addressed the officers of the ship a letter of grateful acknowledgment. The last mail received at Pocotaligo previous to the army taking up its march for the interior, brought the following reply :

U. S. S. WINONA,
Port Royal, S. C., Feb. 3d, 1865.

DEAR SIR: Your favor of the 9th ult., enclosing a card of thanks to the officers of this vessel, has been received.   In reply we would say, that we feel gratified to know that our endeavors to make your recent trip from Savannah to Beaufort an endurable one were successful.   Our vessel not being adapted to the service in which we were then engaged, and our accommodations limited, it was not in our power to offer you such quarters as we would have wished, nor such as you deserved.   But the knowledge that our efforts were appreciated is very agreeable, and we are happy to have the acquaintance of a portion of that army whose glorious progress we have watched with such interest, while we have been comparatively inactive.   Be assured that we shall watch your future steps with renewed interest; and may we be permitted to hope that the "big guns" of the navy may have a voice in some of your future conquests.   But however that may be, the officers of the "Winona," and yourself and comrades, will have no dispute as to precedence; on the contrary, our toast at all times shall be "The *Army* and Navy forever," while war lasts and in happier times of peace.

Please accept for yourself and your comrades the kind regards and good wishes of the officers of this vessel, and believe me, very truly,

E. H. SHEFFIELD.
Acting Master and Exec. Officer.

The same mail also brought the following personal letter, which is quoted to show what friendly relations frequently sprang up between Union soldiers and Southerners. It was written by Z. N. Warren, an ardent supporter of the "confederacy," whose sad history and unhappy death have been narrated in a preceding chapter :

SAVANNAH, GA., Jan. 19th, 1865.

MY DEAR ——— :   *   *   My wife and self are truly rejoiced to learn that your vessel escaped "the perils of the sea."  We were both very anxious on your account, knowing that you had encountered unusually boisterous weather.  We sincerely desire that you may escape all perils of land and sea, and long live to be an ornament of society, and a useful and honored member of the republic.  We greatly miss the com-

pany of yourself and Capt. ———.  Give him our kindest regards,
* * My health is very poorly indeed; I am suffering greatly
to-day, but try not to despair.    *    *

Believe me, very truly, your friend,

Z. N. WARREN.

In the same package with this letter is one penned
by a lady residing on a plantation on Black river, in
the rear of Vicksburg.  It was just after the end of
the siege that the fortunes of war made a Union
soldier for a time an occupant of her house.  She was
a widow, with two daughters, one of whom was
receiving her education in an Episcopal seminary in
New Jersey, and had barely reached home before the
Mississippi was closed to travel at the outbreak of the
war.  Three sons were with the rebel army in Virginia.  Nothing had been heard of them for months,
and the anxiety of the poor women was pitiable.  All
the plantation hands had abandoned the place, and the
family was utterly destitute, but refined and proud.
In this strait it was the privilege of the Union soldier
to relieve their immediate necessities during his stay.
They were profuse in their expressions of gratitude,
and, soon after the close of the war, wrote of their
efforts to re-establish their broken fortunes, and the
sad news that two of the three boys had fallen on
Eastern battle-fields.

Friendships formed under such circumstances were
not uncommon, and were sometimes marked by incidents as romantic as ever penned by novelist.

Memory recurs at the moment to that same plantation not far from Vicksburg, and to bright-eyed Mollie, the dear creature, bitter little rebel that she was. How she delighted to throw open her windows, so that the soldiers about might hear her play "Stonewall Jackson's Way," and how loudly and exultantly her voice would ring out in "The Bonnie Blue Flag," and "Dixie!"

Being not less a woman, however, she did not repel the delicate attentions of a young Union soldier; and the two spent many happy hours over the chess-board and at the piano. The girl was not greatly to be blamed for so amusing herself. Her lover was with Lee, in Virginia, and there were no mails to bring tidings from him. But her companion, being in constant communication with a fair girl at home in Illinois, was less excusable. The young rascal probably never made confession to her of the pleasant flirtation.

One afternoon Mollie wished to go outside the lines to visit friends. The young soldier proposed to escort her, and his company being gladly accepted, they rode out on horseback.

At the picket-line, the soldier gave the countersign, and was cautioned to be careful that the rebel cavalry did not capture him. But he was so engrossed with his fair companion that he gave little heed to the advice.

Their destination, two miles beyond, was soon reached. The horses were hitched at the fence, and Mollie and the soldier entered the house, where both were cordially received.

An hour later Mollie was loitering with one of her friends near the gate, when suddenly she looked up the road and shouted excitedly to her escort, "O! here are our soldiers coming!"

The soldier was not a moment in reaching his horse. A hurried glance revealed a cloud of dust, and in the wrong direction for friends. He thought himself drawn into a trap by the fair rebel, and he put his foot into the stirrup, determined to make a desperate ride for liberty. But before he could reach the saddle, Mollie was by his side. "Don't go without me!" she exclaimed.

She never looked more bewitching than at that moment, and the soldier could not distrust the anxiety for his safety which stood revealed in her tear-dimmed eyes and quivering lips. To assist her to the saddle required but an instant, and, urging the horses to their utmost speed, the two flew down the road. They were none too soon—the enemy, a score or more in number, were but a few hundred yards behind. Faster and faster flew pursuers and pursued, the former gaining, until at a turn in the road, the soldier was delighted to meet the advance guard of a body of Union cavalry. A hurried explanation was

23

given; a moment later a company of gallant troopers dashed by, and a rattling volley from their carbines gave assurance that the pursuit was checked.

The soldier and his fair companion soon passed through the picket lines in safety; and to this day he holds her in grateful remembrance for having saved him from capture, if not death. Doubtless, the only reason for his not being fired upon by the rebel cavalry was the fluttering of Mollie's riding-skirt at his side.

A few weeks later, orders came for the troops to abandon the line of Black river, to engage in the attempt against Atlanta. The young soldier delayed his departure until the last of his comrades had gone and the enemy's cavalry was in sight, and then leaped into the saddle. At the bend in the road which was to shut out his view of the place where he had spent so many happy hours, he turned and waved his handkerchief in farewell. The signal was returned from an upper window, and Union soldier and Southern damsel had parted forever!

## CHAPTER XXXVII.

### THROUGH FIRE AND WATER.

 FTER four days of hard marching and sharp skirmishing, the army reached the Salkehatchie, a considerable stream, which, o u t s i d e i t s banks, broadened into an immense swamp. All the bridges having been destroyed, the enemy had plainly made up his mind that this route was impracticable beyond question, and so it would have been to troops led by a less determined chief than Sherman. But his restless energy and indomitable resolution were reflected in his men, rendering them superior to all circumstances, no matter how disadvantageous, and their triumph at the Salkehatchie, although comparatively bloodless, was one of the most conspicuous in their all-conquering career. To Giles

A. Smith's and Mower's divisions of the Seventeenth Corps fell the severest labor and the greatest credit.

The swamp at the point chosen for forcing was perhaps three miles wide. It was such as Moore described :

> "Tangled juniper, beds of reeds,
> And many a fen where the serpent feeds,
> And man never trod before."

A dog could scarcely make his way through the swamp, much less a horse; and the mounted officers abandoned their animals for the time to travel in the same way as the soldiers in the ranks.

At the command, the troops plunge into the timber. So immense are the trees, and so thickly set, that the eye can not reach half pistol range; and they are so abundantly covered with foliage that the light of day is shut out. No matter for this, however. The sun has not been seen to-day and a cold drizzling rain is falling. The progress of the men is slow and laborious. They force their way through the dense undergrowth, tearing their clothing, and scratching face and limbs. Treacherous vines trip them, and they catch at bush and tree to save their footing. Cypress-knees concealed beneath the water wound their feet at almost every step. Now the water grows deeper and deeper, as the heart of the swamp is approached. It comes up to the waist, and the men take off their cartridge-boxes and suspend them from the muzzles of their guns, above their heads, for they must keep their ammunition dry, no matter what else befalls. The water becomes deeper yet. Those who have watches, diaries or money, place these valuables within their hats. Now the water reaches to the arm-pits, and occasionally all that can be seen of a short man is his head sticking out of the water. Here and there are soldiers sitting upon fallen trees or stumps, exhausted or taken with cramps. The surgeon seeks them out, and, satisfying himself that their distress is not simulated, he directs the hospital steward to serve to the sufferer a " tot " of whisky from the hospital liquor-cask, which at such times, he carries strapped upon his shoulders. The administration of the stimu-lant tells how complete is the exhaustion of the patient. A half-pint of the fiery liquid is swallowed without affecting brain or limb. The human mercury is almost at zero, and the large dose only avails to restore the system to an approximation of its normal condition.

This incident was only unusual in degree. Indeed, there were days and days when the soldier was drenched on account of rains or swamp-wading, and found no opportunity to dry himself save as the sun shone for a few hours, and dried his clothing on his body; or when he shivered over the camp-fire at night, alternately turning front and rear of his person to the blaze. These were the exposures which wrecked

health in countless instances, yet left no mark.   Here
it was that the soldier must do and endure, for he
would not die.   He drew on his reserve energy, and
to-day he suffers with diseases and weaknesses which
cause him to feel an age, and a degree of infirmity,
that face and voice and gait fail to reveal.   Thousands suffer who are unable to locate the date or exact
circumstances which have caused nature to claim her
own, in after years visiting a severe penalty for the
violation of her laws ; and of such the pension list is
necessarily silent.   There are those of whom the writer knows, whose remarkable experience it was to fight
and march the war through, from Cairo to Washington;
who gave to the cause nearly five years of their life,
and how many of their vigor can not be told; who
passed through many actions without a wound; and
whose pride and resolution would not admit of their
going to a hospital.   They had their aches and pains,
but they braved them out.   It would be better to-day
if, in war-times, they had experienced worse fortune
or shown less pluck.   A wound then—always pre-
mising that it was not too severe—or a brief sojourn
in a hospital, would, in all probability, have afforded
nature a breathing-spell, and left them physically
better men.

But to return to the passage of the Salkehatchie.
After a journey of more than three hours, the troops
emerged from the swamp and put foot on solid ground.

The movement was eminently successful, the enemy abandoning his works which had been thus turned.

From the 4th to the 12th, the enemy gave ground rapidly until he reached the Edisto river, behind which lay the little city of Orangeburg. The conditions there were nearly identical with those of the Salkehatchie.

The road leading into the city was a narrow causeway made of corduroy, straight as an arrow, built through the swamp. At the farther end were stout fortifications mounted with heavy guns. It was a veritable Death's bowling alley. Down its two-mile length the enemy could pitch his cannon-balls at any human tenpins that might be set up. The distance to be traveled to reach the battery was so great that the direct attack would have involved terrible loss of life. This route being out of the question, Giles A. Smith's division was designated to force a passage of the swamp below the works, and near them, while Mower's division made an effort still farther down the stream.

As soon as the head of Smith's column appeared at the foot of the causeway, the enemy commenced a warm cannonading. The troops were massed in the shelter of the heavy timber at the side of the road, and out of view of the enemy, and when all was ready they rushed helter-skelter to the same kind of shelter on the other side. Then they deployed and waded through the swamp, in the same manner as at the Salkehatchie, until they came to the Edisto proper, which was exceedingly deep and narrow, and ran with a rapid current. This was bridged by felling large trees, and over these the men scrambled to the farther side, the enemy giving way before a sharp musketry fire. The first regiment across, on this part of the line, was the 32d Illinois, led by Lieutenant-Colonel Rider. The second in command was Major Smith Townshend, a gallant officer and most genial and companionable comrade. He had been a private in the 1st Kansas, at Wilson's Creek, where Lyon fell. There he was wounded, and on recovering was commissioned as a lieutenant in this regiment, rising through the various grades to that of major. After the war he became a clerk in the War Department, studied medicine in his leisure hours, and in a few years entered upon practice in Washington City. Afterward he was appointed Health Officer of the District of Columbia, a position he yet fills. He was the first physician to reach the side of President Garfield after Guiteau's murderous assault, and administered the first treatment.

Returning to Orangeburg : As soon as the troops emerged from the timber into the open ground, the enemy, finding his works turned, abandoned them precipitately. The skirmish line was less than a quarter-mile from the railroad when the last train ran out, loaded with frightened passengers. A number of shots were discharged at it, but without effect, so far as was ever heard.

When the troops entered the city, they found the business portion of it in flames, the effect of the enemy's suicidal folly in setting fire to large quantities of cotton piled in the streets. W. Gilmore Simms, the famous Southern author, had his home at this place. Whether his premises were destroyed or not, the author does not know; but many books from his library, bearing his autograph, found their way into camp, and were carried away by the men as mementoes.

The pursuit of the enemy continued during the 13th and 14th, the federal advance constantly skirmishing with his rear guard. The march on these two days was particularly uncomfortable, and at times dangerous. The route lay along a narrow country road, through an immense pine forest. The trees had been tapped for turpentine, and the resin coated them thickly where they had been denuded of their bark, ten to twenty feet upward. A fire was started, perhaps accidentally, perhaps intentionally, by the enemy, and the entire forest was ablaze. The thick, resinous smoke rose in dense clouds, blinding the sight and choking the lungs, while the fierce heat blistered faces and scorched clothing. The horses of the wagon and ammunition trains and artillery were so frightened that it was a difficult task to coax or force them through the roaring flames, which raged on either side. Frequently a burning tree fell across the road, halting the column until it could be cut up and the pieces dragged away. The sticky, pitchy, black vapors soon changed the complexions of the men, and an Illinois mother might have come into camp and, taking her own son for a pure-blooded negro, have inquired of him the whereabouts of the white troops. Worse yet, no soap was to be had, and it was many a long day before the men regained their normal hue of countenance.

WADING THE SALKEHATCHIE.

See page 357.

# CHAPTER XXXVIII.

## CAPTURE OF COLUMBIA.

EBRUARY 15th, the Seventeenth Corps made a march of fourteen miles, and the next day twelve, halting on the west bank of the Congaree river, just below the confluence of Saluda and Broad rivers. On the opposite side, on ground gently sloping to the river, lay Columbia, its wide streets, wealth of ornamental trees, and handsome buildings, making a picture charming to the eye. The imposing walls of the new capitol, yet unfinished, rose in massive beauty ; the white marble of column and cornice — each stone was said to have cost a round thousand dollars — glittering in the sunlight like immense gems. Near this magnificent edifice stood its less conspicuous neighbor, the old capitol, dingy and forbidding.

Until the 6th it was not known to the troops that the column would reach Columbia at all, the direction appearing to be toward Augusta. But on that date, when Midway was passed, it was discerned that Columbia lay in the line of march, and the fact was regarded by the army with peculiar interest. All recognized that city as being of a verity " the hot-bed of the Rebellion," the birthplace of nullification, out of which came secession as a legitimate fruit ; and they looked upon its occupation as a triumph even more significant than the capture of Richmond itself.

The 32d Illinois Regiment led the advance that day. As this command reached the edge of the almost perpendicular bank overlooking the river, the adjutant turned out to allow the column to change its direction, and form a color-line parallel with the stream. He was mounted on a fine horse, well nigh milk white, which his faithful " bummer " had acquired some days before. A water-mill on the opposite shore, and the bushes which fringed the river near it, proved to be full of the enemy's rifle-men, who found an unusually attractive mark in the white horse, and opened a sharp fire, which moved the troops, in filing past, to exhort the rider to send his "—— white horse to the rear." Without doubt he desired very much to comply with the requests so earnestly expressed, but he had a duty to perform, and honor required that he should not leave his post until it was completed. However, he "sighted" his color-line in much less time than usual, and sent the danger-inviting animal to the rear, but not before three men in his vicinity had been wounded by the fire which he had provoked. He never rode such an animal again ; the ordinary war-risk was hazardous enough, without offering any special inducements to the enemy.

Attracted by the firing, a section of Clayton's First Minnesota Battery of Rodman guns was brought up, and a few shots knocked the water-wheel of the mill to pieces, and sent timbers flying so lively that the riflemen scampered away like rats from a burning barn. About the same time a battery of Parrott guns threw a few shells into the city, dispersing a crowd of people plundering the rebel commissariat.

It was while these events were transpiring that General Sherman rode up, and, after examining the city through his glass, remarked to General Belknap, who commanded the brigade in line at this point, that he "would appreciate the men who first made a lodg-ment in Columbia." General Sherman then rode away, and General Belknap set his wits to work to take advantage of the hint his superior had dropped.

That night, the Fifteenth Corps passed to the left of the Seventeenth, under orders to effect a crossing of

Broad river, three miles above, and to enter the city from the north.

While this movement was in progress, General Belknap dispatched a party to make search for a boat, and Captain H. C. McArthur, of his staff, was so fortunate as to find a leaky old scow. He had been a carpenter, and, assisted by several soldiers, by dint of hard work all night, succeeded in so repairing the craft as to make it tolerably seaworthy.

About 9 o'clock on the morning of the 17th, the frail bark was successfully launched, and a party of thirty men, belonging to the 13th Iowa Regiment, volunteered to cross over. Lieutenant-Colonel Kennedy was in command, and he was accompanied by Captain McArthur and Lieutenant Goodell, of General Belknap's staff. A number of natives who stood about in open-mouthed wonder, warned the men against the dangers of the rocky channel and swift current, and some of the soldiers declined to take the risk. Twenty-one, however, and the officers named, embarked and essayed the passage of the stream. It was a desperate undertaking; the current of the Congaree was very swift, and the channel was broken by dangerous rapids which would have deterred less determined spirits. But energy and courage were strong in these gallant men, and, after several narrow escapes from wreck on the rocks, they landed in safety on the Columbia side. Ascending the slope to the town on a double-quick, at a distance of a couple of squares from the river, the party intercepted a rebel officer hurrying off in a buggy.  The officers and the color-bearer took possession of the vehicle, and drove rapidly toward the capitol buildings, directing the squad to follow as fast as possible.  When within a few hundred yards of their destination, the officers in the buggy were fired upon by the retreating rebel cavalry, but without effect.  Seizing the only gun in the party, McArthur jumped out and fired at the enemy, unhorsing one of their number.  Upon the arrival of the remainder of his men, Kennedy went to the capitol buildings, and displayed the national flag from the old State house, and his regimental banner from the new one. From the dome of the old building could be seen the skirmishers of the Fifteenth Corps, nearly a mile away.

About three-quarters of an hour later, Lieutenant-Colonel Kennedy and Captain McArthur were standing in the rotunda of the old State house, when an officer with a first-lieutenant's strap upon his shoulder, and a flag in his hands, rushed in, and with an almost breathless voice asked, " Which is the way out to the dome ? "

" What do you want ? " inquired McArthur.

" I want to put this flag out ! "

" Well," said McArthur, " you're just too late by

24

three-quarters of an hour, and we've had our flags on both buildings for that time ! "

" Who in —— are you ? "

" From General Belknap's brigade of the Seventeenth Corps ! "

The officer gave vent to an expressive but impolite ejaculation, and in response to a question addressed to him, said that he was from the 9th Iowa, of Colonel Stone's brigade, Fifteenth Corps.

Shortly afterward, Kennedy's color-bearer reported that his national flag had been stolen from the dome. It was not recovered until the army reached Cheraw, when it was returned by a member of the 30th Iowa, Colonel Stone's brigade.

Immediately after Lieutenant - Colonel Kennedy's party had crossed the river, a detachment of the 32d Illinois Regiment, also from General Belknap's brigade, made a crossing, and placed their colors upon the city hall.

While there is no question of the first occupation of Columbia by General Belknap's troops (Third Brigade, Fourth Division, Seventeenth Corps), the truth of history demands the statement that the formal surrender of the city was made to the Fifteenth Corps.

At dawn on the morning of that day, Colonel Stone's brigade of the Fifteenth Corps, threw pontoons across the river above Columbia, working under a heavy fire. Five companies of the 30th Iowa Regiment, under command of Major Cramer, passed over, and as soon as a sufficient supporting force had crossed behind them, advanced and made a charge upon the enemy, capturing thirty prisoners, in the outskirts of the city. Major Cramer's command then moved forward on the main road leading to the city, and soon encountered a carriage bearing a white flag, driving towards them. Major Cramer rode forward and hailed the occupants, one of whom proved to be the mayor of Columbia. A surrender was demanded, which was promptly made. Colonel Stone, commanding the brigade, afterward rode up, and to him the mayor made a more formal surrender. Colonel Stone and Major Cramer then took seats in the mayor's carriage, and in company with him drove into the city.

The part taken by the 13th Iowa Regiment was suitably recognized by General Giles A. Smith, the division commander, who wrote the following letter, the original of which is before the writer of this narrative:

HEADQUARTERS, 4th DIVISION, 17th A. C.,
NEAR COLUMBIA, S. C., Feb. 17, 1865.

*Brig. Gen. W. W. Belknap, Commanding 3rd Brigade:*

SIR : Allow me to congratulate you, and through you Lieutenant-Colonel Kennedy, 13th Iowa Veteran Volunteers, and the men under his command, for first entering the city of Columbia on the morning of Friday, February 17th, and being the first to plant his colors on the capitol of South Carolina.

While the army was laying pontoon bridges across Saluda and Broad rivers, three miles above the city, Lieutenant-Colonel Kennedy, under your direction, fitted up an old worn out flat-boat, capable of carrying about twenty men, and accompanied by Lieutenants H. C. McArthur and W. H. Goodell, of your staff, crossed the river in front of the city, and boldly advanced through its streets, sending back the boat, with another procured on the opposite side, for more troops, and on their arrival, with seventy-five men in all, drove a portion of Wheeler's cavalry from the town, and at 11.30 a. m. planted his colors, one upon the old and the other upon the new capitol.

The swift current of the Congaree River, and its rocky channel, rendered his crossing both difficult and dangerous ; and the presence of the enemy, but in what force unknown, rendered the undertaking still more hazardous. Lieutenant-Colonel Kennedy and his regiment are entitled to great credit for its successful accomplishment.

GILES A. SMITH,
Bvt. Major-General Commanding.

General Sherman, however, had forgotten his remark that he "would appreciate the men who first made a lodgment in Columbia." His report acknowledged the formal surrender of the city to Colonel Stone, and only incidentally stated, that "about the same time a small party of the Seventeenth Corps crossed the Congaree in a skiff and entered Columbia from a point immediately west."

A pleasant incident marked the occupation of Columbia. Among the prisoners there liberated was Lieutenant Byers, of the 5th Iowa Regiment, who while in prison wrote the following, one of the most stirring lyrics of the war :

### SHERMAN'S MARCH TO THE SEA.

Our camp-fires shone bright on the mountain
  That frowned on the river below,
As we stood by our guns in the morning,
  And eagerly watched for the foe ;

When a rider came out of the darkness
    That hung over mountain and tree,
And shouted, " Boys, up and be ready !
    For Sherman will march to the sea."

CHORUS.—Then sang we a song of our chieftain,
    That echoed o'er river and lea ;
    And the stars in our banner shone brighter
    When Sherman marched down to the sea.

Then cheer upon cheer for bold Sherman
    Went up from each valley and glen,
And the bugles re-echoed the music
    That came from the lips of the men.
For we knew that the stars in our banner
    More bright in their splendor would be,
And that blessings from Northland would greet us,
    When Sherman marched down to the sea.

CHORUS.—Then sang we a song, etc.

Then forward, boys ! forward to battle !
    We marched on our wearisome way,
And stormed the wild hills of Resaca—
    God bless those who fell on that day !
Then Kenesaw proud in its glory,
    Frowned down on the flag of the free ;
But the East and the West bore our standard,
    And Sherman marched down to the sea.

CHORUS.—Then sang we a song, etc.

Still onward we pressed, till our banners
    Swept out from Atlanta's grim walls
And the blood of the patriot dampened
    The soil where the traitor flag falls ;
But we paused not to weep for the fallen,
    Who slept by each river and tree,
Yet we twined them a wreath of the laurel,
    As Sherman marched down to the sea.

CHORUS.—Then sang we a song, etc.

Oh proud was our army that morning,
    That stood where the pine darkly towers,

When Sherman said, " Boys, you are weary,
　　But to-day fair Savannah is ours ! "
Then sang we a song of our chieftain,
　　That echoed o'er river and lea,
And the stars in our banner shone brighter
　　When Sherman camped down by the sea !

CHORUS —Then sang we a song, etc.

## CHAPTER XXXIX.

### DELENDA EST CARTHAGO.

ANY accounts have been written about the destruction of Columbia, notably that from the pen of the distinguished Southern author, William Gilmore Simms. This, in common with others, is founded upon information acquired at second-hand, and is wide of the truth in many important particulars. The writer was with the earliest troops in the city; he saw the beginning and remained until the end. In certain particulars the narrative is not entirely creditable to some of the Union troops; but, at the same time, it will be shown that much undeserved blame has been bestowed upon them.

As stated in a preceding chapter, Columbia was first occupied by a company from the 13th Iowa

Regiment of General Belknap's brigade, Seventeenth Corps. This detachment planted its flag upon the capitol buildings.

Immediately upon that command reaching the Columbia side of the river, Adjutant Hedley, of the 32d Illinois Regiment, who was in conversation with General Belknap at the moment, asked permission to take a company over. The request was readily granted, and the Adjutant sent an orderly for the color company of his own regiment. This command, headed by Captain Tip Richardson, responded promptly, and double-quicked to the river. The men embarked in the rickety old scow which was used by the 13th Iowa detachment, and had been brought back by some negroes. To pole it across the stream was a task of great difficulty, and no little danger, the current being very swift, and broken into rapids which threatened every moment to wreck the craft upon the rocks. On reaching the Columbia shore the men scrambled out and set off up the slope toward the city at the top of their speed; but they had not gone far when they were met by several negroes carrying buckets full of whisky, which they offered with great cordiality. The troops, however, had more pressing business on hand at the moment, and thrusting the hospitable blacks aside, started for the city hall at rapid pace. On reaching the building, the color-guard ascended to the tower and displayed its colors. Meanwhile Adjutant Hedley and Captain Richardson halted in the mayor's office, on a lower floor, and entered into conversation with several citizens, one or more of whom represented themselves to be members of the city council. These gentlemen were in great distress, fearing that the city would be utterly destroyed, and called attention to a large quantity of baled cotton in flames in the main business street, near the city building; also, to the fact that some of the business houses were already being pillaged. They said that the mayor had gone out to meet General Sherman and surrender the city, but they feared it would be too late to save it from destruction. They were assured that a force adequate to preserve order and protect property, would soon enter, and were advised to hold their fire engines in readiness to fight the flames in case of necessity. The suggestion was acted upon, and an engine was run out upon the pavement from the engine-room on the first floor, in readiness for action.

It is here to be noted that this detachment of the 32d Illinois were the first federal soldiers in that part of the city, the company from the 13th Iowa having gone to the capitol building. When the former entered the place, as before stated, the cotton piles in the street were in flames, and negroes, in that part of the city, as well as some white citizens, asserted that Wade Hampton's rebel cavalry had fired them on retreating. There was at the same time some pillaging going on, the depredations being committed by negroes belonging in the place, and white men in civilian's dress, or "butternut" jeans ; some of the latter were federal prisoners, confined in public buildings, who had been released by the negroes while the enemy was vacating and the federals entering. As to the pillaging, it will be borne in mind that the 32d Illinois detachment was met at the river's edge by negroes carrying liquor by the bucket-full. These negroes, and after them some of the prisoners whom they had released, evidently began the depredations.

While the officers named were yet in conversation with the citizens in the mayor's office, a soldier from the 13th Iowa Regiment, occupying the capitol building, entered the room and said that the colors of his regiment had been stolen, presumably by troops who had more recently entered the city. Hedley and Richardson at once ascended to the tower to see whether they had suffered like misfortune, but fortunately their colors were still in place, and in custody of the color-guard. As a precaution against loss, and to ensure the presence of the color-guard, they fastened with a bolt, on the under side, the trap-door leading into the tower. Then, descending to the mayor's office, they noticed that the head of the Fifteenth Corps had stacked arms in front of the building and established a provost-guard.

Shortly afterward an officer of the provost-guard made complaint of the men in the tower firing wildly up the street, and, upon investigation, it was found that some of the color-guard, finding themselves locked up in the manner described, and not relishing the idea of losing their share of the liquor that was being consumed upon the street, had cut the bell-rope and let it down upon the outside of the building, with the request that a jug of whisky be sent up. The liquor was accordingly supplied by some sympathetic comrades, and one of the soldiers became so excited by frequent potations that he evidently imagined himself to be a beleaguered garrison resisting an attack. Fortunately, his aim was wild, and no one was injured by his reckless firing. The color-guard was at once relieved, and, with the remainder of the company, directed to rejoin the regiment. Before leaving the building the party took two flags from the mayor's office — one, the rebel "stars and bars," made of some coarse woolen stuff, now in the possession of Adjutant Hedley; the other, a handsome silk state flag. Captain Richardson tendered the latter to General Belknap, who directed him to keep it, which he does to this day.

Up to the time of the arrival of the Fifteenth Corps and the establishing of a provost-guard, not a building had been fired, and reasonably good order prevailed, considering the circumstances. Very many men, some soldiers, but mostly negroes and escaped prisoners, were somewhat intoxicated, and did some pillaging, mainly in liquor houses and a military furnishing store. These depredations were soon stopped by the provost-guard.

Shortly afterward, the jail building just in rear of the city hall was fired, but the flames were soon suppressed. This seems to have been the first fire alarm. Simms, the Southern historian, does not charge this deed upon the troops, but upon the escaped prisoners before mentioned.

Somewhat later, General Sherman rode into the city. It was a sight for a painter, the smile which overspread his features as his eyes fell upon one of his "bummers," who was just crossing the street in front of his horse's head. The fellow was far gone in liquor, his gait being wonderfully irregular. He wore a handsome silk dressing-gown reaching nearly to his feet, and outside of it were buckled his accoutrements. He carried his musket at a loose "shoulder shift." In place of his military head-gear, he wore a shiny "plug" hat, tilted well back, and around his neck were strung a number of epaulettes, evidently part of the stock of some military furnishing store. A moment after, he was in the clutches of the provost-guard.

Somewhat later in the day, a jolly party met in the old senate chamber, where, thirty-three years before, the legislature of South Carolina proclaimed its hostility to the federal union. A mock senate was organized, and a vote of censure was passed against John C. Calhoun, the great nullificationist, whose states' rights doctrines had found their logical sequence in the existing wicked and unhappy rebellion. His marble bust, a conspicuous ornament of the hall, was made the target for inkstands and spittoons. The secession ordinance was repealed, "John Brown" was then sung with great enthusiasm, and the "senate" adjourned to re-assemble at Raleigh, North Carolina.

The magnificent government arsenal was a place of great interest. On the grounds, mounted upon pedestals, were several fifteen-inch shells, trophies of the war, presented to the state by General Beauregard. One bore the inscription: "This shell was thrown into Fort Sumter by the Abolition Fleet." Another, "This shell was fired into Charleston by the Abolition Batteries." The use of the word "abolition" bespeaks the venom of the traitor who presented the relics, and his determination to recognise in no manner whatever the government he so bitterly hated. In the arsenal grounds were also some famous old pieces of artillery, several being revolutionary war relics bearing the legend, "Georgius Rex, 1770," surrendered by Cornwallis at Yorktown. Also a fine Blakeley gun, made in England, bearing a brass plate with an inscription to the effect that the piece was "Presented to the

Sovereign State of South Carolina by one of her sons residing abroad." This fine specimen of ordnance is now in the gun-yard at the Rock Island Arsenal. Inside the Arsenal buildings were many new Enfield rifles from English workshops, evidences of that British "neutrality" of which so much was heard in those days. On leaving the building, the writer brought away with him as mementoes a pair of elegant spurs, which he yet retains ; and a set of "Hardee's Tactics, Compiled for the Use of the Confederate States Army." They were in three volumes, and were printed on paper not much lighter in hue or finer in texture than ordinary brown wrapping paper. This valuable relic he had the great pleasure of presenting in person to General Robert Anderson, the hero of Fort Sumter, some months later. A portrait of the General, and an autograph acknowledgment of the gift, were given in return, and are among the most highly prized of the owner's war relics.

The visit to the capitol and arsenal occupied the afternoon almost until evening, and up to the late hour of departure from the latter building, reasonably good order prevailed in the city. There was some drunkenness, and at times a little pillaging, but the provost-guards managed to keep down any general tumult, and prevented destruction of property.

Towards dusk the writer was one of a number of soldiers who repaired to the principal hotel, the name

IN FRONT OF COLUMBIA.

See page 366.

of which is forgotten, and called for supper. Some federal officers were already seated when the party entered the dining room. The servants were intolerably slow, and when, after much delay, they brought in the meal, it was found to consist of fried side-meat, corn-bread and rye "coffee." Before this food was dispatched, the alarm of fire was raised, and it was discovered that the hotel was in flames. The proprietor, servants and guests, departed hastily, neither waiting to render nor pay a bill. How this fire originated has never been stated.

Many of the business houses on Main Street were now in flames, and the fire was spreading rapidly. There had been a high wind for a couple of hours, and it was now blowing a hurricane, carrying to all directions flakes of burning cotton from the huge piles of blazing bales in the street. As soon as possible, large details of troops engaged in an attempt to stay the tide of destruction, making almost superhuman efforts, but their task was a hopeless one. They might as well have attempted to stop a fire in a powder magazine. The very elements had conspired for the destruction of the city; and human means were futile. The fire apparatus was old and wornout. One rickety engine had been wrecked, and the hose chopped to pieces by drunken negroes and escaped prisoners.

The street was soon a seething mass of flame on both sides, and from end to end. Then the real work

25

of pillage began. Some, wild with drink, and others, sober enough, who conceived that property abandoned by its owners to destruction was flotsam and jetsam, belonging to whomsoever might have courage to rescue it, entered the burning buildings and took what suited their fancy.

The attempt to save the city was abandoned, and the soldier-firemen and the provost-guards exerted themselves to the saving of human life. There were many so intoxicated as to be in danger from the falling walls, and in some instances it was necessary to carry them out of harm's way. Notwithstanding all this effort, some lives were lost.

Meanwhile, there were those who were applying the torch elsewhere in the city. A half-block of frame shanties of the most disreputable character were fired in malicious mischief. A similar fate befell the fine residence of Wade Hampton, who commanded the lately retreated rebel cavalry; also that of Mr. Trenholm, the rebel Secretary of the Treasury, and of other high dignitaries. The incendiaries in these cases evidently regarded the destruction as justifiable and praiseworthy.

It is beyond question that in some instances private premises were plundered and individuals robbed. The writer, however, has this only on hearsay; he witnessed no such disgraceful scenes. There were some ghouls in this army, as in all others, no matter how civilized the age, or righteous the cause ; and a very few such in the midst of thousands of honest and conscientious soldiers, could readily bring reproach upon all. But the author does not know, nor, after diligent inquiry, has he been able to find any soldier who was in Columbia at that time, who knows of any such vandalism as was attributed to Sherman's army by William Gilmore Simms, in his pamphlet, " The Burning of Columbia," published in 1865. He says :

" Ladies were hustled from their chambers — their ornaments plucked from their persons, their bundles from their hands. It was in vain that the mother appealed for the garments of her children. They were torn from her grasp and hurled into the flames. The young girl striving to save a single frock, had it rent to fibres in her grasp. Men and women, bearing off their trunks, were seized, despoiled ; in a moment the trunk burst asunder with the stroke of the ax or gun butt, the contents laid bare, rifled of all the objects of desire.

" ' Your watch !' ' Your money !' was the demand. Frequently no demand was made. Rarely was a word spoken, where the watch, or chain, or ring, or bracelet, presented itself conspicuously to the eye. It was incontinently plucked away from the neck, breast, or bosom. Hundreds of women, still greater numbers of old men, were thus despoiled. The slightest show of resistance provoked violence to the person.

" The venerable Alfred Huger was thus robbed, in the chamber and presence of his family, and in the eye of an almost dying wife. He offered resistance, was collared and dispossessed by violence.

"We are told that the venerable ex-Senator Colonel Arthur P. Hayne was treated even more roughly.

\*　　\*　　\*　　\*　　\*　　\*　　\*　　\*

"Within the dwellings, the scenes were of a more harsh and tragical character, rarely softened by any ludicrous aspects. It was in vain that the woman offered her keys, or proceeded to open drawer or wardrobe, or cabinet or trunk. It was dashed to pieces with ax or gun butt, with the cry, ' We have a shorter way than that ! '

\*　　\*　　\*　　\*　　\*　　\*　　\*　　\*

"Nor were these acts those of common soldiers. Commissioned officers, of rank so high as that of colonel, were frequently among the most active in spoliation, and not always the most tender or considerate in the manner and acting of their crimes; and, after glutting themselves with spoil, would often utter the foulest speeches, coupled with oaths as condiment, dealing in what they assumed, besides, to be bitter sarcasms upon the cause and country."

These are some of the passionate assertions of a bitter partisan, who was not within fifty miles of Columbia at the time of its destruction, and whose information is wholly second-hand, and unsupported by evidence. But even William Gilmore Simms challenges his own assertions when he says : " The western troops, including those from Illinois, Iowa and Indiana, were frequently faithful and respectful.

"and many of the houses which escaped sack and fire, owed their safety to these men."

Who, then, did all the diabolical mischief spoken of by Simms ? The "western troops," of whom he makes mention as being in Columbia that dreadful night, outnumbered all others ten to one, and the provost-guard was an Iowa brigade.

The moral responsibility for the destruction of Columbia, and for the personal suffering which fell upon its people, rests upon the confederate authorities themselves. With criminal recklessness they fired immense stacks of cotton in their principal business streets. It was criminal because it was pure waste, being only destruction of property of which the federals could make no use, and if fired, could only jeopardize the buildings of people in sympathy with their cause. The fearful winds which spread the flames in every direction, and wiped out the principal part of the city, that is, the main business street and those adjoining on either side, were not an invention of the hated Yankee. The comparatively few fires elsewhere in the city, kindled by incendiaries, besides nearly all the pillaging, were perpetrated by negroes and released prisoners, the latter acting as if in bitter revenge for the hardships they had undergone while in the hands of the enemy. For these excesses the confederate authorities were mainly responsible. All might have been readily prevented, or at least restrained, by the federal troops in custody of the city, had not the enemy's own recklessness produced conditions which no human power could control.

When morning came it was found that three-fourths of the city had been destroyed. It was pitiful to see homeless families, grouped in the stunted pine groves adjacent to the city, surrounded by the few poor household goods they had managed to save from the flames. General Sherman left them a large quantity of provisions, taken from his wagon train at the expense of the troops, who were already on short rations in a sterile country, while many of the soldiers divided the contents of their haversacks with the poor people — a measure of liberality which historians of the Simms stripe never acknowledged.

Columbia was more nearly identified with the immediate causes of the war than any other southern city, and her destruction was incomparably greater than that of any other. A Praise-God-Barebones of a couple of centuries ago would have ascribed her downfall to a judgment of God. As it was, there were those who, while they wielded no torch, and deplored the sad misfortune of those who suffered, looked upon her fate as well-deserved.

It is gratifying to note that a fine monument, erected to the memory of the "Palmetto Regiment" which fought in the Mexican war, escaped destruction. This beautiful work of art was a palmetto tree of iron, so skillfully made that only the closest scrutiny revealed the fact that it was not a living tree. It was mounted upon a fine marble pedestal, in which was set a brass tablet bearing suitable inscriptions.

Many years afterward, the "Burning of Columbia" was made subject of enquiry by the British and American Mixed Claims Commission, in the cases of claims for cotton burned, brought against the United States by British subjects. General Sherman's evidence was direct and emphatic, fixing the responsibility entirely upon the confederate authorities. He said, "Cotton was burning in the streets of Columbia at least twelve hours before any soldier belonging to my army had gotten within the limits of the town of Columbia. . . I saw it with my own eyes."

An effort was made by the counsel for British claimants, to show that the Union army was guilty of unusual depredations. General Sherman's evidence is conclusive upon this point, and not devoid of humor :

"Question—General, it is alleged that Von Moltke has said that your army was an armed mob ?

Answer—Von Moltke was never fool enough to say that. I have seen Von Moltke in person ; I did not ask him the question, because I did not presume that he was such an ass as to say that.

Question—You deny that statement, do you ?

Answer—Our army was as good an army as the Prussians ever had ; and Von Moltke is a man of too good sense to have made any such statement as was attributed to him. . . . The Prussian army did learn many a lesson, and profited by them, from our war, and their officers were prompt to acknowledge it.

Question—General, I have often heard your enemies in the South admit the perfect discipline of your army?

Answer—We could not have done what we did do, unless we had kept them under good discipline.

Question—Can you tell me anything about the Fifteenth Corps?

Answer—Yes, indeed, I can ; I know all about it ; they were as fine a body of men as ever trod shoe leather.

Question—They had the reputation of doing their work well?

Answer—Yes sir; thoroughly.

Question—Had they not a reputation in Mississippi for leaving their mark upon the country ?

Answer—Yes, sir ; they left their marks wherever they went.

Question—You were aware of this ?

Answer—Perfectly.

Question—They were a wild set, were they not ?

Answer—No, sir; they were composed of first-rate men—farmers and mechanics, men who are to-day as good citizens as we have in our country, but who went to war in earnest ; they were mostly western men.

Question—They were good men for destroying property ?

Answer—Yes, sir; when told to do so, they destroyed it very quickly.

Question—When not told to do so, if they thought they might do it, and it not be objectionable to their officers —

Answer—They could do their work very thoroughly when they undertook it.

Question—Were they in the habit of destroying property ?

Answer—No, sir; I do not think they were, more than was necessary; they were a very kind set of men, and I have known them frequently to share their rations with citizens and people along the country ; I have often seen it done.

Question—Do you mean to say that you were not aware that the Fifteenth Corps was a corps distinguished for the marks they left upon the country through which they passed ?

Answer—I may have known it, and very likely I did; I generally knew what was going on.

Question—I asked you, did you know it? Were you not aware that the Fifteenth Corps was remarkable for the manner in which they left their mark upon the country through which they passed ?

Answer—Explain what you mean by 'mark.'

Question—Devastation.

Answer—They killed every rebel within range of their guns, and left their dead bodies to mark the ground.

.    .    .    .    .    .    .

Question—Do you not believe that individuals assisted in spreading the conflagration at Columbia?

Answer—My own judgment was that the fire originated from the imprudent act of Wade Hampton

in ripping open the bales of cotton, piling it in the streets, burning it, and then going away ; that God Almighty started wind sufficient to carry that cotton wherever He would, and in some way or other that burning cotton was the origin of the fire.    .    .    .
Some soldiers, after the fire originated, may have been concerned in spreading it, but not concerned at all in starting it.  .  .  .  It would not surprise me if some vagabond did it without orders, and merely for deviltry.  It would not surprise me if some of our escaped prisoners, or some of our own soldiers, aided in spreading the flames.  .  .  .  I would not believe, upon the mere say so, or even the oath, of any person in Columbia that night, when he would state that he saw a fire kindled in a house, or in a shed, unless it were confirmed by some of my own people."

## CHAPTER XL.

### NEARING THE END.

HE army was now pushing on in the direction of Cheraw, South Carolina, and found itself on the very trail of the contending armies of the Revolutionary War. This fact lent additional interest to the campaign, and, in camp or on the march, the troops eagerly pored over such maps as were available, and ransacked their brains for school-day recollections of stories of adventure and battle in the early days of the nation. Day after day they marched and skirmished upon ground made famous by contests between the British rough-riders under Tarleton, and the dashing partisans of the patriots Marion and Sumter. In these days of immense armies and thorough organization, such warriors would be known as "bushwhackers" and "bummers." Orangeburg and Winnsboro lay on the route, and these places had been the head-quarters of Cornwallis at various times. The Fif-teenth Corps found on its line of march the old town of Camden, near which Cornwallis defeated Gates. This was the most disastrous reverse the Americans suffered during the Revolutionary War. Here they lost eighteen hundred men, with all their artillery; and here, too, Baron DeKalb fell. The battle was once regarded as a stupendous struggle, but Sher-man's army boasted a record which justified it in regarding that as nothing more than a respectable skirmish. It had fought a score of such, many far more serious, during the march between Chattanooga and Atlanta.

Somewhat later, a portion of the Army of the Tennessee fought a skirmish near the old revolution-ary battlefield of the Cowpens; but notes at hand neither note the precise locality nor the date.

Leaving the vicinity of Columbia on February 19th, the army reached Winnsboro on the 21st, and there learned that Charleston had been abandoned by the enemy after withstanding siege for nearly four years. The operations of Sherman's army having severed their communications with the headquarters and interior of "the Confederacy," led them to be-lieve that city to be the objective point of the cam-paign.

This recalls the incident that, when in the vicinity of Branchville, well in the rear of Charleston, some days previous, Sergeant Barker, of the 32d Illinois, found among some papers which had been sent out from the city by the enemy, presumably for safe keeping, a requisition dating somewhere back in the '40's, calling for thirteen loaves of bread for the garrison at Fort Moultrie, and signed, " W. T. Sherman, 1st Lieut. 3d Artillery." The dingy little piece of paper was regarded as quite a curiosity, in view of the changed condition of the officer whose name was appended.

March 3d found the army at Cheraw, South Carolina, on the Great Pedee river. The distance traveled during the eleven days' march was something more than one hundred and twenty-five miles, over inconceivably bad roads. As soon as they had emerged from the mud of the swamps, the troops found themselves anchored in the stiff clay hills, which the heavy rains had worked into the proper consistency to hold feet and wagon wheels as if they had grown there. The labor of building roads and pulling wagons and guns out of the quagmires was very severe. To add to the discomfort, this region was almost barren, and little provision or forage was to be found, making it necessary for the troops to subsist upon the greatly abbreviated rations issued from the supply trains. Three days' rations of meat and bread had to suffice for ten days.

At Cheraw large quantities of commissary stores were found, and issued to the troops or loaded into the wagon trains. They also secured several thousand stand of small arms, and about twenty-five pieces of heavy artillery. The former were destroyed, the latter were utilized in a novel way the next day.

March 4th was made a day of jubilee. The last news received from the outer world was that of the re-election of President Lincoln; and this was the day upon which he was to be inaugurated. The event was celebrated in as grand form as the surroundings would permit. At noon, when it was supposed the ceremonies were transpiring at Washington, a national salute was fired from the captured artillery, large sea-coast pieces. In order to make as much noise as possible, and at the same time destroy the guns, which could not be carried away, they were charged to the bursting point, and when the salute was ended, the work of destruction was found to be complete. In the meantime, the lusty lungs of thousands of wildly exultant men added to the din.

March 9th, General Kilpatrick figured in a comical scene which afforded amusement for the army for many days. This dashing rough-rider, commanding a division of cavalry, with a battery of light guns, always moved on the exposed flank of the army, and could be depended upon to attack or resist almost any force, apparently regardless of consequences. So restless was he, so continually in motion, that he went by the name of "Kill-Cavalry." He was of medium height, but compactly built; his face, adorned with side-whiskers, expressed at once affability and great determination. A peculiarity of his dress was a solid silver star worn upon the shoulder in lieu of the brigadier's strap prescribed by the regulations.

Late at night Wade Hampton's rebel cavalry made an unexpected attack upon Kilpatrick's camp, dispersing the command and surrounding a house occupied by the General and one of his brigade commanders, Colonel Spencer, afterward a senator from Alabama. These officers, in anything else but uniform, managed to run the gauntlet and reach the woods near by. Here they rallied their troopers, and after a brisk fight drove away Hampton, regaining their camp and artillery.

March 11th, a beautiful day, the army was marching toward Fayetteville, North Carolina, at a rapid pace and in good spirits, Giles A. Smith's division of the Seventeenth Corps in advance. The adjutant, riding a "captured" horse whose high mettle was stimulated by a sudden blast from a brass band immediately behind, found himself unable to restrain the ambitious animal, and was borne past the head of the column toward a squad of soldiers exchanging shots with the enemy on the opposite side of Cape Fear river. The Union skirmishers turned out to be "bummers," whose zeal for adventure had led them to outdo the regular advance. As soon as they discerned an officer galloping down the road—not knowing that he had no more business there than themselves, but was only present on account of the self-assertion of an unruly horse—they raised a shout, "There goes an officer! Let's follow him and save the bridge!" At once all dashed forward in the direction of the river, but the enemy had piled large quantities of resin upon the bridge, and it was already in flames and past saving when the squad reached it; besides, a rebel battery· was playing across the river. This combination of circumstances, and the fact that his horse was winded by its mad run, caused the officer to halt, and, with the soldiers, seek cover until the arrival of the main column. The wild rider was warmly praised by his superior for courage displayed, but the compliment was coupled with a profane reflection upon his want of sense.

Shortly after the troops entered Fayetteville, a United States dispatch boat ran up to the wharf—the first vessel flying Union colors that had ascended the stream since the war began — the brave little craft making the venture because of the abiding faith of the Government in Sherman's assurance that he would be there at that time. The boat was insignificant enough, scarcely larger than a yawl. It brought no letters, no papers — nothing but a bag of dispatches for the General. But for all that, it was hailed with unbounded enthusiasm. It was the first courier from the outside world since the army left Beaufort, nearly two months before. It spoke no word; but the bright, familiar bunting at its peak seemed to be a personal message to every member of the grand army, telling him the Government at Washington yet lived, and the great heart of the nation confided in his patriotism and courage. No wonder he hailed the flag with as warm delight as thrilled the heart of the patriot in days gone by, when, imprisoned within hearing of a deadly conflict, and after a night's weary vigil, he looked out across the waters from his cell, at the first gleam of dawn, and gave eloquent expression to his joy:

> " On the shore, dimly seen thro' the mists of the deep,
> Where the foe's haughty host in dread silence reposes—
> What is that which the breeze o'er the towering steep,
> As it fitfully blows, half conceals, half discloses?
> Now it catches the gleam of the morning's first beam,
> In full glory reflected now shines on the stream,
> 'Tis the star-spangled banner! Oh, long may it wave
> O'er the land of the free and the home of the brave!"

At Fayetteville an expedition was organized to march down the banks of Cape Fear river to the sea coast, with a cloud of negroes and white refugees who had attached themselves to the army as it moved along. The plantations on the line of march had gen-

26

erally been abandoned by their owners, and when the
slaves concluded to follow the army north in search of
"white wheat bread and a dollar a day," they considered themselves licensed to appropriate whatever of
massa's or missis's finery they could lay hands on.
The white refugees and freedmen traveled together
in the column, and made a comical procession. They
had the worst possible horses and mules, and every
kind of vehicle, while their costuming was something beyond description. Here was a cumbersome,
old-fashioned family carriage, very dilapidated, yet
bearing traces of gilt and filagree, suggesting that it
had been a very stylish affair fifty years before. On
the driver's seat was perched an aged patriarch in
coarse plantation breeches, with a sky-blue, brass-but-
toned coat, very much out of repair, and his gray grizzled wool topped off with an old-fashioned silk hat.
By his side rode mater-familias, wearing a scoop-
shovel bonnet resplendent with faded ribbons and
flowers of every color of the rainbow; a silk or satin
dress of great antiquity, and coarse brogans on her
feet. The top of the carriage was loaded with a
feather-bed, two or three skillets, and other "plunder." From the glassless windows of the clumsy
vehicle peered half a score of pickaninnies of all sizes,
their eyes big with wonder. Elsewhere in the column
a pair of "coons" rode in a light spring wagon, one
urging the decrepit horse to keep up with the proces-

REFUGEE TRAIN.

See page 402.

sion, while the other picked a banjo, and made serious attempts to sing a plantation song, which was almost invariably of a semi-religious character. Those who traveled on foot, men and women, of all colors from light mulatto to coal black, loaded down with bedding, clothing and provisions, were legion. Occasionally a wagon was occupied by white refugees, who, being unionists, had been despoiled by the confederates. These were sad and hopeless. The colored people, on the contrary, were invariably gay hearted, regarding their exodus as a pleasure trip, and evidently strong in the faith that their lot, on "gittin' to freedom," was to be one of bliss.

The fine government arsenal at Fayetteville, which had been used by the confederates, was completely destroyed, General Sherman remarking that he did not believe the Government would ever be so foolish again as to entrust such property to a rebel state.

March 14th, the army moved in the direction of Goldsboro, the march becoming slower on account of the concentration of the enemy's forces in front. Johnston, who was displaced by Hood before Atlanta, had been again called to oppose Sherman, with the relics of Hood's army, and the various garrisons made available by abandonment of the sea-coast line. The Union troops looked for a severe struggle; some felt that there was a strong probability of having to fight a part of Lee's army as well as Hood's, but all were hopeful, believing that the end was drawing near.

March 19th, the Twentieth Corps was caught in flank by the enemy, and had a sharp little engagement. Later reports indicating that it had found in its front the entire rebel army, with General Johnston at its head, the Seventeenth Corps was diverted from its course to go to its assistance, and made a hard night's march over a miserable causeway built through the swamp. Rain fell in torrents all night long ; the lightning was fearful, and one bolt struck a portion of the column, severely shocking several men. The Fifteenth Corps had a scarcely less unpleasant journey, on the same errand, over a different road, and one possibly a trifle better—it could not have been worse.

On the 21st, the army went into line of battle near Bentonville, North Carolina. Notwithstanding the evident hopelessness of their cause, the enemy fought desperately, and Sherman's army won fresh laurels in defeating them.

Giles A. Smith's division of the Seventeenth Corps deployed a skirmish line made up, in part, of the 32d Illinois. This portion of the line was under orders to make a strong demonstration to create a diversion in favor of Mower's troops, who had gone into action farther to the right with so much energy as to be in danger of being overwhelmed. Unfortunately, the ground and the conditions were unknown, and Smith's skirmishers, particularly those of Belknap's brigade, suffered severely. At the word, they advanced through a heavy pine forest, the line of battle being in near support, moving on until they encountered the enemy's works, and some of the men actually fell upon the parapet. One of these, a gallant young lieutenant of the 32d Illinois Regiment, was left for dead. A few days afterward, he overtook the command on the march, and was looked upon as a modern Lazarus. He was scarcely recognizable, for his uniform was horribly dilapidated, and he wore a large patch near his nose, and a bandage around his head, a rifle ball having passed through his cheek, making its exit behind the opposite ear. It is to be hoped that he is now enjoying good health and a liberal pension.

In the charge, one poor fellow, a drafted man (for which class the veteran volunteers manifested a supercilious contempt), bent over the ground as the line came well under fire. " You —— ' connie ' (conscript), come on and fight!" yelled an officer. " Wait till I tie my shoe, and you'll see how a ' connie ' will fight !" was the answer. He finished tying his shoe, for that is what he was really doing, regained his position, and fell dead on the enemy's works.

The line was forced back from the works, but occupied its advanced rifle-pits. Early the next morning the enemy retreated, having been pressed hard at other points. He was never to fight another battle. But that was not known then.

The part taken by a portion of his brigade was suitably recognized by General Belknap, in the following letter to Captain Jeff Dunn, who commanded the skirmish-line :

HEADQUARTERS 3D BRIG., 4TH DIV., 17TH A. C.,
IN THE FIELD, March 22d, 1865.

CAPTAIN : I take the first opportunity that offers to thank you for your gallant conduct on the skirmish-line near Bentonville, N. C., March 21st, and to express the appreciation I have for the skillful manner in which you handled your men. Your line, weak as it was, at a moment's notice, not only charged the rifle-pits of the enemy, but advanced on his entrenched line-of-battle, and only fell back before greatly superior numbers. At night, when relieved by the first brigade of this division, you remained with your men on the skirmish-line, and faithfully did more than your duty, although you could with perfect propriety have brought in all your men. I have the satisfaction of knowing that the men of Iowa, as well as those of Illinois, honor you for your conduct, and I will commend to those of my command your example as worthy of imitation.

I am, Captain,

Yours, very respectfully.

W. W. BELKNAP, Brig.-Gen.

March 22d, the army entered Goldsboro, and was again in communication with the northern homes of the soldiers. Heavy mails, which had been accumulating for more than two months past, were awaiting them ; and, to make their happiness as nearly complete as a soldier's may be, they were served with unstinted army rations.

# CHAPTER XLI.

### A JOYOUS INTERLUDE.

MMEDIATELY after the army had entered Goldsboro, the adjutant was an actor in a chapter of experiences, which, recalled to mind after the lapse of a score of years, might seem to have existence only in dreamland. But a package of military orders, a bundle of letters, and a few photographs, lying upon his desk, assure the reality of the narrative.

Colonel Cadle, General Frank P. Blair's adjutant general, an old and well-known friend, gave hint to the adjutant of some military events soon to occur. Sherman was to crush Johnston, and then move upon Lee, whom Grant was holding as in a vise. Those in high place were so well assured of the successful issue of these operations, that the end of the war, and the transfer of General Sherman's army to the national capital, for final review and disbandment, were regarded as near at hand. General Blair was anxious that his command (the Seventeenth Corps) should make as presentable an appearance as possible, when that event should occur. The Fourth Division (General Giles A. Smith) was without a brass band ; but among the recruits received were several musicians, and one who represented himself as having been a band-leader. These men were to be organized as a band, and the adjutant was ordered to go to New York, taking the leader with him, to purchase instruments, the required funds having been contributed by the officers of the division.

March 26th, the necessary orders were made, and the adjutant and his companion began their journey, traveling by rail to New Berne, thence by boat through the Dismal Swamp and canal to Fortress Monroe and Baltimore. From the latter place they proceeded by railway.

The business in New York was speedily discharged, and the band-master sent back to his command with the instruments. To dismiss this part of the subject, once for all, it is only to be remarked that the " band " proved to be the very worst in the army, and the alleged " leader " a most stupendous fraud. It is perhaps to the credit of the latter, that he never murdered but one tune. It was the only one he ever attempted— " The Roll of the Stirring Drum," from " The Bohemian Girl."

The adjutant availed himself of a saving-clause in his orders, to remain in New York for a few days and enjoy a season of recreation. One evening, soon after his arrival, he stood in the lobby of the Metropolitan Hotel, in the midst of a large throng of army and navy officers, engaged in discussing war questions with considerable spirit. It was evident that all were Eastern men, for they magnified the achievements of the army in Virginia, and of the fleet on the sea-coast ; not forgetting to disparage somewhat their comrades of the West. This was natural enough, from their standpoint ; but it was exceedingly irritating to the adjutant, who finally spoke, with anger and indignation, in vindication of his own army. His hot sentences had scarcely passed his lips, when his hand was grasped by one in the uniform of a naval officer, who excitedly asked, "For God's sake, are you one of Sherman's men?"

Being answered in the affirmative, the stranger introduced himself as Acting Master Gibson, of the gunboat "Marmora," belonging to the Mississippi flotilla. He then pointed to his disfigured face—the cheek-bone had been crushed by a fragment of shell while passing the forts at New Orleans in one of Farragut's wooden vessels.

The two, strangers alike to the throng about them, became close friends on the instant. The Eastern men, hearing their conversation, at once made the *amende honorable*, protesting they meant no disparagement of their comrades in arms, and were unaware that any of General Sherman's army had yet reached the North. They were very sincere and cordial, and proved to be most companionable gentlemen.

Standing well back at the side of the lobby, noting the' altercation and the explanations, but taking no part, was an elderly man, whose whitish hair crept out from beneath a fatigue cap. A military cloak concealed all evidence of rank. Approaching the adjutant, he said that he had heard the conversation, and was surprised that any of General Sherman's command should have reached the North so soon. Then he presented a card bearing his name, and requested the writer to become his guest. The speaker was General Anderson, who, as a humble major, held Fort Sumter against the first treasonable assault in April of 1861. His invitation, at once a high honor and a command, was promptly accepted. The General's carriage was at the door, and the two were soon at his residence on Fifth Avenue. It was now quite late, and the guest was at once shown to a room, with an injunction that he must be prepared to do a great deal of talking on the morrow.

At breakfast next day the guest met Mrs. Anderson and her children. The latter conversed with each other and with their parents in French, the General explaining that it was to assist them in acquiring fluency in the language, which they were diligently studying. After breakfast, all repaired to the library, and the adjutant was desired to give a narrative of the campaigns of General Sherman's army, beginning with the march out of Atlanta. Never did speaker have more attentive auditors, and their deep interest put him so much at his ease that he told his story with considerable enthusiasm, the General frequently calling a halt to ask pertinent questions, or to comment, as the narrative progressed. The morning was thus spent, and the interview suspended for the time.

In the morning of the next day the narrative was resumed and the subject tolerably well exhausted, when General Anderson complied with the solicitations of his guest, and gave a vivid description of the attack upon Fort Sumter and the occurrences preceding it. He told how, with his little band of eighty men, he was virtually besieged in Fort Moultrie, Charleston harbor ; how, upon his own responsibility, and with the positive conviction that President Buchanan would disapprove his action, he abandoned the position by night and occupied

Fort Sumter, the key to the harbor; how at noon on the following day he assembled his command at the foot of the flagstaff, and all knelt, while the chaplain invoked a blessing upon the nation and their own feeble effort ; after which the General (a major then) with his own hands ran up to the head of the staff the flag he had brought away from Moultrie, while the band played "Hail Columbia," and the men broke into cheers.   Then he told of the attack upon the relief-ship "Star of the West," and its driving off; of the summons to surrender the fort, of the fierce cannonading from the rebel batteries, and of how, with his wooden buildings in flames from the enemy's shells, his ammunition and provisions exhausted, he saluted his flag, hauled it down and evacuated the fort.

General Anderson was now looking forward, with the ardent anticipation of a gallant soldier and noble patriot, to a scene which he regarded as a fitting close to his public life.   The fortress he was compelled to surrender to the domestic enemies of the Government, had been conquered and recovered by the national forces, and it was to be his glorious privilege to again raise over the ramparts he had so well defended, the very flag he himself had been obliged to lower.   He had but recently received from the War Department orders prescribing the ceremonies, and announcing April 14th, 1865, the fourth anniversary of the surrender, as the date. General Anderson was to raise the flag precisely at noon, and it was to be saluted with one hundred guns from Fort Sumter, and with national salutes from every fort and battery which fired upon it in 1861. At a later day the newspaper accounts showed that these arrangements were fully carried out, and that an appropriate oration was delivered upon the spot by the Rev. Henry Ward Beecher.

The author has often regretted that he failed to take notes of his conversations with General Anderson, while they were yet fresh in mind. As it is, only the salient points linger in memory. The General spoke with entire freedom, and took a pardonable pride in his military history. He told how he entered the army, and served on the staff of General Scott, and was wounded in Mexico. He expressed his great admiration for General Sherman, and his pride in the success of that officer, whom he referred to as "one of my boys," Sherman having been a lieutenant in his battery, on being commissioned, early in the '40's. He bade his guest call upon General Sherman on rejoining the army, and convey to him his compliments and good wishes. Then the General asked for a souvenir of the great march, whereupon the writer, with outward pleasure but inward reluctance, presented him with three volumes of "Hardee's Tactics, Compiled for the Use of the Confederate States Army," which he had taken from the arsenal at Columbia, South Carolina, having first, at the General's request, inscribed upon a fly-leaf his name and a statement of the circumstances under which they came into his possession. In return, the General handed him a card photograph of himself, upon the back of which he wrote :

To Lieut. Hedley, of Gen. Sherman's army, from an admirer and lover of his old comrade, Gen. W. T. Sherman, with the regards of
ROBERT ANDERSON,
Major General, U. S. A.

On rejoining the army, the adjutant made good his promise to call upon General Sherman. He was received kindly, and the warm - hearted general expressed great pleasure at the incident, speaking in high terms of his old commander, and relating several anecdotes with reference to their early comradeship. At a later day he addressed to the writer a note, in which he said :

The episode with reference to Gen. Anderson is certainly most interesting to me, who esteemed him so highly. I think these anecdotes of the period should be treasured, because time is passing rapidly, and with it the memories of the days which tried the courage and patriotism of our people. I hope you and all others of my old soldiers may live long and attain all the honor and prosperity to which they can aspire.
Truly, your friend,
W. T. SHERMAN,
General.

The morning before leaving New York, the adjutant had occasion to visit Wall Street. He was standing upon the topmost step of the sub-treasury build-

ing, when a bulletin was posted, announcing that Lee was asking terms of Grant. To this moment there was not more than the usual bustle on the street, but in less time than it can be told, the scene changed, and the thoroughfare was packed from end to end with a dense mass of wildly exultant people. It was the beginning of the end. The tidings had flown fast. No need now of telegram or printed sheet. Men saw the glorious news in each other's faces, and felt it in the grasp of the hand. Then, while the vast crowd cheered and cheered again, there went up to the very summit of old Trinity Church, at the head of the street, the triumphant flag of the nation, regal in a splendor it had never worn before; while underneath, from the cross high up in air, to the very ground, were flags and flags, nothing but flags, until the spire was a mass of bright bunting, bathed in the sunshine of God's own peace. Then, exhausted with their own joyous effort, a great hush came over the vast assemblage, and the voices of the birds were heard among the folds of the flag, as might Noah's dove among the olive-branches, where it found rest and peace. And then those glorious chimes rang out that old "Old Hundred," which has been Christendom's Te Deum through so many generations, and the vast concourse, with streaming eyes, and tremulous voices, took up the gladsome words, forever wedded to the music, "Praise God, from whom all blessings flow!"

There was no discord in that vast volume of thanksgiving. All differences as to how this end should have been reached, or by whom should have come deliverance, were forgotten, and there was no thought of aught but joy that strife had ceased, and that God's messenger of peace had indeed come to reign upon earth.

# CHAPTER XLII.

## A KNOT OF CRAPE.

ETURNING from New York to the front, a magnificent panorama presented itself to the eye at Fortress Monroe. Napoleon had begun his designs upon Mexico; and, in view of possible complications, every maritime power in Christendom had sent one or more war vessels into the spacious harbor, whence they might reach Mexican waters without much delay, if necessary. Here were the flags of all nations, and war-vessels of all types, but among them none looked so trim and ready for action, nor did any fly such beautiful colors, as our own. Here were the battle-scarred "Monitors," which for three years had lain under a ceaseless storm of iron hail from the batteries at Charleston ; and swift, heavily armed cruisers, battered by tempest while pursuing blockade-runners,

and blockading rebel ports.   Towering over all, rose
the wall-like sides and lofty spars of a famous old
three-decker ship of the line, a surviving relic of the
naval architecture of half a century ago, made obsolete
by steam and iron, and three-hundred-pounder guns.
In its wake, in curious contrast, somewhat resembling
the little dog-cart of the circus clown following close
upon the heels of the elephant, lazily floated one of
the most diminutive stern-wheelers of the western
river class.   It looked strangely out of place on salt
water, and was regarded with contemptuous curiosity
by the genuine old tars of the salt-water navy, who
persisted in calling it "the wheelbarrow."

At Norfolk, Virginia, it became necessary to leave
the ocean-going steamer and take passage upon a little propeller which ran to New Berne, North Carolina.
The craft was not more than forty feet long, and about
ten feet wide, with only sufficient deck-room to shelter
the machinery and the four men who made up
officers and crew.   The only passengers aboard were
the writer and a civilian, Mr. Segar.   An acquaintance was speedily formed, and Mr. Segar proved to be
a most companionable old gentleman.   He was a
native of Virginia, and a man of considerable note.
As a member of the convention assembled to vote Virginia out of the Union in the early secession days, he
took a leading part in the deliberations of that body,
bitterly opposing its revolutionary and rebellious

spirit, and voting against the ordinance of secession. He was loudly denounced by the mob, and at one time a rope was actually placed about his neck, and he would have dangled from a lamp-post had it not been for the intervention of prominent secessionists, who were his warm personal friends. Thereafter it was not safe for him to live within the rebel lines, and he was kept employed by the federal government in various confidential missions.

The route through the Dismal Swamp lay along the edge of Drummond Lake, a wild and lonely region which recalled the tradition so well told in verse by Moore. It was night, and the moon was at its full, the light increasing, by contrast, the gloom of the lake, which was almost entirely concealed by the dense foliage fringing its banks. Here and there straggling moonbeams crept through, and their fitful glint upon the dark waters far away seemed as if it might be the fire-fly lamp of the phantom Indian maiden, and one almost expected to catch a glimpse of

> " The lover and maid so true,
>     Seen at the hour of midnight damp,
>   To cross the lake by a fire-fly lamp
>     And paddle their white canoe."

But more suggestive reminiscences clung to the lonely region. It had been made even more famous by Mrs. Harriet Beecher Stowe in her powerful novel "Dred," vividly depicting the iniquities of slavery.

The book, once widely and eagerly read, was a power in building up that sentiment under which the system finally sank, but it is almost unknown to the younger generations who have grown up in the past quarter of a century.

Morehead City was reached April 15th, and there, on the day following, was received news of the glorious consummation of General Anderson's mission to Fort Sumter, of which he had advised the writer some days before. The joy of the troops there stationed, on receiving the news, was unbounded, but it was of short duration. The hurrahs had scarcely died out, when the intelligence came, on the evening of the same day of victory and gladness, almost before the echoes of the joyful guns at Sumter had ceased to roll, that Lincoln, the beloved and true-hearted, had fallen by the hand of the assassin.

To those who were on the stage of action at that time, the recollection of the horrible crime comes as a dreadful nightmare. Those of a younger generation can not possibly imagine the terrible sensations, the awful forebodings, it awoke.

It is but a few years ago that the nation was overwhelmed with grief because of the murderous taking-off of the second martyr-President, Garfield. The two events are in no wise comparable. The latter crime was in days of profound peace; the former was in time of fierce war. With Garfield dead, " the government

at Washington still lived," and the smooth, continuous
movement of the machinery of law and order was not
to be interrupted.  When Lincoln fell, the hosts of rebellion were yet in arms, and men dreaded lest the assassin's bullet might consummate that crime against civilization which lines of battle had for years unsuccessfully
struggled to accomplish.  The overwhelming sorrow,
and fear of possible evil to follow, fell upon the nation
like a pall.  It was so much, so unexpected, that men
were stunned, stupefied.  They wandered about in an
aimless, irresolute way, with voiceless lips and blanched
cheeks.  The ordinary concerns of life, the routine
duties which, through long continued habit, had come
to be performed mechanically, were forgotten.  Then,
as the mind slowly grasped the horrible reality, stupor
gave place to fierce rage and an intense desire to be
revenged upon somebody—anybody.  Women, fearful
that all who bore the name of Southerner would be
visited with destruction of property and perhaps of
life, left their homes and came to the military headquarters, bringing with them their children, and plead
in tears that their lives might be spared.  Their fears
were idle, their prayers unnecessary.  It is the highest
tribute that can be paid to the self-control and magnanimity of the soldiers of the Union, that their rage
was expended with their breath, and that neither bullet nor torch was sent upon its deadly work.  It is
wonderful to record that no soldier committed a deed

of excess—a single one might have drenched the land in innocent blood, and covered the name of American soldier with undying shame.

The next day, April 17th, the adjutant arrived at Raleigh, to which point the army had advanced during his absence. The news of Lincoln's assassination had not yet reached the troops, and when he informed the members of his mess, they were incredulous, regarding it as one of the canards which were so numerous in those days. But later in the day, General Sherman gave authenticity to the sad story by the publication of an order in which, after reciting the circumstances, he said :

" Thus it seems that our enemy, despairing of meeting us in open, manly warfare, begins to resort to the assassin's tools.

" Your General does not wish you to infer that this is universal, for he knows that the great mass of the confederate army would scorn to sanction such acts, but he believes it the legitimate consequence of rebellion against rightful authority.

" We have met every phase which this war has assumed, and must now be prepared for it in its last and worst shape, that of assassins and guerrillas ; but woe unto the people who seek to expend their wild passions in such a manner, for there is but one dread result ! "

Then occurred scenes more remarkable than those witnessed at Morehead City.

Sherman's army was confronting that of Johnston.

Both were drawn up in line of battle, only a few hundred yards apart, but peace negotiations were in progress, and white flags along the lines proclaimed a truce. Many of the men forgot this state of affairs in their thirst for revenge ; and, here and there, squads and detachments grasped their arms, and without thought of orders, and unled by officers, moved to the front. A single gun might have opened a conflict involving the whole army, in which no quarter would have been asked or given. Wiser counsels prevailed. and the hot-headed went reluctantly to the rear.

The next day General Sherman and General Johnston met to consider terms for the capitulation of the rebel army. The conference was held midway between the lines, and was regarded by the Union troops with great misgiving. They were fearful lest their General should be slain through treachery, and there was much alarm and nervousness until he had returned in safety within his own lines.

Over in the corner yonder, is an old rusty saber, companion in these campaigns the narrative portrays. In its hilt is a frayed and dust-stained fragment of crape, twined therein under War Department orders requiring the army to wear mourning for six months, in memory of the lamented President. The period had not expired when the war ended, and he who wore it was mustered out of service ; and he leaves the mournful emblem in the sword-hilt to this day — the most saddening and sacred of his war relics.

## CHAPTER XLIII.

### VICTORIA

PRIL 17th Generals Sherman and Johnston met to arrange for the capitulation of the last of the rebel armies. The former knew, but his men did not, that Lincoln had been assassinated. Other conferences followed, but as to their result the Union troops knew nothing.

The people at home were aware that, for some reason or other, the terms offered Johnston by Sherman had been overruled at Washington, but this was not known to the army.

The two armies lay in idleness, under flag of truce, until the 24th, seven days after negotiations had been opened, when General Grant suddenly

ACTION AT BENTONVILLE.

See page 407.

appeared upon the scene. His coming, taken in connection with the protracted delay, when all expected the declaration of a lasting peace, was painfully suggestive, and the troops concluded that Sherman's course was not satisfactory to the Government, and Grant had been sent to supersede him. There was no warrant for this conclusion, but the men believed it to be the fact, and so implicitly did they trust Sherman, that, ignorant of the merits of the case, they looked upon Grant, their former commander, with suspicion and jealousy, while under other circumstances they would have been overjoyed to see him. This feeling was intensified when, on the day of General Grant's arrival, orders were issued for the termination of the truce, and the renewal of hostilities, at the expiration of the agreed forty-eight hours' notice. The men had supposed the war was over, their mission accomplished ; but they now felt that the wisdom and honor of their chief had been called in question ; and they were inclined to resent the interference. Happily, however, before the expiration of the truce, another conference was held by the opposing commanders, terms were arranged, and Johnston's men laid down their arms forever.

The struggle was ended, and the curtain was now about to fall upon the final scene, a most fitting one, which was to shed added glory upon the gallant Sherman and his victorious hosts.

Here is the Line of Blue which marched out of Cairo nearly four years ago and pressed on from victory to victory, every halt adding one more to its list of heroic achievements. It invested Fort Henry, and stormed and carried Fort Donelson. It snatched victory from defeat at Shiloh and Stone River. Vicksburg fell before its dogged determination, and Lookout Mountain succumbed to its impetuous assault. Atlanta was literally hammered to pieces under its terrible blows. Then it defiantly marched eight hundred miles through the heart of a hostile territory, demanding and receiving the surrender of its foe at the very gate of his capital. It was the victor! It had the power and the right to exult! Its bands might play and its artillery thunder jubilant volleys! Well might its columns march with proud and arrogant step in sight of the enemy it had conquered! Now for the scenes honored in days of chivalry! The disdainful look of the victor, the bended knee of the vanquished! The surrendered swords! The grounded muskets! The pillage of the camp! "To the victors belong the spoils!"

No! nothing of this. The Line of Gray grounds arms in the seclusion of its own camp, and furls its ill-starred banners. The Line of Blue stacks arms in its own quarters. There is neither blare of band nor peal of cannon. But there is the outstretched hand, and with it the canteen and haversack!

It was pitiful to look upon those men in Gray. Engaged in a cause which had a great wrong—a crime against humanity and civilization—for its foundation, yet were they bone of our bone and flesh of our flesh. They had the same hardy manhood and the same stern devotion to what they misguidedly deemed to be right. As soldiers, they had won a right to be admired and honored. Ever in retreat, they made stout battle at every stopping-place. Defeat did not dishearten them, and to the very last they fought with conspicuous courage. In their butternut jeans, which by courtesy was known as a uniform, and their broad-brimmed, gray slouched hats, they looked anything but soldierly. That they should be such in reality was wonderful. Theirs had been a losing game from the first. The vast majority had not received tidings from their families for many months; they only knew that the war tempest had swept over their homes; and their fearful anxiety as to the fate of their loved ones was unappeased. They were poorly provisioned, and their medical department was worse than their commissariat; the two great necessities of the field hospital, quinine and morphine, were rarely to be had. Yet amid all these hardships and discouragements they were courageous, self-reliant, even hopeful. All praise for their true soldiership! But shame and everlasting disgrace be upon the base conspirators who imposed upon them so desperate an undertaking in so unholy a cause!

The terms granted by General Sherman were most magnanimous. Field transportation and artillery horses belonging to the enemy were lent to them (such were the terms of the articles of agreement; practically it was a gift outright) for their march to their homes, and for subsequent use in industrial pursuits. Each brigade or detachment was allowed arms for one-seventh its numerical strength, to enable those in charge to preserve order.

There were those who criticised General Sherman severely for granting such favorable terms, which were, however, certainly in accord with the sentiment of his troops and the spirit of the age. It is highly probable that the censure visited upon him would have had no existence, had it not been for the unfortunate animadversions of War Secretary Stanton and General Halleck with reference to the terms first submitted by General Sherman, which were overruled at Washington. The rejected portions of this memorandum provided for the disbanding of the rebel army, the conduct of the men to their respective states, there to deposit arms and public property in the state arsenals; the recognition, by the federal government, of the various state governments, on their officers and legislatures taking the oaths prescribed by the constitution of the United States; the people and all the in-

VICTORIA ! 435

habitants of the (rebel) states to be guaranteed, so far as the Executive could, their political rights and franchises; and the executive authority of the United States not to disturb any of the people by reason of the late war, so long as they lived in peace and quiet, abstaining from acts of armed hostility, and obeying the laws in existence at the place of their residence.

These conditions were properly overruled by the authorities at Washington, but Secretary Stanton and General Halleck seemed to lose their heads, and the former authorized a semi-official "statement" which was an argument against the agreement. It asserted that the agreement practically acknowledged the rebel government, undertook to re-establish rebel state governments, relieving rebels from the effect of national victories, and placed in their hands arms and munitions of war which might be used, as soon as the national armies were disbanded, in a renewed effort to overthrow the national government and subdue the loyal states.

It is remarkable to look back to that time, and note how high feeling rose against General Sherman, who the day before was regarded as a demi-god. A leading paper, which had never faltered in its devotion to the cause, and had bestowed the most unstinted praise upon General Sherman, was led by Secretary Stanton's "statement" to make a bitter assault upon that officer. It said that "in reading the compact, one is

at a loss to know which (Johnston or Sherman)
agreed to surrender." These "infamous concessions"
were "intended (sic) not only to secure full amnesty
to every class of rebel offenders, but to open the way
for the re-establishment of slavery." This "ignoble
instrument might have become the Magna Charta of
American slavery." The act of General Sherman was
one of "dangerous insubordination."

General Sherman contended that the agreement, by
its very terms, and by every principle of law, could
not be valid unless approved by the President; that in
fact it was but a basis. He explained that he had
taken extraordinary precautions to lay the matter before the President in all its fullness, sending a staff
officer to Washington, and enjoining upon him to
avoid spies and informers, and say nothing to anybody
until the President should make known his determination. A few days later, in a letter to Secretary Stanton, in answer to the disapproval of the Government,
General Sherman said : "I admit my folly in em-
bracing, in a military convention, any civil matter."
So late as March 3d, he supposed that all the discussion which had grown up between himself and the
Government was in the nature of privileged communications, unknown to the general public; but on that
day he read in the public prints of April 24th the
"statement" of Secretary Stanton, together with the
newspaper comments based upon it, and he exclaimed

with righteous indignation : "It does seem strange to me that every bar-room loafer in New York can read in the morning journals 'official' matter that is withheld from a General whose command extends from Kentucky to North Carolina."

Meanwhile, General Halleck was further complicating matters by ordering troops under his command to invade General Sherman's territory, and renew offensive operations, disregarding the truce existing between Sherman and Johnston, pending discussion of the terms of surrender. At a fortunate moment Halleck's order was revoked, and none too soon, for two bodies of federal troops were on the eve of collision.

It is one of the most painful recollections to a soldier who bore arms in those days, that two officials so high in the esteem of the nation, each so necessary to the triumphant vindication of its authority, as Secretary Stanton and General Sherman, should have been so completely estranged by these unfortunate events, that, even in the hour of triumph, when the victorious armies of the nation marched before them, as they stood almost side by side on the Presidential reviewing stand in the national capital, neither recognized the other, and that one of the two went to his death, unforgiving and unforgiven, so far as the world can ever know.

## CHAPTER XLIV.

### SOCIETY OF THE ARMY OF THE TENNESSEE.

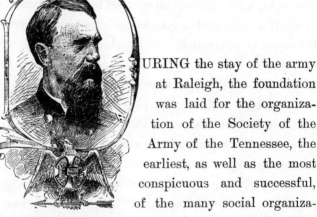

URING the stay of the army at Raleigh, the foundation was laid for the organization of the Society of the Army of the Tennessee, the earliest, as well as the most conspicuous and successful, of the many social organizations which have grown out of the companionships of camp and field. Its membership represents an army which had for its General, in turn, Grant, Sherman, McPherson, Howard and Logan. The achievements of that command were as brilliant and remarkable as the lives of its chiefs. Its nucleus was a half-dozen regiments which occupied Cairo when the first gun was fired. The little army grew to be seventeen thousand men, when it invested Fort

Henry, and afterward stormed and carried Fort Donelson.   Farther on, its numbers were swelled to
forty-two thousand men, who fought at Shiloh and
Corinth under General Grant.   It invested and conquered Vicksburg, being then seventy-three thousand
strong, comprising the Thirteenth Corps, McCler-
nand's; Fifteenth Corps, Sherman's; Sixteenth Corps,
Hurlbut's, and Seventeenth Corps, McPherson's.   Its
Fifteenth, Sixteenth and Seventeenth Corps, thirty-two
thousand men, under General McPherson, participated
in the campaign against Atlanta.   Later, the Fifteenth
and Seventeenth Corps, thirty-seven thousand men,
under General Howard, marched to the sea, and afterward through the Carolinas, while its Thirteenth and
Sixteenth Corps were fighting on Red river, in Missouri, at Nashville, and Mobile.   Few of its many
regiments traveled less than six thousand miles in
their wanderings during the war; many of them all
but doubled this distance.   Its roll of dead was ap-
palling.

If the history of this Army was phenomenal, the
organization of the Society which sprang from it was
dramatic.   It was literally born amid the clash of
arms; and the sound of the enemy's guns was the
accompaniment to the songs of the camp at its first
meeting.

April 14th, Sherman's forces were grouped about
Raleigh, North Carolina, under orders to move against

the enemy the next morning. Later in the day,
General Sherman received from General Johnston a
letter proposing a truce, with a view to a cessation of
hostilities, but this was not known to the army until
afterward.

That evening a number of officers of the Army of
the Tennessee met in the senate chamber at Raleigh.
All were in high spirits, for General Sherman's order
had just been issued, in which he announced the surrender of Lee's army to General Grant, adding:
"Glory to God and our country, and all honor to our
comrades in arms, toward whom we are marching.
A little more labor, a little more toil on our part, the
great race is won, and our government stands regene-
rated, after four long years of war!"

Among the company was General Frank P. Blair.
He was in his happiest mood, and made a brilliant
impromptu speech, congratulating his comrades upon
the speedy conclusion of the war, and suggesting the
organization of a Society " to preserve the recollections
and renew from year to year the companionships of
camp and field." A committee, with General Blair as
chairman, was appointed to draft a plan for organization, and the meeting adjourned subject to call. At
that very hour, President Lincoln fell at the hand of
the assassin, but the sad intelligence did not reach the
army until three days later.

A further meeting was held April 25th, when

General Blair reported a constitution, which was adopted. That paper embraced the following provisions :

"I. The association shall be known as 'The Society of the Army of the Tennessee,' and shall include every officer who has served with honor in that army.

"II. The object of the Society shall be to keep alive and preserve that kindly and cordial feeling which has been one of the characteristics of this army during its career in the service, and which has given it such harmony of action, and contributed, in no small degree, to its glorious achievements in our country's cause.

"The fame and glory of all the officers belonging to this army, who have fallen, either on the field of battle or in the line of their duty, shall be a sacred trust to this Society, which shall cause proper memorials of their services to be collected and preserved, and thus transmit their names with honor to posterity."

General John A. Rawlins, General Grant's adjutant-general, was elected president, and Colonel L. M. Dayton, General Sherman's aide-de-camp, secretary.

At the time of this meeting, the army was under orders to move upon the enemy on the following day, General Sherman's negotiations with General Johnston having been overruled at Washington.

In November of the same year, the war being ended, and the army disbanded, a large number of members of the Seventeenth Corps met in Chicago, and organized the Societies of the "White Arrow" and "Blue Arrow," supposing that the organization at Raleigh had been abandoned. Their membership was composed of ex-officers of the Third and Fourth Divisions, and their titles were taken from their distinctive badges in the field. The two organizations united in a banquet at the Briggs House, and addresses were made by General Belknap, General Gresham, Colonel Dayton, and others. They adjourned to meet at Indianapolis, in November of the following year ; but, in the meantime, the president of the Society of the Army of the Tennessee issued his call for a meeting of that body at Cincinnati, about the same time, and the Division Societies abandoned their organizations.

The meeting of the Society of the Army of the Tennessee at Cincinnati, in November, 1866, the first after the temporary organization at Raleigh, was successful and notable in every way. General Rawlins, the President, since deceased, delivered the annual address, which was an admirable résumé of the history of the Army of the Tennessee ; and an original poem, " Men of the Tennessee," was read by T. Buchanan Read.

At this meeting, an effort was made to modify the constitution so as to admit to membership all enlisted men who had served in the Army of the Tennessee, but without success. It was objected that " the society was formed before the close of the war, not in its pomp

and circumstance, but in the theatre of military movement, and within the sound of hostile guns, and was,
therefore, peculiar.  At that time the discipline of
service did not allow that character of association between officers and men that the constitution of this
society contemplated for its members, and the original
principles and intentions of the Society should be
adhered to." Frequent attempts have since been made
to the same purpose ; but, thus far, unsuccessfully.

After the death of the lamented Rawlins, General
Sherman became President.  He has been re-elected
each succeeding year without opposition, and will
undoubtedly be continued in the position so long as
he lives.  Colonel Dayton, Recording Secretary; General Hickenlooper, Corresponding Secretary; and General Force, Treasurer, were also elected at that meeting, and have been re-elected each year since.

The annual meetings of the Society are notable
events, and attract the presence of the most distinguished civilians, as well as military men, of the
nation.  The orations and responses to sentiments are
worthy of the most cultured audiences of the land,
and the banquets are very grand affairs.

The meeting at Springfield, Illinois, in 1874, was
one of national interest.  Upon that occasion the Lincoln Monument was displayed to the public, the statue
of the great War-President being unveiled by General

Grant, himself President at the time, who delivered a brief but feeling address.

Two years thereafter, the Society met in Washington City, to participate in the observances connected with the unveiling of a monument reared to the memory of Major-General James B. McPherson, third commander of the Army of the Tennessee. This fine work of art was an equestrian statue in bronze, colossal in measurement and effect, the cost of which was defrayed, in greater part, by members of the Society, and altogether through their effort. The orator of the occasion was General John A. Logan, whose eloquent address was read throughout the length and breadth of the land.

In 1879, the Society met in Chicago and there received General Grant, then *en route* east from his journey around the world. This event was made the occasion of one of the finest pageants ever witnessed in Chicago.

This chapter would not be complete without some reference to General Sherman as a presiding officer. In this capacity he is *sui generis*, brusque, nervous, dispatching business at lightning speed, and cutting to pieces parliamentary rules as ruthlessly as he did red-tape in war times, when moving supplies to feed and clothe a vast army. He rarely waits for a motion, but proceeds upon his own suggestion of what should be done, and with a determination to do it. "We

want a committee to select an orator, and I will name
General Jones, Colonel Smith and Major Brown ; all
in favor of the motion say 'aye!' Carried." And so
he pushes along after a fashion, it is fair to presume,
"the boys" would tolerate in no one else. Would-be
orators receive no mercy at his hands. "Yes; speak,
Major; but a very few words. We understand all
about it." "Now, don't make a speech, Colonel; let's
vote," and so on. He cares nothing for popular
applause. As he entered the hall at Minnetonka, the
members of the Society began to cheer. "Stop that
foolishness," said he, "and let's get to business."
Addressing the audience, made up in large part of the
fashionables, he said: "Now, while we are carrying
out this programme, we want quiet. We like to have
these visitors here, but they must understand that
this is a Society meeting, and we are not to be interrupted by applause from outsiders." At the banquet,
where he invariably presides, he said : "It is now
2 o'clock A. M., time for me to quit, and I think you
had better quit too!" At a Society meeting held in
St. Louis, in one of the theatres, in the presence of a
brilliant assemblage of the people of the city, a
fashionable young man, occupying one of the boxes,
took advantage of that stage of the proceedings where
"the boys" call out any of their comrades whom they
desire to hear, to rise in his place and state that
"Several of us would like to hear from Mr. ———,"

naming a civilian of some note. "Sit down, young
man!" thundered the General. "We are willing you
and your friends should stay here and listen; but this
is our meeting, and we propose to run it!"

These eccentricities, however, are but incidents.
General Sherman has a remarkable faculty for inter-
jecting really pertinent comments or suggestions in
course of a debate; and, as an after-dinner speaker he
is inimitable, bestowing words of praise and advice in
epigrammatic language. Upon one occasion he said:

"How we all looked for him (Lincoln) to welcome
us back to our homes, after our long and devious wanderings; but it was not reserved for him, and another
did it in his stead, while the whole nation stood by to
proclaim with shouts of joy, 'Well done, good and
faithful soldiers;' and now I, your old commander,
re-echo the same sentiment, and tell you, you *have* your
reward—not in money or precious jewels, not in lands
or houses, but the consciousness of a noble duty well
done, and in the possession of those priceless memories that will become more and more precious as time
rolls on. The day will come when not a man in this
land of ours but would share with you his wealth
could he say, like you, that he was of the Army
of the Tennessee, and could tell his children that
he had heard the first hostile shot at Fort Henry
and the last boom of cannon at Raleigh.   .   .   .
Our men have returned to their homes in peace
and quiet, and go where I may, I meet them,
all more or less busy at their varied callings.

Turn which way we may, we find our comrades busy, their swords turned into pruning-hooks, each planting his own vine and fig-tree, and no man afraid.   Go, then, I say, and encourage honest industry everywhere.   Have unbounded faith in your country and its flag, and you will win for the Army of the Tennessee a fame in peace equal to that which you won for it in war ; and He who holds the fate of nations in the palm of His hand, will see that your labors are not in vain, and that the glory of your country, for which you battled in war and labored in peace, shall not be tarnished by an insidious foe."

## CHAPTER XLV.

### " ON TO WASHINGTON ! "

T last the army turned its face northward.

" On to Washington ! " Four years before, the words were a war-cry. They were now the glad assurance of victory, peace, and home.

It was an odd experience for the first few days, to jog along the road without stopping here and there to form a line of battle, and to go to sleep at night undisturbed by a midnight call to re-inforce the skirmishers. The occupation of the " bummer " was gone. No straggling or plundering was tolerated, nor was there any disposition in that direction ; chickens and buttermilk were now bought with Uncle Sam's greenbacks, instead of being " cramped." The citizens no longer

fled at the approach of the blue-coated army; but women and children flocked to the road to see them pass;
and, not infrequently, one of Lee's or Johnston's men,
still clad in his "butternut" suit, which had passed
for a uniform, leaned over his gate to crack a joke with
his deadly enemies of a few days before. "Say, Yank!
ain't you 'uns a long way from home?" "You,
Johnny! why in the —— don't you fix up that fence?"
"Say, Yank! you 'uns licked us, but we gin you a
—— of a 'rassle'!" "You bet you did, Johnny!"
And then the two would agree that Sherman's men
and Lee's (or Johnston's, as the case might be) could
together "clean out" (that was their way of expressing it) any nation on earth.

The line of march lay through many points of historic interest, at which the pen insists upon halting
for the moment — down the Boydtown Plank Road,
rendered famous by the brilliant closing engagements
fought by gallant Phil. Sheridan; to Dinwiddie Court-
house, where he fought a fierce battle; and Five
Forks, the scene of what was at once his most brilliant
victory, and one of the most decisive of the war.

Passing by the old farm where General Winfield
Scott was born, the army crossed the Appomattox
river, and entered Petersburg, famous for sustaining a
siege comparable only to that of Vicksburg.

Two days afterward, Manchester was reached, on
the south side of the James river, immediately oppo-

29

site Richmond. Here were first met Custer's gallant troopers, who, despite their hard riding and stout fighting, were so often near to their base of supplies, that they were generally able to appear very presentably. They wore paper collars, and affected long scarfs which fluttered from their necks, each brigade wearing a distinguishing color. These evidences of excessive "style" were regarded by Sherman's ragged roysterers with great contempt, and their sharp comments were extremely irritating to the victims.

Across the river lay Richmond, the rebel capital, which had been, for four years past, in a state of siege. General Halleck was in command here, and between him and Sherman some unpleasantness had arisen, growing out of the discussion with reference to the peace negotiations at Raleigh. Halleck issued an order requiring Sherman's army to pass in review before him at Richmond. Sherman refused, whereupon Halleck forbade the army entering the city at all. The bridge across the river had been destroyed, and a pontoon, laid in its place, was guarded by Halleck's troops. The cranky and contemptuous order by that officer, with reference to Sherman's army, soon became known to the men of that command, and they determined to go into Richmond at all hazards. Accordingly, a large body, unarmed and without officers or orders, made a charge across the bridge, overpowering the guards by sheer weight of numbers. No one was

HALT ON THE MARCH.

See page 283

hurt, but some of Halleck's bridge guards were unceremoniously dumped into the river, whence they scrambled out as best they could. The affair was entirely irregular and unmilitary, but that Sherman enjoyed it in a quiet way is not to be doubted.

The next day the army entered Richmond in regular order. Many points of interest were noted with keen curiosity, especially the mansion so long occupied by Jeff Davis, the civil chief of the " Confederacy," and the state capitol, which had been the quarters of the Confederate congress. These and other public buildings were heavily draped in mourning for President Lincoln, by order of the Union authorities. The capitol grounds were rich in statuary. Here was Houdon's magnificent statue of Washington, and near it a fine marble bust of Lafayette. The finest work of art, however, was Crawford's bronze equestrian statue of Washington ; and, grouped about it, the figures of John Marshall, Thomas Jefferson and Patrick Henry. More than half of the city was in ashes, having been fired by the retreating enemy, just before the national forces entered.

Libby Prison was viewed with a mournful interest. It was an immense building, three or four stories high, once used as a tobacco warehouse ; but, since the beginning of the war, as a prison for federal captives, who were crowded into it until there was absolutely no room for more. The walls were covered with inscriptions written by the unhappy occupants, all breathing an air of hopeless despondency, yet full of bitter hatred for the rebels, and lurid with blasphemous anathemas. Among them was one, said to have been composed by Parson Brownlow, a rather doubtful statement, inasmuch as he never boarded at Libby, and was a clergyman besides. The words had been set to music, and it was said that the prisoners were accustomed to sing them with great vigor, howling the refrain at the top of their voices, sometimes aggravating the rebel guards on the outside to such a degree as to cause them to fire a few shots at the upper windows, in the vain hope of putting a stop to the disturbance. The verses were as follows :

> O ! may that cuss, Jeff Davis, float,
>     Glory, Hallelujah !
> On stormy sea, in open boat,
> In Iceland's cold, without a coat,
>     Glory, Hallelujah !
>
> No rudder, compass, sail, or oar,
>     Glory, Hallelujah !
> A million miles away from shore,
> Where myriad briny monsters roar,
>     Glory, Hallelujah !
>
> May shark devour them, stem and stern,
>     Glory, Hallelujah !
> A whale then gulp them down in turn,
> And the devil get the whole concern,
>     Glory, Hallelujah !
>
> In burning brimstone may he be,
>     Glory, Hallelujah !
> While little devils dance in glee,
> And lock the door, and lose the key,
>     Glory. Hallelujah !

And 'mid his roars and frantic cries,
   Glory, Hallelujah !
O make eternal ashes rise,
And blow forever in his eyes,
   Glory, Hallelujah !

The floors of Libby were marked off with checker-boards and faro lay-outs, testifying to the efforts made by the prisoners to kill time. These species of amusement, however, were only available in the early war-days ; later on, the building was too crowded to admit of anything of the kind. The remains of the celebrated tunnel under the wall, made by Colonel Straight, in his effort to escape, were yet visible.

After crossing James river, the army passed by Hanover Court-house. This famous old building was erected in 1732, and many of the original oak benches yet remained. Within these walls Patrick Henry pleaded his first case in behalf of the people, against the privileged clergy under the British crown, and won a grand victory. He was borne out of these doors in triumph upon the shoulders of the people, and was famous from that instant.

Near at hand was an old church, which afforded a relic of peculiar interest — an old folio Bible, containing the service of the Church of England. In the printed text of the prayer for civil rulers, the name of " His Gracious Majesty, George the Third," had been marked over with red pencil, and immediately above it, well nigh faded out, were the words, written in ink, " The President and Congress of the United States."

From Richmond on, the line of march lay through a country bristling with field-works, and strewn with the débris of vast camps. At one place was quite a thicket of young peach-trees, which a farmer living near by said had grown up from seeds thrown away by the soldiers after eating the canned fruit.

Crossing the Pamunkey and Mattapony rivers, the army passed through Fredericksburg, and halted on the farther bank of the Rappahannock.

This was the range occupied by Burnside that disastrous day in December of 1862. It was quite high, well nigh destitute of timber, and commanded a fine view for miles to right and left. Across the stream lay the village, scatteringly spread over ground sloping to the river's edge ; and just beyond the town was visible a heavily wooded ridge, partly crowned with the stone fence which served the confederate army to so good purpose. It required but little imagination to fill out so suggestive a landscape with batteries and troops, and paint that dreadful battle scene. From the point of observation, two hundred pieces of federal artillery discharged their terrible volleys across the stream, into and through the streets of Fredericksburg, and shot for shot was hurled back by Stonewall Jackson and Longstreet. Under this fire, pontoon bridges were laid by the federals, one at a point immediately before us, where Sumner and Hooker passed over. They assaulted Longstreet immediately opposite this very ground. The enemy was silent until the gallant troops were within short musket-range. Then they opened fire — Longstreet said the gaps made in the Union column by his artillery could be seen a half-mile off. But the boys in blue manfully struggled on toward the stone fence they were never to reach. From behind it leaped a very hell of flame from small arms, and batteries right and left poured in an enfilading fire of grape and canister, that human flesh and blood could not withstand. The Unionists were compelled to retreat. Their comrades on the left fared no better, and the battle was lost.

Fredericksburg cherishes, as one of its greatest treasures, the grave of Edward Heldon, who was a contemporary of Shakspeare, and one of the pall-bearers at the funeral of the immortal bard.

Marching via Stafford Court-house and Acquia Creek, the army entered Alexandria, inseparably connected with the memory of the gallant Ellsworth, whose murder early in 1861, caused a profound sensation throughout the North, and drew thousands of men into the Union army. The story was once familiar, but is probably new to many of a younger generation.

In 1860, young Ellsworth, a clerk in a business house in Chicago, interested himself in organizing and drilling an independent military company, known as "Ellsworth's Zouaves." This corps soon became noted for its admirable drill, particularly in the manual of arms, which abounded in fancy movements not recognized by the books, and the bayonet exercise. It gave exhibition drills in all the principal cities, creating a furore of excitement. Ellsworth, soon after his return from this trip, went to Springfield to study law with Mr. Lincoln, and accompanied him on the journey to Washington, being charged with his safe conduct. When the war began, the young officer organized a regiment of volunteers in New York, and became its colonel.

During the early war days, while troops were assembling at Washington, a rebel flag flying at Alexandria was plainly to be seen from the national capitol. Chafing under the insult, Ellsworth determined to capture the flag. With his regiment he marched to Alexandria, where he found the defiant emblem of treason floating from the roof of a hotel. He tore down the offensive colors, and descended with them upon his arm. At the foot of the stairs he encountered the landlord, Jackson by name, who discharged the contents of a double-barreled shot-gun into his breast, the deadly charge killing him instantly, and driving into his body a gold military badge recently presented to him, bearing the significant legend, "*Non nobis, sed pro patria.*" The murder was avenged by Frank Brownell, a member of the regiment, who shot Jackson dead with his minie-

rifle, and the same instant ran him through with his
sword-bayonet.

Ellsworth was buried from the White House at
Washington, with imposing ceremonies. Brownell
was ever afterward known as "Ellsworth's avenger,"
and he is to this day a noted and honored figure at the
many military gatherings he attends. He yet has in
his possession the weapon with which he avenged the
death of his chief. His home is in Cleveland, Ohio,
where he is engaged in the custom-house service.

## CHAPTER XLVI.

### THE GRAND REVIEW.

THE army left Raleigh, North Carolina, April 29th, and arrived at Alexandria, near Washington City, May 19th. The march occupied twenty days, and the distance traveled was fully three hundred miles, an average of fifteen miles a day—pretty fair marching, considering the fact that haste was unnecessary.

At Washington, the troops, under reasonable restrictions, enjoyed the freedom of the city, and explored all the public buildings and other places of interest, to their hearts' content ; and greatly to their credit, they took no undue advantage of the liberties granted them.

May 23d and 24th, the armies passed in final review, previous to discharge.

Never before was such a sublime pageant witnessed by mortal eye — the review of two hundred thousand citizen soldiery, weather-beaten veterans, flushed with victory, fit to conquer a world, yet who on the morrow would doff the habiliments of war, and return to the office, the work-shop, and the farm. The wisest statesmen had dreaded this day. Foreign, but not unfriendly, ministers said: "The United States have easily raised great armies, but will never be able to return to a peace footing. The soldiers are masters of the situation ; they can never be disbanded." Ardent patriots at home feared that the demoralization of life in the field, the utter freedom from restraints of social ties and civil laws during so long a time, would unfit men for taking up the dull routine of peaceful pursuits, and lawlessness would run rampant. There were designing men who, seeking their own advancement, held the same views, and selfishly sought to lead many of the troops into ambitious exploits in anarchical Mexico.

But the soldiers of the Union were no mere adventurers. They at once allayed the fears of friends, and disappointed the hopes of demagogues; proclaiming, by their conduct, their own unimpeachable integrity as conscientious soldiers and inimitable citizens. They laid aside the sword and musket as readily as they had taken them up, four years before.

May 23d, General Meade's grand army debouched upon Pennsylvania Avenue and poured down the broad street in admirable order. Heroes, all! No army, save that gallant, mistaken band it had assailed for four long years, ever stood up so nobly under severe punishment. At times, victims of incompetency and jealousy in high places, sacrificed on many a bloody altar, their courage never failed, their hopes never died out, their faith in the final result never faltered. Here were the men who learned the alphabet of war at the first Bull Run, crushed there only to rise in superior vigor and courage; the battalions which stood up under the terrible seven days' butchery in the Peninsula; the brigades which snatched victory from a haughty foe at Antietam; the survivors of the murdered legions at Chancellorsville and Fredericksburg; the hosts who mined and charged at Petersburg; the victorious columns which compelled rebellion to bow its head at Appomatox! Their colors were riddled by shot and shell; every rent stood for a battle, and scores of human lives. Erect and proud, they strode down the broad avenue, every foot in time, every musket perfectly poised, while a glad people, gathered from all parts of the nation, strewed flowers before them, and shouted themselves hoarse in their praise.

That night General Sherman's army crossed the Long Bridge from Alexandria and bivouacked in the streets entering upon Pennsylvania Avenue. At nine o'clock next morning it began the march in review.

The avenue was literally packed with people on either side; every window was occupied, and the very house-tops were black with humanity. General Sherman and his staff led the way. It was amusing to the troops to note the complete equipment of him whom they had seen almost daily for years in a dingy uniform, carelessly worn, which many a brigadier would have thought disgraceful. His horse's neck was covered with wreaths of flowers by admiring spectators. Then came Howard, the gentle but brave, commanding the Army of the Tennessee; his empty coat sleeve, pinned upon the breast, mutely proclaiming his deeds of courage. Then rode Logan, at the head of his gallant Fifteenth Corps, once Sherman's. None asked his name—he was known of all; swarthy of complexion, with heavy black mustache and eagle eye, he was the image of a born soldier. Then followed his division commanders: Hazen, who stormed Fort McAllister, and Woods, Smith and Rice, with brigade commanders, Tourtelotte, of Allatoona fame; and Clark, so long McPherson's accomplished adjutant-general, and others. Then came Frank P. Blair, the liberator of Missouri, and gallant soldier of many a bloody field, leading the Seventeenth Corps, McPherson's old command. After him were the division com-

manders, Force, Leggett and Smith; with Belknap,
Potts and others, leading brigades.

But who could picture the hosts that followed?
Here were the men who had taught new lessons to the
masters of war. Such terms as "lines of retreat" and
"base of supplies" were not in their vocabulary.
Their strong backs almost made unnecessary commissary and ammunition trains. Their swift limbs out-
ran and outlasted horses. Ten thousand mile posts
marked the roads they had traversed, through every
revolted state save two. They were the men who
fought at Belmont and assaulted Fort Donelson.
They had been crushed at Shiloh; and while the
enemy was reaping the fruits of victory, snatched it
from him. They had fought over every foot of
ground within thirty miles of Corinth. They had
lain in the trenches at Vicksburg for three bloody
months, and when they rose from before that stronghold, the mighty river "went unvexed to the sea."
They had shattered Bragg at Stone River and Chickamauga, and rescued the beleaguered garrison at
Chattanooga, planting their standards above the very
clouds. Foot by foot they had pressed their enemy
back upon Atlanta, and after a well-fought struggle of
nearly half a year, wrested that mighty stronghold
from him. They had dissected the very bowels of the
"Confederacy" by their march to the sea, and bestowed upon the nation Savannah, as a "Christmas

gift." Three hundred miles farther they had pressed their enemy, and received his surrender as they were stripping themselves to give the *coup de grace.*

With heads erect and an air of indescribable *sang froid*, these men of the West stretched down Pennsylvania Avenue with an easy, swinging gait, peculiar to themselves, acquired in long and rapid marches. They wore no holiday garb. The ragged and faded uniforms in which they had slept and marched, through the swamps of the Carolinas, still clung to their bodies, and they strode along as if proud to display them as badges of faithful service. They were so regarded by the tens of thousands of spectators, and cheers upon cheers followed them from the beginning to the end.

There were some very comical features even in the midst of all this grandeur. In the rear of many regiments were the pack mules loaded down with kettles, pans, gridirons, and all the paraphernalia of the darkey cook, who trudged alongside, consciously feeling the dignity of his office; besides squads of "contrabands," who, with their game-cocks, banjos and plantation airs, provoked much mirth.

From the Treasury Department a large concourse of Government servants and others viewed the troops; and high up on the building was displayed the legend, "The only debt the nation can never pay is that of gratitude it owes to its gallant defenders."

30

The grand reviewing stand was erected in front of the White House. Here stood the President and Commander-in-Chief, Andrew Johnson. The troops proudly recognized his presence; but there was not a heart in all that vast concourse of soldiers and spectators which did not ache with sorrow that Lincoln, the loved and true-hearted, had not lived to see this, the consummation of his highest effort and most ardent hopes. Here, too, were Grant and Sherman, and about them, offering heartfelt congratulations and bestowing unstinted praise, the statesmen of the nation, and the bejeweled ministers of every foreign land.

As the grand pageant rises once more before the eye, memory recurs to the hosts who did not live to participate in this great national jubilee. It must have been with similar emotions that Bret Harte wrote that noble bit of sentiment, "The Last Review":

> "And I saw a phantom army come
>     With never a sound of fife or drum,
>     But keeping time to a throbbing hum
>         Of wailing and lamentation;
>     The martyred heroes of Malvern Hill,
>     Of Gettysburg and Chancellorsville,
>     The men whose wasted figures fill
>         The patriot graves of the nation.

> "And there came the nameless dead—the men
>     Who perished in fever-swamp and fen,
>     The slowly-starved of prison pen ;
>         And marching beside the others
>     Came the dusky martyrs of Pillow's fight,

COMMANDING OFFICERS
FOURTH DIV. 17TH A.C.

See page 145.

With limbs enfranchised and bearing bright ;
I thought—perhaps, 'twas the pale moonlight—
    They looked as white as their brothers.

" And so all night marched the nation's dead,
  With never a banner above them spread,
  Nor a badge, nor a motto brandished ;
  No mark—save the bare, uncovered head,
      Of the silent bronze Reviewer ;
  With never an arch save the vaulted sky ;
  With never a flower save those that lie
  On the distant graves—for love could buy
      No gift that was purer nor truer.

" So all night long swept the strange array,
  So all night long, till the morning gray,
  I watched for one who had passed away,
      With a reverent awe and wonder—
  Till a blue cap waved in the lengthening line,
  And I knew that one who was kin of mine
  Had come; and I spake—and lo! that sign
      Awakened me from my slumber ! "

May 30th, General Sherman issued his farewell
order, in which he eloquently rehearsed the achievements of his army, and to which he added some excellent words of admonition. As a matter of fact, most
of the troops had left Washington for their homes
before the order was published, and many an old
soldier will read it in these pages for the first time:

(Special Field Orders, No. 76.)
        HEADQUARTERS, MILITARY DIVISION OF THE MISSISSIPPI,
                Washington, D. C., May 30, 1865.
    The General commanding announces to the Armies of the Tennes-
see and Georgia that the time has come for us to part. Our work is
done and armed enemies no longer defy us. Some of you will go to
your homes, and others will be retained in military service till further
orders.

And now that we are all about to separate, to mingle with the civil world, it becomes a pleasing duty to recall to mind the situation of national affairs when, but a little more than a year ago, we were gathered about the cliffs of Lookout Mountain, and all the future was wrapped in doubt and uncertainty.

Three armies had come together from distant fields, with separate histories, yet bound by one common cause—the union of our country and the perpetuation of the Government of our inheritance. There is no need to recall to your memories Tunnel Hill, with Rocky Face Mountain and Buzzard Roost Gap, and the ugly forts of Dalton behind.

We were in earnest, and paused not for danger and difficulty, but dashed through Snake Creek Gap and fell on Resaca; then on to the Etowah, to Dallas, Kenesaw; and the heats of summer found us on the banks of the Chattahoochee, far from home, and dependent on a single road for supplies. Again we were not to be held back by any obstacle; we crossed over and fought four hard battles for the possession of the citadel of Atlanta. That was the crisis of our history. A doubt still clouded our future, but we solved the problem, destroyed Atlanta, struck boldly across the State of Georgia, severed all the main arteries of life to our enemy, and Christmas found us at Savannah.

Waiting there only long enough to fill our wagons, we again began a march which, for peril, labor and results, will compare with any ever made by an organized army. The floods of the Savannah, the swamps of the Combahee and Edisto, the "high hills" and rocks of the Santee, the flat quagmires of the Pedee and Cape Fear rivers were all passed in mid-winter, with its floods and rains, in the face of an accumulating enemy, and, after the battles of Averysboro' and Bentonsville, we came once more out of the wilderness, to meet our friends at Goldsboro'. Even then we paused only long enough to get new clothing, to reload our wagons, again pushed on to Raleigh and beyond, until we met our enemy suing for peace instead of war, and offering to submit to the injured laws of his and our country.

As long as that enemy was defiant, nor mountains, nor rivers, nor swamps, nor hunger, nor cold had checked us; but when he, who had fought us hard and persistently, offered submission, your General thought it wrong to pursue him farther, and negotiations followed, which resulted, as you all know, in his surrender.

How far the operations of this army contributed to the final overthrow of the Confederacy, and the peace which now dawns upon us, must be judged by others, not by us; but that you have done all men could do has been admitted by those in authority, and we have a right to join in the universal joy that fills our land because the war is over, and our Government stands vindicated before the world by the joint action of the volunteer armies and navy of the United States.

To such as remain in the service, your General need only remind you that success in the past was due to hard work and discipline, and that the same work and discipline are equally important in the future. To such as go home, he will only say that our favored country is so grand, so extensive, so diversified in climate, soil and productions, that every man may find a home and occupation suited to his taste; none should yield to the natural impatience sure to result from our past life of excitement and adventure. You will be invited to seek new adventures abroad; do not yield to the temptation, for it will only lead to death and disappointment.

Your General now bids you farewell, with the full belief that, as in war you have been good soldiers, so in peace you will make good citizens; and if, unfortunately, new war should arise in our country, "Sherman's Army" will be the first to buckle on its old armor and come forth to defend and maintain the Government of our inheritance.

By order of
Major-General W. T. SHERMAN.

L. M. DAYTON,
    Assistant Adjutant-General.

## June 2d, following, Lieutenant - General Grant issued the following :

*Soldiers of the Armies of the United States :*

By your patriotic devotion to your country in the hour of danger and alarm, your magnificent fighting, bravery and endurance, you have maintained the supremacy of the Union and the Constitution, overthrown all armed opposition to the enforcement of the laws and of the proclamations forever abolishing slavery—the cause and pretext of the rebellion— and opened the way to the rightful authorities to restore order and inaugurate peace on a permanent and enduring basis on every foot of American soil. Your marches, sieges and battles, in distance, duration, resolution, and brilliancy of results, dim the lustre of the world's past military achievements, and will be the patriots' precedent in defense of liberty and right, in all time to come. In obedience to your country's call, you left your homes and families, and volunteered in its defense. Victory has crowned your valor, and secured the purpose of your patriotic hearts; and with the gratitude of your countrymen, and the highest honors a great and free nation can accord, you will soon be permitted to return to your homes and families, conscious of having discharged the highest duties of American citizens. To achieve these glorious triumphs, and secure to yourselves, your fellow-countrymen, and posterity, the blessings of free institutions, tens of thousands of your gallant comrades have fallen, and sealed the priceless legacy with their blood. The graves of these, a grateful nation bedews with tears, honors their memories, and will ever cherish and support their stricken families.

U. S. GRANT,
Lieutenant-General.

## CHAPTER XLVII.

### HOMEWARD BOUND !

 HE western troops, a few days after the grand review, moved homeward over the Baltimore & Ohio Railway. The supply of passenger-coaches was altogether inadequate to the great demand, and the men were obliged to put up with flat and box cars for the journey. It was no great hardship, compared with what they had undergone daily during the year past. Fortunately, the weather was unexceptionable, and there was ample opportunity to enjoy the magnificent scenery on that famous route.

At Parkersburg, West Virginia, the troops embarked upon steamboats for Louisville. A serious accident, with collateral comical incidents (what would " soldiering " have been without such ?), befell a por-

tion of the command. The boat bearing the 32d Illinois Regiment was engaged in a race with another
vessel of the fleet, when, just below Blennerhassett's
Island, the former ran into a barge, knocking a hole
in her own bows. Almost as soon as it could be told,
the bottom dropped out of the craft, and she settled on
the river-bed, the water rising so high as to overflow
the cabin-deck. Quick as was the boat to sink, the
negroes and teamsters on the lower deck managed to
cut loose the horses and mules, and they swam to
shore ; while the men who could not swim, straddled
gang-planks, wagon-beds, and anything that would
float, and continued their voyage toward Louisville
upon their own account.

At the time the boat struck, a merry party was
seated at a card-table in the cabin above, immediately
in front of the bar. When the shock came, all jumped
to their feet and rushed to the guards. While they
were making up their minds whether to leap over-
board or not, a sudden jar indicated that the boat had
struck bottom, and they immediately returned to their
game, unwilling to lose time for a trifle. Another
blue-coat took possession of the bar (which had been
left open by the bar-keeper, in his haste to jump over-
board), and insisted upon dealing out free drinks to
all who remained on the craft. Half an hour later, the
shipwrecked passengers were taken off by another boat
belonging to the fleet, which, after repeated stoppages

at islands and clumps of timber on the banks, succeeded in picking up all the soldiers who had abandoned their own sinking craft. Fortunately no lives were lost, but a good deal of personal baggage was never seen afterward.

Soon after reaching Louisville, orders were issued for the dispatch of the troops to their respective states for muster-out. General Logan, commanding the Army of the Tennessee, just before the disbandment occurred, issued the following farewell order :

HEADQUARTERS ARMY OF THE TENNESSEE,

LOUISVILLE, KY., July 13, 1865.

*Officers and Soldiers of the Army of the Tennessee:*

The profound gratification I feel in being authorized to release you from the onerous obligations of the camp, and return you, laden with laurels, to homes where warm hearts wait to welcome you, is somewhat embittered by the reflection that I am sundering the ties that trials have made true, time made tender, suffering made sacred, perils made proud, heroism made honorable, and fame made forever fearless of the future. It is no common occasion that demands the disbandment of a military organization, before the resistless power of which, mountains bristling with bayonets have bowed, cities surrendered, and millions of brave men been conquered.

Although I have been but a short period your commander, we are not strangers ; affections have sprung up between us during the long years of doubt, gloom, and carnage, through which we have passed together; nurtured by common perils, sufferings and sacrifices, and riveted by the memories of gallant comrades, whose bones repose beneath the sod of a hundred battle-fields, nor time nor distance will weaken nor efface.

The many marches you have made, the dangers you have despised, the haughtiness you have humbled, the duties you have discharged, the glory you have gained, the destiny you have discovered for the country in whose cause you have conquered, all recur at this moment, in the vividness that marked the scenes through which we have just passed.

From the pens of the ablest historians of the land, daily are drifting out upon the current of time, page upon page, volume upon volume, of your heroic deeds, which, floating down to future generations, will inspire the student with admiration, the patriotic American with veneration for his ancestors, and the lover of Republican liberty with gratitude to those who, in a fresh baptism of blood, re-consecrated the powers and energies of the Republic to the cause of constitutional freedom. Long may it be the happy fortune of every one of you, to live in the full fruition of the boundless blessings you have secured to the human race.

Only he whose heart has been thrilled with admiration for your impetuous courage and unyielding valor in the thickest of the fight, can appreciate with what pride I recount these brilliant achievements which immortalize you, and enrich the pages of our national history. Passing by the earlier but not less signal triumphs of the war, in which most of you participated, and inscribed upon your banners such victories as Donelson and Shiloh, the mind recurs to campaigns, sieges, and victories, that challenge the admiration of the world, and elicited the unwilling applause of all Europe. Turning your backs upon the blood-bathed heights of Vicksburg, you launched into a region swarming with enemies, marching without adequate supplies, and fighting your way, to answer the cry for succor which came to you from the noble beleaguered army at Chattanooga. Your steel next flashed among the mountains of Tennessee, and your weary limbs found rest before the embattled heights of Missionary Ridge. There, with dauntless courage, you breasted again the enemy's destructive fire, and shared with your comrades of the Army of the Cumberland the glories of a victory than which no soldiery can boast a prouder.

In that unexampled campaign of vigilant and vigorous warfare, from Chattanooga to Atlanta, you freshened your laurels at Resaca, grappling with the enemy behind his works, hurling him back, dismayed and broken. Pursuing him thence, marking your path by the graves of fallen comrades, you again triumphed over superior numbers at Dallas. Fighting your way from there to Kenesaw Mountain, under the murderous artillery that frowned from its rugged heights, with a tenacity and constancy that finds few parallels, you labored, fought and suffered through the broiling rays of a southern midsummer sun, until at last you planted your colors upon its topmost heights. Again, on the 22d of July, 1864, rendered memorable through all time for the terrible struggle you so heroically maintained under discouraging disasters, and, saddest of all reflections, the loss of that exemplary soldier and popular leader, the lamented McPherson, your matchless courage turned defeat into a glorious victory. Ezra Chapel and Jonesboro' added new lustre to a radiant record, the latter unbarring to you the proud Gate City of the South. The daring of a desperate foe, in thrusting his legions northward, exposed the country in your front, and though rivers, swamps, and enemies opposed, you boldly surmounted every obstacle, beat down all opposition, and marched to the sea.

Without any act to dim the brightness of your historic page, the world rang plaudits when your labors and struggles culminated at Savannah, and the old "Starry Banner" waved once more over the walls of one of our proudest cities on the seaboard. Scarcely a breathing spell had passed, when your colors faded from the coast, and your columns plunged into the swamps of the Carolinas. The sufferings you endured, the labors you performed, and the successes you achieved in those morasses, deemed impassable, form a creditable episode in the history of the war. Pocataligo, Salkahatchie, Edisto, Branchville, Orangeburg, Columbia, Bentonville, Charleston, and Raleigh, are names that will ever be suggestive of the resistless sweep of your columns through the territory that cradled and nurtured, and from whence was sent forth on its mission of crime, misery, and blood, the disturbing and disorganizing spirit of secession and rebellion.

The work for which you pledged your brave hearts and brawny arms to the Government of your fathers, you have nobly performed. You are seen in the past, gathering through the gloom that enveloped the land, rallying as the guardians of man's proudest heritage, forgetting the thread unwoven in the loom, quitting the anvil, and abandoning the workshops, to vindicate the supremacy of the laws, and the authority of the Constitution ! Four years have you struggled in the bloodiest and most destructive war that ever drenched the earth in human gore ; step by step you have borne our standard, until to-day, over every fortress and arsenal that rebellion wrenched from us, and over city, town, and hamlet, from the lakes to the gulf, and from ocean to ocean, proudly floats the "starry emblem" of our National unity and strength.

Your reward, my comrades, is the welcoming plaudits of a grateful people, the consciousness that in saving the Republic, you have won for your country renewed respect and power, at home and abroad ; that with the unexampled era of growth and prosperity which dawns with peace, there attaches mightier wealth of pride and glory than ever before to that loved boast, "I am an American citizen !"

In relinquishing the implements of war for those of peace, let your conduct ever be that of warriors in time of war, and peaceful citizens in time of peace. Let not the lustre of that bright name that you have won as soldiers, be dimmed by any improper act as citizens, but as time rolls on, let your record grow brighter and brighter still.

JOHN A. LOGAN,
Major-General.

General Belknap, commanding the Fourth Division of Blair's Corps, at the same time addressed to the writer of these pages a letter, in which he said :

" I am grateful for the friendship ever shown me by the officers and men of your gallant regiment. None better ever served in my command, and they early won my regard by their dutiful obedience, kind consideration, and soldierly qualities. It will ever give me pleasure to meet you or any of your comrades."

## CHAPTER XLVIII.

### A SUPPLEMENTAL CAMPAIGN.

 HORTLY after arriving at Louisville, the Illinois brigade, as it was now known, comprising the 14th, 15th and 32d Illinois Regiments, was embarked upon steamboats for St. Louis. Instead of being landed, and sent to Springfield for muster - out, as they had been led to expect, the troops were dismayed to find the boats continue up the Missouri River to Fort Leavenworth. There they received orders to provide themselves with a suitable wagon-train, and march to Utah, where difficulties existed with both Indians and Mormons.

This was an unforeseen event. What it all meant no one knew. The troops, however, conjectured one of two causes. These three regiments, among the oldest in the service, through casualties of war had become so greatly depleted that the late assignments

of drafted men and recruits, received at Goldsboro'
and Raleigh, made them almost new regiments, the
old soldiers being outnumbered by the "conscripts"
four to one. Forces being needed at the West, these
regiments had been ordered to the duty as being practically new troops. Either this, or the brigadier,
desirous of being retained in the service, possessed
sufficient influence to have a command set off for him,
whether the exigencies of the service made it necessary or not.

The latter was the popular verdict, and the General
was cursed with a heartiness and euphonic originality
which was probably never surpassed, even in the
swamps of the Carolinas. The officers were fully as
much disgusted as the men, and the entire command
was at the very verge of mutiny. The veterans argued
that they were under no moral obligation to obey the
order to go West. They had enlisted early in '61,
"for three years unless sooner discharged," and when
they found that the war was not to be disposed of in
that time, they had re-enlisted. The war was now
over, and in all equity they were relieved of their contract. Nothing was said, in their oath of enlistment,
about serving after the close of the war, or about
fighting Indians or Mormons. They might be ordered
to South America with as much justice. These were
the sentiments expressed by the old soldiers—the
"conscripts" were not taken into the account at all,

and would have received no sympathy if they had been ordered to march to Hades; but they complained as bitterly as the others. The officers, however, and many of the veterans, resented the idea of mutiny, and discountenanced desertion, believing the injustice was so evident that, upon proper representations to the War Department, the order would be revoked and the men speedily mustered out. Furthermore, they were determined that no act of theirs, no matter what the provocation, should cloud their long and honorable record. Accordingly, a statement of the case and a remonstrance was prepared and telegraphed to Washington, over the signatures of a number of the field, line and staff officers.

July 21st arrived, the day set for the beginning of the march, and no reply having been received from Washington, the command left camp, their faces turned westward, following a New York cavalry regiment and a battery of artillery, as much out of humor as themselves.

The Illinois Infantry Brigade numbered nearly two thousand men, and was commanded by Brigadier-General C. J. Stolbrand, who had attained distinction as General Logan's chief of artillery, an arm of the service in which he had been trained in Europe, and of which he was a thorough master. The writer was his adjutant-general.

The line of march lay along the old Government

31

trail via Fort Kearney.    It was only about twenty
years ago, but it was "old times" for all that.    There
was not a foot of railroad iron west of the Missouri
river, and each day Ben Halliday's heavy overland
stage coaches rolled by, coming and going, escorted
by a guard of cavalry; and the fleet-footed "pony
express" sped past as if on lightning wings.    Here
and there "doby" houses (made from sun-dried bricks,
after the Mexican fashion), changing-places for the
stage teams and pony-express horses, were the only
visible evidences of civilization, or, more correctly
speaking, of human existence.    It was wearisome enough
to ride or walk, day after day, over those uninhabited
plains, ascending and descending with the roll of the
ground, reaching the summit of one hillock, hoping to
see a house, or a tree, or a human being, only to
behold the summit of another hill outlined against the
sky still further on.    The monotonous scenery and
want of incident in the march begot in the breasts
of the men great repugnance to the untamed West,
and many gave expression to the conviction that the
good Lord never intended that region for aught else
than Indians and buffaloes.    They consequently re-
frained from being millionaires to-day, by contemptuously refusing to pay thirty-seven and a half cents
an acre for what is now some of the most productive
and thickly populated land in Kansas and Nebraska.

Game was abundant along the route, and on

several occasions the troops halted for a day's hunt. They had all the comical experiences of the "tender-foot" on the plains, including the attempt to run down the supposed crippled jack-rabbit, which hobbled off on three legs, but, when crowded a little, put down his fourth, and soon distanced the fleetest dog. Antelope and elk were very numerous. Great strategy was necessary to ensure a successful shot at the former; but the latter traveled in great droves, and were hunted more successfully. At one time everybody in the brigade who owned a horse, or could borrow an animal of any description from the wagon-train, went into a grand skirmish line; and by keeping on the hills, managed to surround a large drove of elk in the valley between. A fierce fire was opened all along the line and a quantity of game killed; but the experiment was rather disagreeable to the hunters, balls from the long-range Springfield rifles on the opposite side of the circle of hunters, whistling un-pleasantly near, entirely too much after the fashion of old times in Georgia.

August 7th, the command reached the Little Blue river, in Nebraska—a territory then—something more than two hundred miles from Fort Leavenworth, and seventy-five from Fort Kearney. This had been the scene of the Indian uprising which desolated the beautiful valley and made necessary the presence of troops. Just one year before, the Government made a payment to the Pawnees and Cheyennes for ceded lands, and the Indians took great offense because it was made in paper money instead of coin. They made a concerted raid upon the settlements, and murdered great numbers, women and children as well as men, and drove away two regiments of cavalry. On the Cottonwood the destruction had been fearful, and pathetic evidence of the sufferings of the settlers was visible in the ruins of their burned cabins, and door-yards where flowers reared by woman's hand yet peeped through the weeds which had overgrown them since the work of murder and rapine was accomplished.

Each night that the brigade went into camp, some of the dissatisfied soldiers deserted and took the road homeward. Each morning the column was shorter than on the day previous. The total number of deserters during the march was about five hundred. Many threats upon the life of the General were made, for he was supposed to be responsible for the march. One night, a canteen of gunpowder was exploded at the entrance to one of the headquarters tents, wrecking it and driving the occupants out-doors amid an eruption of fire and smoke. The adjutant had made every effort to place reliable guards over the General's quarters during the entire march, but even they often deserted. In one instance, he went to his former company and detailed as officer of the headquarter guard, a trim, soldierly sergeant who had been his comrade from the very day of enlistment, and with whom he would have risked his life. Upon this trusted soldier he placed a special obligation, confiding to him the General's security, and perhaps his life. Even this sergeant, least expected of all others, deserted the second night he went on duty. The General, probably looking upon the personal risk as entirely too hazardous, although he did not lack courage, as a long and honorable service amply testified, finally relinquished his command, and rode back to Fort Leavenworth with a small detachment of troops passing in that direction. He was succeeded by Brevet-Brigadier-General Cyrus Hall, Colonel of the 14th Illinois, a brave and tried officer, and extremely popular with his men.

August 10th, the brigade arrived at Fort Kearney, twenty days out from Fort Leavenworth. The garrison was very friendly, and several days were spent in hunting and preparing to continue the march.

From this place further explanations and remonstrances were telegraphed to Washington, and a few days later, orders were received in response, directing the command to retrace its steps and proceed to Springfield for muster-out.

On the 14th, the homeward march was begun. As the command neared its destination, many of the deserters hastened to rejoin, resuming their place in the ranks in time to be properly discharged. Many more, however, failed to appear, and their record is just now being " whitewashed " by an act of forgiveness contained in a recent act of Congress.

It was so recently as last August, at the reunion of the Society of the Army of the Tennessee, at Lake Minnetonka, that the writer, in conversation with General William T. Clark, former Adjutant-General of the Army of the Tennessee, learned that the Illinois Brigade was sent West solely because troops were needed. It was only the ill luck of this command that the errand fell to its lot instead of some other. As a matter of fact, many veteran troops were sent to the Mexican border at the close of the war, and remained in service until the April following, six months after the muster-out of the Illinois Brigade.

## CHAPTER XLIX.

### THE LAST PARADE.

N September 20th, the regiment whose wanderings we have so long followed, drew up in line for its last parade, and muster-out, on the banks of Clear Lake, where its ranks were first formed, upwards of four years before.

The line is shorter now than it was then. Four out of every five of the old faces are missing. The uniforms, once bright and trim, are ragged and travelworn. The flags, whose folds shone with resplendent beauty, are rent by bullet and shell, and stained with dust and smoke of march, camp and battle, until their hues are scarcely distinguishable.

The arms are stacked, and the colors folded. The men break ranks — once more they are free. There are fervent hand-shakings, hurried farewells, and a parting which is forever! The old battalion will respond to the "assembly" never again!

And so they go out into a world which has become new to them. They were school-boys, many of them, when they enlisted. They left their books unfinished, but are too old now to begin again at the turned-down page. Some had occupation four years ago, but they come home to find that others have stepped into the work they began. Old avenues are closed to them, old ambitions are dead, and they walk as in a dream— as strangers in a strange land.

To some, by-and-by, come new aspirations, leading them to embark in ventures they would not have dared but for their experience in days of hardship and conflict. They take up the struggle against Fate and those who, having refused to do duty for their country, have thus far outstripped them in the race of life, but despite the odds against them, they push forward to honorable distinction. They lead the van-guard of civilization in the unexplored places of the land, building up communities and creating states, planting everywhere the school-house and the printing-press, and leading into channels of thrift and enterprise all who gather about them. North and south, they pass the confines of their own land, and travel beyond seas, spreading commerce and introducing invention, to the advancement of their country and their own fortunes.

Others, broken in body and weary of spirit, stoop their shoulders to the burden which lies nearest them, though it be a heavy one. Poor they are in this world's goods, yet are they rich — rich in a life of noble effort, of heroic deed, of patriotic unselfishness, of broadened manhood, of conscientious citizenship. God bless them! The harpies who coined wealth out of their blood and tears, leave no such heritage to the children of their selfishness !

But now, side by side with the skeleton battalion, the old regimental line, as it stood on parade a thousand strong, before shot and shell tore through its ranks, before disease had done its deadly work, rises before memory's eye. It is peopled with faces once familiar — those of our boyhood's comradeship — whose bones are now the milestones marking the bloody road from Cairo to the Gulf, to Atlanta, to Savannah, to Raleigh and Mobile. Others, yet in the land of the living, are bending under an age older than their years, their limbs stiffened by weary march and exposure on tentless camping-ground, or maimed by cruel shot and shell. All these, the comrades of long ago, are again young. They stand erect of form, their eyes gleam with undaunted courage. Not one is missing !

*Present* — ARMS ! A thousand muskets flash in

the sunlight. How smartly the men handle their pieces ! One can hear the sharp snap as the guns respond to the command !

The sergeants march to the front and report :  *All Present !* They return to their posts.

The company officers meet on the center, close upon the adjutant, march forward, and salute their commander. Even while he returns the greeting, the flag on high flutters to the ground, and the sunset gun booms over the waters of the lake.

*Parade is Dismissed !* and the old battalion marches silently back

> " To the camping-ground of ghosts,
> Where the spectral guides have led
> To the white tents of the dead."

Comrades, Brothers !  Hail and farewell!